Writing the History of Crime

WRITING HISTORY

The *Writing History* series publishes accessible overviews of particular fields in history, focusing on the practical application of theory in historical writing. Books in the series succinctly explain central concepts to demonstrate the ways in which they have informed effective historical writing. They analyse key historical texts and their producers within their institutional arrangement, and as part of a wider social discourse. The series' holistic approach means students benefit from an enhanced understanding of how to negotiate the contours of successful historical writing.

Series editors: Stefan Berger (Ruhr University Bochum, Germany), Heiko Feldner (Cardiff University, UK) and Kevin Passmore (Cardiff University, UK)

Published:

Writing History (second edition), edited by Stefan Berger, Heiko Feldner and Kevin Passmore
Writing Medieval History, edited by Nancy F. Partner
Writing Early Modern History, edited by Garthine Walker
Writing Contemporary History, edited by Robert Gildea and Anne Simonin
Writing Gender History (second edition), Laura Lee Downs
Writing Postcolonial History, Rochona Majumdar
Writing the Holocaust, edited by Jean-Marc Dreyfus and Daniel Langton
Writing the History of Memory, edited by Stefan Berger and Bill Niven
Writing Material Culture History, edited by Anne Gerritsen and Giorgio Riello

Forthcoming:

Writing History (third edition), edited by Stefan Berger, Heiko Feldner and Kevin Passmore
Writing Queer History, Matt Cook
Writing Transnational History, Fiona Paisley

Writing the History of Crime

PAUL KNEPPER

Bloomsbury Academic
An imprint of Bloomsbury Publishing Plc

B L O O M S B U R Y
LONDON · OXFORD · NEW YORK · NEW DELHI · SYDNEY

Bloomsbury Academic

An imprint of Bloomsbury Publishing Plc

50 Bedford Square	1385 Broadway
London	New York
WC1B 3DP	NY 10018
UK	USA

www.bloomsbury.com

**BLOOMSBURY and the Diana logo are trademarks of
Bloomsbury Publishing Plc**

First published 2016

British Library Cataloguing-in-Publication Data
A catalogue record for this book is available from the British Library.

ISBN: HB: 978-1-4725-1853-8
PB: 978-1-4725-1852-1
ePDF: 978-1-4725-1854-5
ePub: 978-1-4725-1855-2

Library of Congress Cataloging-in-Publication Data
Knepper, Paul.
Writing the history of crime / Paul Knepper.
pages cm. – (Writing history)
Includes bibliographical references and index.
ISBN 978-1-4725-1853-8 (hbk) – ISBN 978-1-4725-1852-1 (pbk)
1. Crime–History. 2. Crime–Historiography. 3. Criminology–Methodology.
4. History–Methodology. I. Title.
HV6233.K64 2015
808.06'6364–dc23
2015011001

Series: Writing History

Typeset by Deanta Global Publishing Services, Chennai, India
Printed and bound in India

CONTENTS

Introduction

The arrival of the 'new social history' in the 1970s turned the writing of history inside out. The topics which had been so important to traditional history, such as great politicians and their plans, military campaigns and diplomacy, lost their privileged position, and rival topics, including the working class, women, cities and the everyday lives of ordinary people, became important. 'What was once at the center of the profession', as Gertrude Himmelfarb put it in 1987, 'is now at the periphery. What once defined history is now a footnote to history.'[1] Crime was one of the topics to emerge from the outside. Criminals joined workers, women and city dwellers as those interested in labour history, women's history and urban history redefined what it meant to be a historian.

The social history revolution was not only about topics, but also about the role of theory, sources of evidence and how to use them, and the purpose of writing about the past. Traditional history had emphasized scrutiny of documents in archives. Historians searched for materials originating in the period of interest and tried to interpret them according to what was possible at the time. The aim was to uncover what happened on the assumption that history meant a unique sequence of events. The new social history borrowed statistical techniques from economics and produced social science history. Urban historians, also keen to use quantitative techniques, carried out analyses of populations living in cities and changes in occupations, families and migration. Marxist historians insisted that in writing about the past, it was impossible to avoid politics. They pursued economic change, class divisions and collective organization. Feminist historians charged that women had been 'hidden from history'. They sought to recover the lives of women, their role in family and work, and their relationships to wider society. There were also psychohistory, which brought techniques of psychoanalysis to historical figures, and microhistory, which emphasized reconstruction of individual lives and forgotten events.

Social historians had a difficult time convincing those committed to traditional history that they were on to something worthwhile. But as it turned out, traditional history was not the primary obstacle. In the 1980s, a counter-revolution began in the form of the 'new cultural history', and an approach to the past inspired by linguistics and literary theory. Post-structuralism (or postmodernism) said that the past could only be understood in the language of discourses and narratives. Fact could not be separated from fiction. Philosopher-historians such as Michel Foucault rejected any pretence of 'science' in history. The quantitative historians were deluding themselves in their belief that numbers got historians any nearer the truth. The Marxists had got it wrong in their adherence to a one-dimensional view of exploitation and dreams of political revolution. Feminist historians championed women when they should have concentrated on the critique of gender and sexuality. Social historians in general missed the importance of culture in mistakenly committing themselves to the belief that society was a 'thing' worth studying.

All of this influenced crime history. Historians writing about violence, theft, prisons, police and other topics emerged within social and cultural history. Quantitative historians developed models and trends from court records, police files and national crime statistics. Urban historians examined the impact of urbanization and industrialization on crime; they looked into policing, delinquency and the underclass. Marxist historians pointed to inequality in the rule of law and considered crime as a primitive form of revolution. Feminist historians found women who murdered family members and stole where they shopped; they also wrote about women who founded prisons and did policing. In a sense, this book is about the generation of crime historians that emerged in the 1970s. Much of the discussion covers what they were trying to do in social history and the challenge they faced from cultural history.

But as important as the new social history has been to crime history, crime history is more than social history. Crime had been part of legal history since the Victorian era. Lawyer-historians produced multi-volume histories of law which led to crime as a topic of study. From the perspective of social history, legal history offered an unsuitable platform for crime. To make crime a suitable topic for social history, it had to be more than a legal concept, something other than what lawyers knew about. But legal history did yield a 'law and society' approach to crime, and studies of courts and procedures which have given substance to criminal justice. More recently, crime has become part of the history of empire.[2] There had been a narrow sort of colonial history, the 'old imperial history' which perceived the British Empire as separate from British history, but the 'new imperial history' insisted that one was part of the other. Of course, no other nation, not even the United States, ever had an empire on the same scale. But the message is clear enough: it is a mistake to assume that 'society' and 'nation' mean the same thing. To focus on national or more local places is to miss the larger picture; national patterns fit into hemispheric and global patterns.

Crime history is also less than social history. Along with historians, criminologists have been interested in crime. 'Historical criminology' has emerged with the new social history, but its practitioners are not really interested in the past. It is less than history in the sense that the aim is not to find out what happened, but to produce practical knowledge for understanding the problem of crime in society. Criminologists do not try to understand the past for its own sake, but the future. Historical criminology wants to create models that explain the past well enough that they can be projected into the future and guide policy decisions in the present.[3] All historians have some interest in the present. But packaging the lessons of the history for politicians in this way makes academic historians uncomfortable.

This book examines how historians have gone about writing the history of crime. It examines the formation of crime as a topic of historical study: the problems crime historians want to solve, the theories they use to understand them and the methods they use to investigate them. The discussion explores trends in historical writing that have shaped the writing about crime in the past. I offer some references to wider historiographical traditions so that leading crime historians can be located on the wider grid of historical writing. At the same time, I try to keep historical issues which have little to do with crime as such to a minimum, preferring instead to include discussion about what has been said about crime topics. The result, I hope, will have something to offer historians who want to know about crime and criminologists who want to know something about history.

Each chapter covers an approach to crime history. Roughly, this includes legal history, quantitative history, biological and psychoanalytic theories, Marxist approaches, urban history, cultural studies, gender history and colonial history. Each chapter explains the starting points, initial questions, insights and ideas, and the methodological preferences, the sources, evidence, techniques and strategies. Much of the discussion covers controversies, debates and disagreements. Writing the history of crime is a grand conversation about what to examine in the past, how to study it and why it matters. My purpose is to explain why historians disagree – how theories lead to questions, guide the methods and enable satisfying conclusions. Rather than tag crime historians according to rival theoretical commitments, I try to provide enough detail about the arguments and the evidence to show what the conflict is about.

Of course, even this will leave out a great deal. There is, in fact, too much crime to cover in a single book. For this reason, I do not offer a survey of the literature. The amount of historical scholarship on homicide, prostitution, delinquency, police, prisons and a dozen other crime-related topics would require a book on their own.[4] Not only could the topics of chapters become separate books, some already have. Shani D'Cruze and Louise A. Jackson have written a book about the historiography of women, crime and justice, and they deal only with England.[5] There is a vast amount of crime history from the United States; this pertains not only to the histories written on a national scale, but also to some gems in the national treasury contributed by state and regional history journals. And, in addition to the history published in English language, there is extensive work in French and German. I have included some of the scholarship on South America,[6] but at the end of the day, the discussion here largely concerns Europe, Britain and the United States.

A word about sources. Quite a few of the books discussed here have appeared in multiple editions. My strategy has been to cite the first edition (or the first English edition) to see what people found interesting at the time. In other words, to recall what was in those first editions that led to the second and third. To find these, I have benefitted from the resources and staff at several great libraries: the British Library, both in London and Yorkshire; the Bodleian Library at Oxford; the New York City Public Library and the Regenstein Library at the University of Chicago.

Some of the people cited here I know personally, many I only know from their work. To both friends and colleagues, I would like to say thank you for such interesting and inspiring work. My thanks to Stefan Berger, Heiko Feldner and Kevin Passmore, the editors of the *Writing History* series, for giving me a chance to contribute.

Notes

1　Gertrude Himmelfarb, *The New History and the Old: Critical Essays and Reappraisals* (Cambridge, MA: Belknap Press, 1987), 4.

2　Barry Godfrey and Graeme Dunstall, eds, *Crime and Empire 1840-1940: Criminal Justice in Local and Global Context* (Cullumpton, Devon: Willan, 2005).

3　Paul Lawrence, 'History, criminology and the "Use" of the past', *Theoretical Criminology* 16 (2012): 313–28.

4　Paul Knepper and Anja Johansen, eds, *The Oxford Handbook of the History of Crime and Criminal Justice* (New York: Oxford University Press, 2015).

5　Shani D'Cruze and Louise A. Jackson, *Women, Crime and Justice in England Since 1660* (London: Palgrave Macmillan, 2009).

6　Ricardo Salvatore, 'Criminal justice history in Latin America: Promising notes', *Crime, History and Societies* 2 (1998): 5–14.

CHAPTER ONE

Legal history

The first historians to write about crime were lawyers who saw it, not so much as a subject of history, but as an aspect of law. During the Victorian era, lawyer-historians penned multi-volume and wide-ranging histories of law which regarded crime as part of broader legal history. Later generations of historians expressed some doubts about their contribution. They criticized the legal historians for their preoccupation with the origins of legal doctrines and for being too closely guided by the interests of the contemporary legal profession. During the late twentieth century, advocates of the 'new social history' rejected the legal approach as narrow and trivial. They anchored the history of crime, not against the framework of law, but against social theory.

It would seem that to develop as an area of historical writing, crime history had to break free of legal history. The emphasis on law had to give way for a wider history of crime in society to emerge, and when crime became the property of social history, it developed rapidly and in multiple directions. Within a few decades, there were studies of crime trends, cities and crime, women and crime, crime in popular culture and colonial criminality. But it is worth asking how far to take this separation. Judging from some of the exchanges between lawyers and historians in the 1980s, it would appear that both sides would be happy to proceed without the other. To what extent, or in what ways, does crime history still need legal history?

This chapter reviews the conversation between lawyers and historians over the years. Part 1 recalls the weighty multi-volume histories of English law, such as that of Leon Radzinowicz, to see the Whig tradition at work. Part 2 examines the 'internal' approach to legal history pursued by John Langbein. Part 3 considers the law in society perspective championed by Lawrence Friedman and Part 4, the law and social theory perspective initiated by E. P. Thompson, Douglas Hay and the British Marxists. Part 5 introduces the law and culture perspective and particularly the influence of Carlo Ginzburg and microhistory.

Whigs and lawyers

Writing the history of crime as a specialization within the study of law has a long provenance. In 1753, William Blackstone began offering a course of lectures at Oxford that became his *Commentaries on the Law of England*. No author's copy of the manuscript has survived, but the structure of the book follows the lectures. Although the lectures were intended to teach about the law, he suggested a historical approach that had not been seriously undertaken before. History supplied the raw material from which to construct the principles of law.[1] For this, Blackstone has been regarded as the founder of legal history.

The *Commentaries* present a theory of natural law connected with the process of history. Blackstone founded this on two contradictory positions. First, he offered the idea of primitivism. The laws of nature amounted to the rules which human beings were free to disobey, so it was important to study them to make the world more like its ideal. Primitivism represented the original state of human nature, which had embodied goodness, and to recover the past was to glimpse the lost innocence of humanity. Since then, humanity had degenerated, which brought about the rise and fall of civilizations. Second, he presented the idea of providence. Humans were ultimately subject to the laws of God, and no action could prevent humanity from reaching its final destination. History represented the movement forward, inevitable progress towards the preordained end of the world. Blackstone fitted these two dissonant themes together into an argument for keeping English law as it was, which he hoped, would serve as a warning against rash attempts to improve it. Contemporary institutions, he believed, represented the inevitable culmination of 'the accumulated wisdom of the ages'.[2]

If Blackstone planted the seed of the Whig view of the past, the Victorian lawyers who wrote legal history cultivated it to full flower. The technological, economic and social changes of the nineteenth century fascinated and frightened the Victorians, and they imposed the idea of progress on the past to reassure themselves about the future. The Whig view of history (the name that Herbert Butterfield would give to it) began with the assumption that the present state of society represented the inevitable outcome of past trends. Whig historians searched the past for the pattern of development behind the success of modern England; some identified stages of progress, others a particular feature responsible for success, such as geography.[3] The Victorian lawyers who produced multi-volume histories equated England's legal heritage with the advance of civilization, and laying down this history in a comprehensive manner confirmed its top position among the great empires. It was history for lawyers, a celebration of the present, history as a preface to the success story of English law.

A History of the Criminal Law of England (1883), by Sir James Fitzjames Stephen, revealed this approach. Stephen was a high court judge for whom writing history was leisure. Strange though it seems, he produced his nearly 1,500 pages as a diversion from the strain of the bench. In three volumes, he covered the history of criminal law from the thirteenth century to the nineteenth century: the organization of courts and their jurisdiction, judicial proceedings and rules of evidence and procedure, along with sections on legal punishments, mental illness and foreign legal practices.[4] The book, Stephen wrote in his preface, had turned out longer and more elaborate than he planned. The difficult part was to find a way to present a coherent account of scattered fragments. There was no continuous set of changes that could be identified in the course of the criminal law as a whole; rather, each part came together at a various speeds at particular places. He made sense of it by portraying a gradual progression of legal traditions built up over the centuries. He remarked at 'how the crude, imperfect definitions of the thirteenth century were gradually moulded into the most complete and comprehensive body of criminal law in the world'.[5]

The Whig view involved celebration, but there was a nervousness as well. Britain's expanding empire confirmed the advance of civilization, but crowded cities, political strife and economic slumps suggested that things could go wrong. So the Whig view included a look for evidence of decline, activities that would indicate society had taken the wrong road, and crime was one of the clearest signposts. Luke Owen Pike, a London barrister interested in history, realized this in the 1870s. At first glance, his two-volume *A History of Crime in England* (1876) seems to be the work of an antiquarian, not a historian. He offered a wide-ranging discussion of legal changes, moral beliefs and social customs from the period of the Roman invasion to the reign of Queen Victoria. His commentary wanders from the Star Chamber to the poor law; treason, drunkenness and transportation; the origins of police; and introduction of science in fighting crime. But Pike revealed the method behind his meandering when he explained that while other historians had offered 'histories of civilization', he was the first to offer the reverse.[6]

The first paragraph of the first volume of Pike's history begins with a question: 'What is crime?' He did not furnish an answer, although he suggested that 'prevailing sentiments' were important. Crimes could not be exhibited in their true light without 'some knowledge of the surrounding social conditions'.[7] So, in addition to material from statutes, records of trials, parliamentary papers and review articles, he included discussion of population growth and the expansion of wealth – the social and political effects of increasing commerce. By the end of the second volume, he was ready: crime could be defined only by criminal law. 'Crime, then – the crime with which the historian is concerned – is that which the law declares to be a crime.'[8] In other words, crime gradually came into existence only with the slow march of civilization itself, from a code of conduct as it developed from ancient to modern Britain. The history of crime could not have been written at an earlier period, or in another place, because it was only in the present period of English history that the necessary legal foundation had been built to identify and measure it as an aspect of society.

Although William Holdsworth did not begin his seventeen-volume *History of English Law* until 1903, he was more Victorian than Stephen or Pike in his thinking about the past. Holdsworth studied at Oxford and taught at University College London before returning to Oxford in 1922 to take up the Vinerian chair (that had been held by Blackstone). Holdsworth used present legal categories as his framework for organizing legal developments from the medieval period. If he had presented the law as it looked to a lawyer prior to the eighteenth century, it would have resulted in an unsystematic, even random, arrangement. But because Holdsworth wrote his history for lawyers in his own time, he used subject headings of English common law from the twentieth century. He described his approach as 'the professional tradition of English legal history', an approach that regarded legal history as a means for distilling legal principles. Searching the past revealed ancient sources of the law, that when appreciated by lawyers as such, could reveal correct principles to apply to individual cases in the present.[9] The professional approach, Daniel J. Boorstin pointed out, was less historical investigation than 'legal embryology', a search for rudimentary forms of the fully formed system. 'The present becomes the culmination of all the past, and the present forms of institutions seem to be their inevitable forms. The past is thus closed to the infinite possibilities of history.'[10]

While Holdsworth was still at work, Leon Radzinowicz started his five-volume English legal history. Radzinowicz, a Polish émigré, became the first Wolfson professor of criminology at Cambridge in the 1930s. To write this history, he consulted some 1,250 reports of commissions of inquiry, 3,000 accounts and papers, 800 annual reports and 1,100 volumes of parliamentary debates. He covered 300 years, from the eighteenth century to the early twentieth century. *A History of English Criminal Law and its Administration from 1750* (1948) examined the senténce of death, from the extension of capital statutes in the 1750s, to the 1780s when some members of Parliament began to voice objections. Radzinowicz took the story forward with four more volumes, the last of which, co-authored with Roger Hood, covered Victorian and Edwardian criminal justice policy. Radzinowicz and Hood wrote 800 pages of annotated text built up from primary sources, and in the process brought many sources, published and unpublished, to the attention of historians.[11]

Radzinowicz found the motivation for his labour in the belief that it was essential to the future. He aimed to 'look upon criminal law as an instrument of criminal policy' and to regard the criminal law as a 'historical category evolving within the social, political and moral context of society'.[12] At the start of his project, he explained that English law occupied the pinnacle of an enlightened, rational approach, and the nation should take pride in its basic principles and practical achievements. A detailed and comprehensive study would demonstrate what England had achieved. Legal reform could not be adequately planned, and mistakes were likely to be made, unless this legacy was taken into account. Reforms made at the spur of the moment, in response to sensational cases or to further political objectives, could reverse progress that had taken centuries to put into place.[13] To maintain a proper perspective, it was necessary to understand how the main features had been founded on the reform movement that began in the eighteenth century, and to pay close attention to changes in the second half of the nineteenth century, when the essential structure had been established. Radzinowicz became the king of Whig history when he stated in his preface to volume 1: 'Lord Macaulay's generalisation that the history of England is the history of progress is as true of the criminal law of this country as of other social institutions of which it is part.'[14]

Geoffrey Elton so disliked the view of legal history Radzinowicz stood for that he did not want to be known as a legal historian. Elton held a chair at Cambridge in English Constitutional History, and he certainly contributed to legal history. He wrote about the early modern period in England, particularly Parliament, but also about courts, procedures and doctrines. But as far as he was concerned, historians trained in law suffered from disturbing tendencies: a narrow focus on technical details, reliance on legal documents as if they were privileged sources and portrayal of law as divorced from political and social contexts.[15] The lawyer's view of history encouraged a preoccupation with the present and jeopardized any meaningful study of the past. As Elton put it, the lawyers writing legal history gave the impression that the purpose of historical inquiry was to explain the present rather than the past. They read the records of the past in the light of modern doctrine, which guaranteed that they missed any historical context. In doing so, they had fallen into the Whig interpretation of history, that is, of regarding the past as a story of progress leading to the present.[16]

Elton is drawing on historicism, the view of historical writing established in Germany by Leopold von Ranke. He insisted that the past should only be understood in the context of time, place and circumstance, and that circumstances unfolded in a chronological manner. Historians should proceed by scrutiny of primary documents to learn what people at the time thought about what was going on. Through a reconstruction of events, the great forces which have shaped history would become apparent. One of the implications of this was a belief that time is a river. History flowed once in the way it had; it does not repeat itself in a series or cycle predictable by philosophy. Another implication is that historians will find the course history has taken through traces left in documents. Historical research *is* archival research.[17]

Internal legal history

The five volumes of Radzinowicz on English law represent what Robert Gordon referred to in 1975 as 'internal' legal history. It is an approach that regards the law as the story of legal rules, principles and doctrines. The sources are primarily legal materials: statutes, decided cases, and the like, and the sources reveal the work of legal minds, judges and lawyers writing about statues and cases. Written by historians trained as lawyers, this work appeals primarily to other lawyers. This approach differs from 'external' legal history which is the history of law in practice, of legal institutions and their work in society rather than legal rules and the court environment. External history seeks to explain legal practices, doctrines and institutions in relation to wider change in society. Gordon borrowed these terms from the history of science. The internal history of science regards scientific knowledge as cumulative, built up from discoveries, so that the present understanding amounts to the most accurate or true understanding. The external view tries to understand the political, economic, cultural and other influences on the pursuit of scientific research, acceptance of findings and understanding of 'scientific truth'.[18]

'Running throughout this work', Martin Wiener explains of volume 5 of Radzinowicz's history, 'is an underlying framework of "progress," as defined by modern professional opinion, and a complementary focus on formal policy formation and application, leaving blurred the social and psychic fabric within which policy is embedded and from which it derives its meaning.'[19] The book seems to be intended to serve not only as a contribution to modern British history but as a guide for present-day policymakers as to how their predecessors handled similar problems. The trouble here, Wiener explains, is that penal policy is dealt with in a self-contained and self-explicable sphere whose history can be accessed by working backward from later twentieth-century professional perspectives. Radzinowicz and Hood 'pass over the wider instrumental and symbolic roles of criminal policy' and avoid what would otherwise 'take them into deeper waters of politics, social relations and culture'.[20]

John Langbein succeeded Radzinowicz as the foremost practitioner of the internal view of English legal history. Langbein, professor of law at the University of Chicago, has written about the origins of the adversarial system, the distinguishing feature of Anglo-American criminal court procedure. The adversary system was initially devised in the late seventeenth century as a special procedure for cases of treason, intended to compensate for special hazards such as proceedings imposed on defendants. From the late seventeenth century to the mid-eighteenth century, lawyers for prosecution and defence had minor roles in court proceedings. In the early eighteenth century, judges began to allow the defendant to have the assistance of counsel for examining and cross-examining witnesses. Gradually, the defence counsel became more common, and by the late eighteenth century, lawyers came to dominate the felony trial. Procedures devised for protecting aristocrats in special cases extended to common people accused of stealing sheep or breaking into a shop.[21] In writing about courts, Langbein made a substantial contribution to criminal justice history. Much of the work that can be defined as criminal justice history has concerned police and prisons, and this was especially true when Langbein began.

Nevertheless, in taking the internal view, Langbein drew fire from the advocates of social history. Douglas Hay criticized the historical portrayal of law in society as the achievement of a small clique of remarkable individuals trained in law.[22] Any history which did not inquire into the dynamics behind the legal process led to hasty and erroneous generalizations, and to the conclusion that little had changed over the centuries. Legal history assigned too much weight to the attitudes and opinion of a few legislators, judges and lawyers from previous centuries. The social history approach aimed to uncover popular beliefs as well as these professional views, to explain the beliefs not only of legislators, judges and lawyers but also of victims of crime, prosecutors, criminals, potential criminals, the public, spectators at executions and children who acquired legal folklore through oral tradition. There could be no privileged views, no hierarchy of sources on which to examine the relationship between law and crime.[23]

Hay's indictment of 'history for lawyers' contained five counts. (1) Moralism: the assumption that state law reflects a moral consensus, roughly the same across all social classes. (2) Presentism: working from present concerns to past origins, a formula for false analogies and mistaken conclusions. (3) Identity: the idea that legal behaviour has legal causes, a habit of thought that tends to become self-reinforcing. (4) Rationalism: the idea that legal judgements derive from a narrow range of prescribed or authorized sources, which does not allow for the intrusion of unexamined assumptions, derived from class, gender and ethnicity. (5) False dichotomies: framing questions of crime in relation to law, such as, did the criminal law express the interest of elites or common people? The issue is framed as an either/or when it would be both.[24]

Hay's critique is so comprehensive that it is difficult to see the value of the internal view. But Langbein built up his picture of the adversary trial from a source known as the *Sessions Papers*, and in thinking about this, we can see the importance of legal knowledge in writing crime history. The *Sessions Papers*, or *Old Bailey Proceedings* as they are also known, provide accounts of the trials at the Old Bailey, the court with jurisdiction over cases of serious crime in London. The first of these appeared in the 1670s and were published until 1913, although the content and format changed considerably. When first published, they amounted to journalistic pamphlets featuring sex, violence and intrigue for the public, but later in the eighteenth century, they received the sponsorship of the City of London and became more of an official source of the court's business. Langbein recalled having seen these papers for the first time at the Bodleian Law Library where he had gone looking for other materials.[25]

Since Langbein's work appeared, the *Sessions Papers* have become readily available. Robert Shoemaker and Timothy Hitchcock converted them to digital form in 2003 through their Old Bailey Proceedings Online project. They received funding to convert over 1,000 published editions of the *Sessions Papers* into digital images that could be accessed electronically. At first, the proceedings extended from 1674 to 1834, and then, following release of further funding in 2005, this was extended to the period from 1834 to 1913. The material can be searched in different ways: by name, crime type, punishment, crime location, date, and defendant and victim occupations.[26] The digitization of the *Old Bailey Proceedings* has made it remarkably easy to carry out research. This is a valuable project and a positive good. But, as Shoemaker and Hitchcock are well aware, the most accessible sources are not necessarily the best sources. They caution against reliance on the digital source 'at the expense of possibly richer sources which are not so easily accessible'.[27]

The Old Bailey Proceedings Online website can generate a wealth of information for a social analysis of crime because most of the cases concern the lives of ordinary people. But making the most of any social analysis of legal records requires an understanding of the legal institution and its procedures that generated them. To draw reasonable conclusions from the Old Bailey Proceedings Online, it is necessary to have some knowledge of the court and its organization. The court as an agency of criminal justice changes from 1674 to 1913. The roles of victim, of defence lawyers, of evidence – the sorts of topics presented by Langbein – are very relevant. External changes took place in London from the late seventeenth century to the early nineteenth century, but so too internal changes in the administration of criminal justice. Historians of crime have been interested in the origins of police and prisons, in why criminal justice emerged when it did. But before taking on the 'why', it is necessary to have a grasp of the 'what'.

Charles Donahue insists that what legal historians did in the past is no longer practised today. It *was* possible to talk about legal history and social history as separate forms, as the difference between an internal view and an external view of the law. But neither can proceed without the other. Pure external or pure internal are both likely to be 'bad history' or the very least, incomplete history. Most lawyers, Donahue says, have by now given up the idea that the law is autonomous, but recognize that legal specialization in periods of wider history is 'semi-autonomous'. Historians of the law, whether trained in law or history, are interested in the interaction between law, politics and culture. The biggest difference is the starting point. Those trained as lawyers start 'inside the box' and move outward. Those trained as historians start with a wider view of society and seek to locate the law within it. But any historian who tries to stay 'outside the box' makes a mistake, because what happens inside affects the outside.[28]

Law and society

The external view of legal history originated in American law schools in the early decades of the twentieth century. Roscoe Pound, head of Harvard Law School, advocated a philosophy of law founded on knowledge from economics, sociology and political science. His 'sociological jurisprudence' maintained that law was not a mental process but a concrete phenomenon that included institutions of government, their actual operation and their effects. After the war, legal scholars pushed for an expansion of the scientific approach, to include not only the social sciences, but behavioural sciences, such as psychology, as well. Karl Llewellyn and Jerome Frank began the 'realist movement' which urged the importance of understanding the personality of the judge as the means of analysing decisions. Pound, Llewellyn and Frank shared a belief that judicial decision-making could be improved by avoiding artificial legal logic and turning instead to empirical studies of law in society. They equated science with progress and advocated social planning based on scientific expertise. They urged research into the actual operation of agencies of government and how their activities interacted with social and psychological contexts.[29]

Jerome Hall, professor of law at Indiana University, brought sociological jurisprudence to the history of crime. In *Theft, Law and Society* (1935), he stated that it was of no use to recall a legal concept without examining how this language entered the law. Legal history represented the aggregate of events, and to understand how any law came about, it was necessary to identify the specific events that led up to it. There were two general categories of historical legal analysis: (1) Legal changes occurring over a long period, which made it possible to separate legal from social influences on lawmaking and (2) legal changes over a short period, in which it was easier to examine the institutions as a combination of social and legal factors. As Hall explained, 'In each development of the law, the particular step taken was a result of forces determined largely by social and economic conditions, the existing sanctions, the whole body of precedent, and the established judicial techniques.'[30] To write a history of theft, it was necessary to look at England during the period of the Industrial Revolution because it was here that almost the entire law of theft was written. But in looking at legal change in this period, he found many references to an event that took place three centuries earlier.

The event was the 'Carrier's Case', decided by the Star Chamber in 1473. The case involved a defendant who had been hired to carry some bales to the port of Southampton who, instead of taking them to Southampton, took them to another place, broke them open and took the contents. The legal dilemma arose because larceny assumed trespass: the carrier could not have stolen bales of which he had lawful possession. The economic dilemma was that secure transportation was a requirement of the commercial economy. In the end, the judges settled for some legal legerdemain. To avoid jeopardizing the commercial interests at stake, they decided that the carrier had possession of the bales, not the contents, and declared the event as a theft. The carrier trespassed the moment he broke open the bales. Hall was well aware of the wider social history surrounding the law of theft. He audited the political and economic conditions leading to the judges' decision, drawing not only legal materials, parliamentary debates, committee reports and comments of philosophers, but also sources of social and economic history. Hall provided an interesting perspective because he emphasized that the source of legal change – doctrine, practice, etc. – was not found within the law itself.

James Willard Hurst did not write about crime or criminal justice as such but had an influence on the writing of crime history because one of his students, Lawrence M. Friedman, did. In the 1950s and 1960s, Hurst established the 'Wisconsin School' of American legal history. He wrote about the history of lawmaking agencies, not only courts, but executives, administrative agencies and the bar. He regarded governmental activity, the work of agencies, as 'law', essentially a term of convenience without any boundaries. He wanted to find out why the law had permitted the timber industry to saw thirty million acres of forest into exhaustion. This coincided with the Wisconsin idea that social science research should lead to social reform through legislation. The answer had to do with social and cultural traditions, short-term vision of lawmakers, and fragmentation of enforcement agencies. Only a small portion of Hurst's detail concerned the doctrine and procedure that made up traditional, internal legal history.[31]

Friedman brought Hurst to the history of criminal justice. 'I have surrendered myself wholeheartedly to some of the central insights of social science,' Friedman declared at the start of *A History of American Law* (1973).[32] He offered a wide-ranging history of law in American history from 1776 to 1900, including chapters on crime and punishment. The law was 'not a kingdom unto itself' or the 'province of lawyers alone', but a 'mirror of society'. The legal system worked like 'a blind insensate machine' that did the 'bidding of those whose hands are on the controls'.[33] Nothing about it was autonomous; everything was moulded by the economy and politics. In other words, there is no difference between the pace of legal change and social change. Legal practices and institutions are not really conservative institutions, reluctant to change, resistant to outside forces. Rather, lawyers have synchronized their watches with those in business, politics and the press. 'The strongest ingredient in American law, at any given time, is the present: current emotions, real economic interests, and concrete political groups.'[34]

'This is a *social* history of crime and punishment', Friedman says at the start of his popular history of American criminal justice (italics as in the original), 'this is not a history of "criminal law" as lawyers would conceive of it.'[35] Friedman chronicled developments in criminal justice from the Salem witchcraft trials to the surge in violent crime in the decades after the Second World War. He said that the shape of the system did not follow from a philosophical or intellectual tradition, but from 'social *structure*' and 'social *norms*' that interacted with the legal context. The story of crime and punishment over four centuries is a story of changes in culture, changes in the structure of society, and changes in the economic, technological and social orders. And it is a story told without a political message. 'I have tried to tell an honest story. It would be silly to claim total success. Bias is inevitable.'[36] Recalling the history of criminal justice afforded the ability to suggest some solutions to the problem of crime. Crime had 'skyrocketed' in the second half of the twentieth century, and a look at criminal justice could suggest why the United States was such a violent society. One possible answer was a mismatch between crime and criminal justice: crime results from broad social and cultural forces, and American criminal justice was a matter of local politics.

Friedman pioneered a kind of legal history that avoided the celebrated cases in the law library for the records of ordinary people in criminal courts found 'in the cellar'. Along with Robert Percival, Friedman gathered statistics of crime from courthouse, prison and police records for Alameda County, California. They built a statistical model of the county's criminal justice system from 1870 to 1910.[37] The empirical study yielded insight into plea bargaining. Plea bargaining was not an organizational solution to a twentieth-century problem. The evidence showed that it was not a recent development, but had occurred since 1880. 'This fact alone', Friedman concluded, 'makes it hard to attribute the practice to crowded dockets of modern cities.'[38] Rather, it was connected with structural and social changes in criminal justice, particularly, the development of professional police and prosecutors. Friedman took the law and society view as far as it could be taken – perhaps too far. Attributing all legal change to social forces reduces law to an artefact of society. Jim Phillips insists that the law has been resistant to outside pressures, and further, that legal innovation represents a source of social change. The law has 'relative autonomy' from social, economic and political influences. Legal institutions can resist change because the law has a life and a logic of its own.[39]

The external approach to legal history strives to discuss the law in practice, the relationship between legal institutions and social, economic and political trends rather than development of legal rules, doctrines and procedures. Allen Steinberg's examination of private prosecution in Philadelphia provides a sense of what we are missing in taking the institutional approach. At the beginning of the nineteenth century, Philadelphia's courts produced a system of prosecution that was 'popular, particularistic, and extremely locally-based'. It was also vulnerable to exploitation and corruption. Steinberg provides a window into the time when the United States was governed locally, before reformers, professionals and experts built urban government and brought in the modern state. He elaborates on themes in Langbein, the gradual disempowerment of the average citizen and the way the new system of state prosecution grew out of the old-world of private prosecution. But he is much more concerned with the 'relationship between law and popular life' and the way in which a legal culture responded to official hostility and massive social change.[40]

Robert Ireland looked at twelve cases of women murderers in the nineteenth-century United States. These were cases involving the 'unwritten law' which held that it was permissible to kill male perpetrators of sexual violence against women. Juries believed that an outraged husband, father or brother had the moral right to kill the man who took sexual advantage of his wife, daughter or sister. Juries were prepared to extend this right to women who killed to avenge sexual dishonour. But they did so more reluctantly and less consistently. In cases involving female avengers, he found that juries did not always forgive the women, and when they did, they did so in ways that activated stereotypes of women as emotional beings. They regarded women as delicate souls prone to madness.[41] Although Americans had always placed a premium on sexual virtue, they valued it even more highly in the nineteenth century than at any other time in history. Women were regarded as the keystone of the family, and the family was the foundation of society. Judging from all the homicide trials involving the 'unwritten law', in cases of men and women on trial, Ireland concluded that forgiveness had as much to do with preserving the honour of men as with women. The doctrine encompassed many myths and hypocrisies of the era, including the double standard of sexual conduct.[42]

As Elizabeth Dale points out, the institutional view of legal history regards popular justice as the exception. The formal workings of criminal law were shaped by popular forces that functioned outside of courts and the law. Popular justice refers to an act undertaken to judge or punish another's act. It may include violence by groups, such as vigilantes and mobs, or individuals, such as crime of passion. It includes actions that are not violent, such as malicious gossip, shaming and shunning, but will involve non-state actors. Dale insists that popular justice should not be regarded as the exception, but a regular part of the legal history, and historians need to understand what such actions tell us about the meaning of justice and informal responses to conflict. The study of popular justice includes ways in which individuals and groups influenced formal criminal justice. In her study of 150 years of criminal justice in the United States from 1789 to 1939, she examines how criminal justice emerged in different states. In the period from 1789 to 1839, it was decentralized, reliant on local community ideas and under popular control. Over the next forty years, the states wrested control, making criminal justice more formal and less responsive to community norms. By 1930, the national paradigm emerged.[43]

Law and social theory

Douglas Hay's critique of legal history grew out of the theoretical history centred around Edward Thompson at Warwick University in the 1970s. The 'Warwick School' drew on the theory of Marx and his critique of capitalist society (Chapter 4). They examined the history of law and crime, not to uncover the origins of present institutions, but to recover class relations in the past, the relationship between aristocrats and the working class. The British Marxists could not accept historicism because it denied patterns, comparison and generalizations. Historicism denied historians the ability to talk about anything other than the case at hand, particularly the present. *Whigs and Hunters*, by Thompson, and *Albion's Fatal Tree*, by Hay and others, replaced law as a framework for the history of crime with that of social theory.[44]

The first chapter of *Albion's Fatal Tree* – Douglas Hay's essay, 'Property, Authority and the Criminal Law' – examined the place of capital statutes in eighteenth-century justice. Between 1688 and 1820, the number of capital offences swelled from 50 to 200, although relative to earlier periods, few people were actually hanged. So why pass so many capital sentences and only execute a few people? This could be seen as a process that did not live up to expectations, a system that did not function as planned. But Hay turned the question around: not carrying out sentences was the point of the system. He argued that the law had much to offer the ruling class, a small elite of gentry, aristocracy and merchants. They used it to maintain the status quo, as a hedge against threats to their privileged position. Not only did they leave it unchanged, they added to the inventory of unenforced capital statutes. They resisted the idea of a regular police force and preferred to rely on the terror of the law. Hay examined how the criminal policy, based on terror, worked, and what it says about the rule of law. For rulers as much concerned with protecting their authority as with protecting their property, courtroom procedures involved spectacle. They were careful to preserve the appearance that the law in England did not allow even the wealthiest defendants to avoid death. In a society divided by rich and poor, the occasional execution of a wealthy villain or victory of a cottager in the courts made a sharp impression. In extending mercy and exercising discretion, English courts sought to reinforce the authority of law. The 'criminal law, more than any other social institution', Hay wrote, 'made it possible to govern eighteenth century England without a police force and a large army. The ideology of the law was crucial in sustaining the hegemony of English ruling class.'[45]

Hay's argument here initiated the study of mercy or discretion in the law. Carolyn Strange brought together a collection of essays concerning the discretionary use of power: the substitution of transportation to Australia for capital punishment, the demise of corporal punishment in England, the use of pardons in Canada and the politics of discretion in Australia and Canada. The study of discretion requires an understanding of the motivations and actions of decision-makers rather than the rationale and institutions set up to enforce rules. Legal doctrines and institutions are important, but only with reference to an understanding of culture and politics. As Strange points out in her introduction, the full array of potential criminal sanctions has never been carried out, not even in periods known for the 'bloody code'. Despite the implications of this for understanding what the criminal law actually means, historians have overlooked this, partly as a matter of evidence: it is easier to find materials about hangings than to document practices that led to commutation. But this is also a matter of commitments: historians of criminal justice seem more interested in grasping the power invested in executions, torture and punishment than that of mercy, forgiveness and compassion.[46]

Jim Phillips examined the operation of the royal pardon in Nova Scotia during the late eighteenth century. Almost two-thirds of those sentenced to death for property offences in this period were spared. He points out that so long as the death sentence dominated the substantive law of crimes and punishments, pardon was essential to its administration. Part of the story is why so many were spared, but also, why a few were allowed to hang. He looked into the cases of 121 men and women sentenced to die between 1749 and 1815. The answer affords a glimpse into the process by which pardons were granted, about the aspects of authority revealed in that process and why pardons were given to most, but not all, property offenders. The answer, he found, had to do with institutional and individual aspects of the proceedings, factors both internal and external to the legal system. To reach his decision, the governor considered the facts of the crime, assessed the character of the accused, and weighed the need for deterrence and the benefit of displaying mercy. The Canadian system appeared to operate along the same lines as the English one: the system 'involved socially and politically significant decisions, not merely formal legal ones'.[47]

The most extensive examination of discretion in eighteenth-century England has been completed by Peter King. His study concerned property crime and the way it was dealt with, defined and perceived; it was based on a detailed analysis of Essex court records.[48] He focused on the period between 1740 and 1820, before repeal of the 'bloody code' and establishment of professional police. It was the high tide of discretionary justice. King charted the journeys of the accused through the proceedings at each decisive point: examining the circumstances in which decisions were made, the social status of decision-makers, the range of choices available to them and the extent to which their decisions were based on formal legal rulings or by informal pressures that the accused and family could bring to bear. He considered the stages on the journey of the accused: pretrial negotiations and commitment proceedings; trial, courtroom proceedings and verdicts; sentencing and pardons; and the death sentence and gallows. King agreed with Hay about the importance of the law in practice but could not accept the emphasis on class. The elite never had the power to control the legal process in the way Hay claimed that it did. The law was not a tool of the rich to use against the poor, but an 'arena of struggle, negotiation, and accommodation' in which the social relations of the eighteenth century were worked out.[49]

Hay wanted to replace law as a framework for crime history with social theory derived from Marx. As a way of understanding the past, the law was not fit for purpose, because the legal definition of crime did not correspond to the attitudes of the majority of the population. English society in the eighteenth century was sharply divided between a small elite of wealthy landowners and everyone else, otherwise known as the labouring poor. The elite had the power to enact laws criminalizing even trivial threats to their position, such as poaching and smuggling, but the majority of people regarded these activities as perfectly legitimate. Within certain communities, other offences, such as wrecking and coining, were legitimate, and at least for some people at particular moments, even sheep-stealing was alright. Historians should not accept legal categories of crime, because these are elite conceptions only, but should pursue the sociological view of crime as a label applied to certain behaviour. It was a mistake to assume that theft was the work of isolated individuals and that there was a consensus about what it meant. To learn about 'ordinary crime', it was necessary to set aside the law.[50]

Elton advised against moving too far away from a historical understanding of law. He was well aware of the need to avoid reifying legal categories. He pointed out that even after the sixteenth century, and as late as the eighteenth century, crime lacked a precise legal meaning. Crime can be seen in this time only as an 'artificial construct', a compound of 'diverse and separate' breaches of the law. The first category of legal offences, the real crimes, comprised treasons and felonies, punishable by death. These included murder, arson and forms of theft, such as appropriating the cargo from a shipwreck. There is also a series of illicit acts, which might be called misdemeanours, such as beatings, cheating and nuisances.[51] It is possible, Elton admits, to treat crime as a social phenomenon rather than a legal phenomenon. This turns crime into a tool for analysing behaviour and offers opportunities for studying social disapproval. But it has the disadvantage of using a category unfamiliar to the people studied. It introduces an anachronistic, ahistorical conception of crime. He proposed a two-step thought experiment. (1) Set aside modern understandings of crime as anti-social activity or social deviance in order to identify legal understandings, or the absence of them, within the historical time of interest. (2) Reintroduce modern concepts in order to learn what criminal activities the strictly legal analysis has left out. Comparing legal categories with social categories will bring clarity to the parameters of the inquiry.[52]

Additional testimony concerning the value of legal definitions in crime history comes from historians working in England and the Netherlands.

James Sharpe has found it useful in his work on early modern England to regard 'crime as illegal behaviour which, if detected and prosecuted, led to a criminal charge answerable in a court of law, and carrying certain penalties'.[53] But he rejects Elton's claim that any legal definition comes close to expressing real crime in the past. While serious crime might appear more real, he advises against narrowing the subject to offences of treason and felony. In modern British society, and others, petty crime was more common, typical and entitled to be known as real crime. In his own book about crime in England from 1550 to 1750, he was determined 'to come to grips with past definitions and to leave the modern layman's definition of "real crime" as far away as possible'.[54] Serious crime merits attention, but trends in less serious crime are revealing. 'Our aim when studying crime in the past, therefore, must be to take as wide a view of the phenomenon as possible.'[55]

Pieter Spierenburg appreciates the legal definition as well. 'There is not a monolithic social unit called "crime," the volume of which and the reactions to which can simply be ascertained.'[56] Crime presupposes the existence of an authority, the State, which is interested in identifying and punishing offences, and because of this, he says that the history of crime properly begins in the sixteenth century. Investigation of crime in the past, through the study of court records, yields an 'institutional' or 'operational' definition, formed partly by accident, and subject to change. Any other definition risks anachronism and the application of an anti-historical value judgement. Nevertheless, the institutional/operational definition has limitations. It conflicts with the intuitive view that in talking about crime, we are talking about actions that involve some measure of seriousness. There should be a distinction between crime in the sense of what the State prosecuted, and 'real crime', that is to say actions that people saw as wrong which the law did not. Further, it makes comparative research particularly challenging. Finding equivalent legal terms in French, German and other European languages is difficult. The English word *crime* is novel in its ability to refer to both a specific individual act and a general social activity.[57]

Law and culture

The advantage of a term like 'external' legal history, Gordon said, is that unlike 'law and society', it included cultural history.[58] Cultural history emphasizes lived experience and interpretations of this experience by the actors themselves. The cultural approach to legal history emphasizes law as a linguistic activity invested with meaning. Working from legal records, the historian's task is to uncover this meaning. Cultural histories of law became increasingly common from the 1980s.

Michael Hindus produced a comparative history of sanctions in Massachusetts and South Carolina from 1767 to 1878 that paid attention to legal culture. 'It would be futile to study crime', he said, 'without knowing something about the legal tradition and legal culture of the locality and of the social tensions that produce both crime and the means of repressing and suppressing it.'[59] The legal systems of these two states originated in a common English legal tradition; both were common law jurisdictions committed to ideals of universal application, procedural rights and neutral judges. But they functioned in different social and demographic contexts; Massachusetts became urban and industrial, and South Carolina developed the plantation system. It would be easy to characterize Massachusetts as an example of a modern, professional system and South Carolina as backward and amateurish. But Hindus saw different systems of authority shaped by differences in legal culture, economic needs and slavery. Massachusetts bolstered formal, bureaucratic legal authority by strengthening courts, establishing police and curtailing extra-legal violence. South Carolina developed an alternative to legal authority that celebrated the personal and individualistic. Plantation owners mocked courtroom procedures, resorted to duelling to settle quarrels, encouraged vigilante organizations and generally expected citizens to respond to conflict without accessing the law.

Martin Wiener wrote a cultural history of criminal policy in England during the Victorian era and Edwardian period.[60] He developed a variety of sources, including novels and newspapers as well as parliamentary proceedings and legal texts, to show how the ideas that drive criminal policy are reflections of, and contributions to, wider cultural understandings. He proposed that in the decades after 1820, policymakers worried about the loss of control. 'Images of the criminal reflected rising anxieties about impulses and will out of control; crime was a central metaphor of disorder and loss of control in all spheres of life.'[61] By the late 1900s, this had changed. Policymakers of the Edwardian era recognized the limitations of a programme of control and increasingly invested their energies into new ways of enabling themselves. They felt less confident about their role, less capable of effecting control. At the same time, they saw criminal offenders as less threatening and less responsible for their behaviour, and turned to a new approach to the treatment of criminality. Wiener acknowledged that he could have offered more. His strategy did not incorporate popular understandings – the cultural universe is far too vast for this, he said – nor did it capture the arguments between institutions – he decided to concentrate on consensus rather than conflict. And, from the point of view of understanding the law in relation to crime, he also offered less. Wiener had little to say about what was happening at the level of the doctrine of the criminal law itself, so we learn only a little about the judicial interpretation of criminal law.[62]

There is a precedent for the study of crime in relation to law and culture in the work of German legal scholar Gustav Radbruch in the sense that he was one of the first to do this. As an academic lawyer before the First World War, he earned a reputation as a legal theorist and served as Minister of Justice during the early years of the Weimar Republic. When the Nazis took over in 1933, he was deemed 'politically unreliable' and dismissed from his professorship at Heidelberg. During the war, he began a book on the history of crime. It offered a novel approach because it pursued a cultural history of crime and not a history of criminal law. For Radbruch, legal history was a form of cultural history. However, *Geschichte des Verbrechens: Versuch einer historischen Kriminologie* (roughly, 'History of Crime: An Attempt at Historical Criminology') was not published until 1951, after Radbruch's death, and was neglected by German legal historians, who took more interest in civil law. It has not been available in English and is virtually unknown outside Germany.[63]

The work of the Italians in the 1970s who used legal records to revive forgotten activities, involving a single event, village or individual, has been more influential. The first examples of Italian microhistory appeared in a series of books by a Turin publisher and the journal *Quaderni Storici*. It was this same intellectual environment that led to Umberto Eco's best-selling novel of historical crime fiction, *The Name of the Rose*. The leading figure has been Carlo Ginzburg, a founding editor of the *microstorie* series. He wrote about the lives of people living in sixteenth-century Rome and Bologna, and he treated them as if they were citizens of another country. Through the intense scrutiny of a few legal documents, especially records of interrogations, he recovered interactions between elite culture and popular culture.[64] Fernand Braudel used the word *microstorie*, originally in a derogatory way, as a synonym for the history of events, which he dismissed as far less significant than the *longue durée*. But Ginzburg gave it a new meaning. The unifying principle in all microhistories is the belief that detailed analysis of a small place or moment in time can reveal meanings previously overlooked. Microscopic analysis can make the smallest events yield far-reaching conclusions.

Edward Muir has done more than anyone else to combine the techniques of Italian microhistory with a wider approach to cultural history. He produced, along with Guido Ruggiero, more than one volume dealing with crime. *Microhistory and the Lost Peoples of Europe* (1991) contains essays set in the sixteenth century about a Jew hiring a mason to destroy the Christian images in another Jew's house, episodes of pillaging property after the death of a bishop or pope, the lives of unwed mothers caught between hospitals and the Inquisition, and how the myth of the armies of dead warriors led to sightings of an apparition.[65] *History from Crime* (1994) presents essays that originally appeared in *Quaderni Storici*. It contains essays on cohabitation, witchcraft, magic, corruption, counterfeiting and infanticide.[66] The events take place in different settings, a seventeenth-century village in north-eastern Italy and early-twentieth-century Vienna. These essays use a particular criminal event as a point of departure for investigating society and culture from the perspective the records can provide.

For the microhistorian, as Muir and Ruggiero explain, 'history begins where justice ends'. After the legal proceedings have ended, and the archivists have stowed away the records, microhistorians can go to work, using these materials for their own purposes. The value of the criminal records is not so much what they reveal about the particular crime but what they reveal about otherwise invisible or opaque realms of experience. Historians have looked at crime in different ways. They have seen criminal events as disrupting social solidarities, as revealing social hierarchies, as demonstrating communication and power. In all cases, the historian must regard the crime itself as a provisional and open-ended example of social interaction situated in a particular time and place. The historian must struggle to avoid being drawn into the judicial process itself or submitting his or her view to that of the states that manufacture the ideas of crime and criminals, criminal desires and criminal class. 'Traditionally', they observe, 'the history of crime has focused on crime itself and how crime was defined, disciplined and perceived in the past.' As microhistorians, they do more. These essays move beyond the specific documents and events to examine effects and contexts related to the broader society and culture. 'Crime opens many windows on the past.'[67]

Wiener used techniques of microhistory in his discussion of the George Hall murder case. George was convicted and sentenced to death in 1864 for the murder of his wife, Sara Ann Smith. She had been a reluctant bride and carried on with another man after her marriage to Hall. When Sara ran away to pursue the affair, George purchased a set of pistols. He met her at her mother's house, persuaded her to walk with him and shot her in the head. To pursue his defence, Hall had the services of a young James Fitzjames Stephen, the man who would become the prominent authority on the history of English criminal law. As Wiener explains, George Hall received a reprieve from the gallows owing to powerful cultural forces in Victorian culture: sentimentalism and populism. He dodged the penalty imposed by the criminal law through 'the unwritten law' that authorized use of lethal violence by a provoked husband. Using newspapers and literary magazines of the period in addition to legal records, Wiener shows 'the sad story' George endured as a result of Sara's adultery. He demonstrates the importance of how an 'extra-legal concept of manliness' led to the legal decision.[68]

Malcolm Gaskill borrowed from microhistory for his history of crime in England during the early modern period. No account would be complete without a 'history of mentalities', the beliefs, ideas and thoughts that animate culture, so there is a need to see 'what the law meant on their own terms using social contexts as a means of communication'.[69] He used court records and the history of criminal justice as the raw material for reconstructing the mental world of English people from the mid-sixteenth century to the mid-eighteenth century. But mentalities have no tangible existence. They leave only 'oblique marks on the written record'. Crime is also useful because the records offer details of social contexts. Gaskill proposed that legal records reveal mentalities at three levels. (1) Normative sources, statutes, proclamations, orders and sermons present the way things 'were *supposed* to be'. (2) Impressionistic sources, literary accounts, broadsides, ballads, newspapers and letters suggest how 'things *seemed* to be' to contemporaries. And (3) administrative and legal sources, which best reflect the lives of ordinary people, indicate the way 'things really *were*'. The assize records contain depositions – information and examination of plaintiffs, witnesses and defendants – which offer a detailed background for the offences recorded and indictments and recognizances.[70]

Benjamin Carter Hett turned to microhistory to write about the criminal trial in Germany before the First World War. *Death in Tiergarten* (2004) focuses on a small number of trials in Berlin from 1891 to 1913, mostly murder trials. He offers a study of the 'culture of the criminal courtroom' – how the lawyers and judges, prosecutors and jurors, criminals and police, reporters and witnesses met and interacted, not only about what they did, but also about what they thought about what they did. The analysis borrows from legal realism and the emphasis on the large difference between the law as written and the way it is applied in the trial courts. But he chose to focus on a few trials to understand the actuality of German justice. What we miss in a broad treatment, Hett emphasizes, is culture. He shows the culture of German criminal justice at work: the treatment of prisoners, psychology of the courtroom, publicity of trials and moral tone in general. He used not only records, but also newspapers to understand why the German legal system failed to put a brake on the Nazi steamroller, and he has looked for continuities across the nineteenth and twentieth centuries. But it is not so easy to read judicial outcomes as political ideology. The judicial mind of imperial Germany cannot be isolated from professional, social and political factions vying for influence over the judicial system.[71]

In a discussion of homicide in the United States, Elizabeth Dale noted the difficulty of making any conclusions about *the* American legal system because there are so many regional, state and local versions. She focused on two murder cases in South Carolina, a state said to have a culture of violence, for insight into American violence. This microhistory approach traded the study of aggregate changes in rates over time for a microscopic examination of meaning. Ordinarily, the culture-of-violence argument saw things in only one direction: creating a culture that would explain higher homicides. But what about the other direction? She proposed examining the role of extra-legal justice in punishment, its function in providing an alternative to the formal legal system. Acquittal did not signal resignation or reluctance to punish, but punishing by social means; for defendants in both cases, legal acquittal meant life-long shame and ostracism. She encouraged historians interested in murder to 'dig deep for the facts that determined outcomes in particular cases' and to 'look beyond the legal outcomes' to see who delivered punishment and the various ways they delivered it.[72]

Conclusion

This chapter has explained what historians do not like about legal history and why crime history still needs lawyers, or at least, law. As a framework for understanding crime in the past, legal history has more than one defect. Whether it is Holdsworth's idea of a professional approach or Radzinowicz's desire to inform policy, there is a preoccupation with the present that leads to misreading the past. Legal historians have been guilty of cheerleading Whig history and of narrow, institutional history. The advocates of social history were quick to jump on these flaws, leading to terrific exchanges in the 1980s with lawyer-historians. The search for alternatives to legal history, such as Friedman's pursuit of law and society, the British Marxists' application of social theory and the microhistorian's approach to law and culture, has broadened and deepened the understanding of crime in society. The rest of this book is in many ways a discussion of how much there is to learn about crime history once we move outside the courtroom.

But, the lawyers and their histories produced the first crime history. As strange and flawed as Pike's view of history is, he was one of the very first, if not the first, individuals to write a history of crime. Lawyer-historians, such as Langbein, have produced valuable work in understanding criminal justice, which after all, is meant to include not only prisons and police (favourites of social historians) but courts. Legal records are a priceless source of historical evidence, and to make the most of them, legal knowledge is vital. Even when incorporating them in social, economic and cultural contexts, we need to know *what* before we can get to *why*. And, despite the limiting and mistaken legal definition of crime used in conjunction with Whig or institutional approaches, the law remains central to historic definition of crime. It is possible to write about deviance, immorality or violence, but it is not possible to write about crime without the law.

What we can say is that, from the standpoint of writing the history of crime, the exchange between the lawyers and their critics has been a great benefit. It has sharpened the views of the contestants and inspired countless spectators. Legal historians brought to the surface a number of basic problems in their pursuit of the criminal past: issues of definition, interpretation, meaning and significance. Although they did not necessarily solve them, their histories inspired other historians to take a look for themselves. Examining crime in legal history yields a deeper understanding of the complexity of crime as a topic of historical inquiry.

Notes

1 Daniel J. Boorstin, *The Mysterious Science of the Law* (Cambridge, MA: Harvard University Press, 1941), 35.
2 Boorstin, *The Mysterious Science*, 63–4.

3 Peter J. Bowler, *The Invention of Progress: The Victorians and the Past* (London: Basil Blackwell, 1989), 3–5.

4 Leon Radzinowicz, *Sir James Fitzjames Stephen* (London: Bernard Quartich, 1957), 39–42.

5 James Fitzjames Stephen, *A History of the Criminal Law of England*, vol. 1 (London: Macmillan, 1883), viii.

6 L. Owen Pike, *A History of Crime in England*, vol. 1 (London: Smith, Elder and Co, 1873), 2.

7 Pike, *A History of Crime*, vol. 1, 6.

8 Pike, *A History of Crime*, vol. 2, 491.

9 William Holdsworth, *A History of English Law*, vol. 1 (London: Methuen, 1903), 2.

10 Daniel J. Boorstin, 'Tradition and method in legal history', *Harvard Law Review* 54 (1941): 429.

11 Leon Radzinowicz and Roger Hood, *The Emergence of Penal Policy in Victorian and Edwardian England* (Oxford: Clarendon Press, 1990).

12 Leon Radzinowicz, *Adventures in Criminology* (London: Routledge, 1999), 159.

13 Leon Radzinowicz, 'Some sources of modern English criminal legislation', *Cambridge Law Journal* 8 (1943): 181–94.

14 Leon Radzinowicz, *A History of English Criminal Law and Its Administration from 1750*, vol. 1 (London: Stevens and Sons, 1948), ix.

15 Clive Holmes, 'G.R. Elton as a legal historian', *Transactions of the Royal History Society* 7 (1997): 268 (267–79).

16 Holmes, 'G.R. Elton', 269.

17 George Iggers, 'Historicism: The history and meaning of the term', *Journal of the History of Ideas* 56 (1995): 129–52.

18 Robert W. Gordon, 'J. Willard Hurst and the common law tradition in American legal historiography', *Law and Society Review* 10 (1975): 10–12.

19 Martin J. Wiener, 'The march of penal progress?', *Journal of British Studies* 26 (1987): 84.

20 Wiener, 'The march of penal progress', 86.

21 John H. Langbein, *The Origins of Adversary Criminal Trial* (Oxford: Oxford University Press, 2003).

22 Douglas Hay, 'The criminal prosecution in England and its historians', *Modern Law Review* 47 (1984): 1–29.

23 Hay, 'The criminal prosecution', 17.

24 Hay, 'The criminal prosecution', 18–21.

25 Langbein, *The Origins of the Adversary*, vii.

26 Tim Hitchcock and Robert Shoemaker, 'Digitising history from below: The Old Bailey proceedings online, 1674-1834', *History Compass* 4 (2006): 193–202.

27 Hitchcock and Shoemaker, 'Digitising history', 199.

28 Charles Donahue Jr, 'Whither legal history?', in Daniel Hamilton and Alfred Brophy, eds, *Transformations in American Legal History* (Cambridge, MA: Harvard University Press, 2009), 327–43.

29 Edward White, 'From sociological jurisprudence to realism: Jurisprudence and social change in early twentieth-century America', *Virginia Law Review* 58 (1972): 999–1028.

30 Jerome Hall, *Theft, Law and Society* (Boston: Little, Brown, 1935), 36.

31 Robert J. Cottrol, 'Lawrence Friedman: The legal historian and the social organisation of criminal justice', *Tulsa Law Review* 40 (2005): 627–38.

32 Lawrence Friedman, *A History of American Law* (New York: Simon and Schuster, 1973), 10.

33 Friedman, *A History of American Law*, 14.

34 Friedman, *A History of American Law*, 14.

35 Lawrence M. Friedman, *Crime and Punishment in American History* (New York: Basic Books, 1993), 6.

36 Friedman, *Crime and Punishment*, 15.

37 George Fisher, 'Historian in the cellar', in Robert W. Gordon and Morton J. Horwitz, eds, *Law, Society and History: Themes in the Legal Sociology and Legal History of Lawrence M Friedman* (Cambridge: Cambridge University Press, 2011), 215, 273–92.

38 Lawrence M. Friedman, 'Plea bargaining in historical perspective', *Law and Society Review* 13 (1979): 247–59.

39 Phillips, 'Why legal history matters', 302–4.

40 Allen Steinberg, *The Transformation of Criminal Justice: Philadelphia, 1800-1880* (Chapel Hill, NC: University of North Carolina Press, 1989).

41 Robert M. Ireland, 'Frenzied and fallen females: Women and sexual dishonor in the nineteenth-century United States', *Journal of Women's History* 3 (1992): 95–117.

42 Robert M. Ireland, 'The libertine must die: Sexual dishonor and the unwritten law in the nineteenth-century United States', *Journal of Social History* 23 (1989): 27–44.

43 Elizabeth Dale, *Criminal Justice in the United States, 1789-1939* (Cambridge: Cambridge University Press, 2011), 170–7.

44 E. P. Thompson, *Whigs and Hunters: The Origin of the Black Act* (London: Allen Lane, 1975); Douglas Hay, Peter Linebaugh, John G. Rule and Cal Winslow, eds, *Albion's Fatal Tree: Crime and Society in Eighteenth Century England* (London: Allen Lane, 1975).

45 Douglas Hay, 'Property, authority and the criminal law', in Douglas Hay, Peter Linebaugh, John G. Rule and Cal Winslow, eds, *Albion's Fatal Tree: Crime and Society in Eighteenth Century England* (London: Allen Lane, 1975), 56.

46 Carolyn Strange, ed., *Qualities of Mercy: Justice, Punishment and Discretion* (Vancouver: University of British Columbia Press, 1986).

47 Jim Phillips, 'The operation of royal pardons in Nova Scotia, 1749-1815', *University of Toronto Law Journal* 42 (1992): 401–19.

48 Peter King, *Crime, Justice and Discretion in England 1740-1820* (Oxford: Oxford University Press, 2000).

49 King, *Crime, Justice and Discretion*, 4.

50 Douglas Hay, 'Crime and justice in eighteenth and nineteenth-century England', *Crime and Justice* 2 (1975): 45–84.

51 G. R. Elton, *Studies in Tudor and Stuart Politics and Government*, vol. 3 (Cambridge: Cambridge University Press, 1983), 290.

52 Elton, *Studies in Tudor*, 291–5.

53 J. A. Sharpe, 'The history of crime in late medieval and early modern England: A review of the field', *Social History* 7 (1982): 188; J. A. Sharpe, *Crime in Early Modern England 1550-1750*, 2nd edn (London: Longman, 1999), 6.

54 Sharpe, *Crime in Early Modern*, 10.

55 Sharpe, *Crime in Early Modern*, 10.

56 Pieter Spierenburg, 'Evaluation of the conditions and main problems relating to the contribution of historical research to the understanding of crime and criminal justice', in European Committee on Crime Problems, *Historical Research on Crime and Criminal Justice* (Strasbourg: Council of Europe, 1985), 64, 51–95.

57 Spierenburg, 'Evaluation of the conditions', 64–6.

58 Gordon, 'J. Willard Hurst', 10–12.

59 Michael S. Hindus, *Prison and Plantation: Crime, Justice and Authority in Massachusetts and South Carolina, 1767-1878* (Chapel Hill: University of North Carolina Press, 1980).

60 Martin Wiener, *Reconstructing the Criminal: Culture, Law, and Criminal Policy in England, 1830-1914* (Cambridge: Cambridge University Press, 1990).

61 Wiener, *Reconstructing the Criminal*, 11.

62 Nicola Lacey, 'In search of the responsible subject: History, philosophy and social sciences in criminal law theory', *Modern Law Review* 64 (2001): 350–71.

63 Herbert Reinke, 'Crime and criminal justice history in Germany. A report on recent trends', *Crime, History and Societies* 13 (2009): 117–37.

64 Carlo Ginzburg, 'Microhistory: Two or three things that I know about it', *Critical Inquiry* 20 (1993): 10–35.

65 Edward Muir and Guido Ruggiero, *Microhistory and the Lost Peoples of Europe* (Baltimore: Johns Hopkins University Press, 1991).

66 Edward Muir and Guido Ruggiero, eds, *History from Crime* (Baltimore, MD: Johns Hopkins University Press, 1994).

67 Muir and Ruggiero, *History from Crime*, 226.

68 Martin J. Wiener, 'The sad story of George Hall: Adultery, murder and the politics of mercy in mid-Victorian England', *Social History* 24 (1999): 174–95.

69 Malcolm Gaskill, *Crime and Mentalities in Early Modern England* (Cambridge: Cambridge University Press, 2000), 20.

70 Gaskill, *Crime and Mentalities*, 21.

71 Benjamin Carter Hett, *Death in the Tiergarten: Murder and Criminal Justice in the Kaiser's Berlin* (Cambridge, MA: Harvard University Press, 2004).

72 Elizabeth Dale, 'Getting away with murder', *American Historical Review* 111 (2006): 95–103.

Further reading

Beattie, J. M. *Crime and the Courts in England 1660-1800*. Oxford: Clarendon, 1986.

Dale, Elizabeth. *Criminal Justice in the United States, 1789-1939*. Cambridge: Cambridge University Press, 2011.

Dale, Elizabeth. 'The role of popular justice in United States History', in Paul Knepper and Anja Johansen, eds, *The Oxford Handbook of the History of Crime and Criminal Justice*. New York: Oxford University Press, 2015.

Dubber, Marcus D. and Lindsay Farmer. 'Regarding criminal law historically', in Marcus D. Dubber and Lindsay Farmer, eds, *Modern Histories of Crime and Punishment*. Stanford: Stanford University Press, 2007, 1–13.

Harris, Ruth. *Murders and Madness: Medicine, Law and Society in the Fin de Siècle*. Oxford: Clarendon, 1989.

Hay, Douglas. 'The criminal prosecution in England and its historians'. *Modern Law Review* 47 (1984): 1–29.

Lemmings, David, ed. *Crime, Courtrooms and the Public Sphere in Britain, 1700-1850*. Surrey: Ashgate, 2012.

Robins, Jane. *The Magnificent Spilsbury and the Case of the Brides in the Bath*. London: John Murray, 2010.

Walker, Samuel. *Popular Justice: A History of American Criminal Justice*. New York: Oxford University Press, 1998.

Wiener, Martin. *Reconstructing the Criminal: Culture, Law, and Criminal Policy in England, 1830-1914*. Cambridge: Cambridge University Press, 1990.

CHAPTER TWO

Statistics, trends and techniques

Counting has generated some of the most significant arguments among historians writing about crime. The nineteenth-century positivists drafted initial plans for quantitative analysis of the past, and in the early twentieth century, the *Annales* school added to the architecture. But it was really in the 1970s, when historians gained access to computers for data analysis, that the quantitative approach took off. Inspired by the techniques displayed by economists, demographers and other social scientists, historians went about building a new social history. Crime historians analysed not only crime statistics as such, but police files, court records, prison registers, coroners' reports, newspaper accounts – anything that furnished 'data' for crime and criminal justice. The debates have been about statistics as a source of evidence, quantification as a historical technique and theories used to interpret trends.

The debates about numbers among historians of crime have taken place within wider conversations about quantification in historical writing. Exchanges have taken place around what the figures actually measure, about whether trends can be discerned and about whether current criminological techniques can be retrofitted to historical statistics. The exchanges hint at an even bigger philosophical issue about the 'use' of history. The application of social science to history accompanied great optimism about what could be achieved. If historians could make use of social science, they could acquire the same level of confidence in their research. Could historians provide knowledge of the past that was truly useful in the sense of guiding government policy?

The aim of this chapter is to examine the usefulness of statistical approaches to crime history as well as difficulties that arise. Part 1 revisits early claims by positivists and *Annalistes*. Part 2 looks at efforts to construct and interpret long-term trends in violence from court records, including arguments about a decline in violence and the changing ratio of violence to theft. Part 3 considers the views of J. J. Tobias on the worthlessness of British crime statistics for the nineteenth century and the response to his arguments. Part 4 samples the ongoing debate about the use of social science techniques for writing history with a look at the exchange over whether the American 'Wild West' was really so wild.

The promise of quantification

The word *positivism* has more than one meaning, but essentially, it has to do with the application of science to society. Positivists believe that the same method that scientists use to study the world of nature – rocks, plants, wind and water – should be used to study people, behaviour and society. In the nineteenth century, technological progress generated enthusiasm. Engineers produced technological marvels in industry, transportation and communication, and there seemed to be no limit to what science could achieve. Auguste Comte proposed his 'new science' of positivism.

The objective of Comte's 'new science' was to discover the natural or unavoidable laws of civilization, as important to human activity as gravitation to the earth's movement. He did not work as a historian, but there was a clear implication that it was possible to construct a universal history of humankind through identifying the natural laws at work. The discovery of the laws was referred to as the 'historical method'. Curiously, Comte did not believe that statistics would be a useful tool. While other positivists, including Adolphe Quetelet and Emile Durkheim, saw in the analysis of statistical data a means of uncovering laws of society, Comte favoured induction. The positivist could intuitively grasp the essential aspects of civilization and then deductively arrive at the processes behind their construction. Positivism had a tremendous influence on the formation of social sciences across Europe through intellectuals in various fields who shared Comte's enthusiasm for the application of science to human activity.[1]

The gentleman-scholar Henry Buckle brought positivism to English history. He proposed a science of history to parallel achievements in the physical sciences. To pursue this, historians would need to abandon their commitments to free will in human affairs in favour of a more scientific view. When an individual performs an action, Buckle explained, it is a consequence of some motive or motives. While these motives cannot be observed, they result from antecedents that can be. So, if we were to inventory these antecedents, we could grasp the laws concerning their movements, and with some confidence, predict the whole of immediate choices of individuals. Individuals shaped, and were shaped by, the natural world, or as he put it: 'What we have before us is man modifying nature, and nature modifying man ... out of this reciprocal modification all events must necessarily spring.'[2]

The challenge was to come up with a method of finding the laws governing this interaction of humanity and nature. And the most promising method was to search for recurring patterns or regularities in history. The possibilities for studying the past, Buckle proposed, were wide. To manage this, historians had divided the past into specific slices of knowledge. He proposed to pursue history on a 'far larger scale' with the 'expectation of discovering regularity in the midst of this confusion'.[3] As an example of the sort of regularities on offer, Buckle pointed to crime. It was a fact, he said, that murders occurred with as much regularity as movements of ocean tides and rotation of seasons. Quetelet had demonstrated that crime statistics captured social behaviour over time. In his analyses of French criminality, he had shown that every kind of offence recurred with clockwork regularity. The number of criminal perpetrators across France from 1826 to 1844 was equal to the number of deaths of men in Paris for the same period. Further, fluctuations in the annual rate of crime were less than that of mortality.[4]

What became known as the *Annales* school affirmed the value of statistics. It began with a journal, *Annales d'histoire économique et sociale* (Annals of Economic and Social History), founded in 1929 by Marc Bloch and Lucien Febvre to promote an interdisciplinary approach to history. After the Second World War, Fernand Braudel joined the group and contributed to a tradition of economic and social history that achieved international renown. The *Annalistes* brought positivism to a new level. They revered numbers: trade figures, birth rates and death rates, textile production and agricultural prices. But they also brought a scheme of interpretation to their techniques of quantification. They wanted to grasp the 'totality' of historical experience, to capture more than the narrative of political events. They believed in 'social determinism', that history was driven by forces beyond the control of individuals, particularly rooted in geography. They saw historical change over a long period of time, the *longue durée*. And to pursue this, they advocated statistical analysis, the 'measurement of whatever can be measured'.[5]

In an essay published in the 1950s, 'History and the Social Sciences', Braudel touted 'social mathematics' to uncover 'unconscious history'. Although people believe they can grasp the significance of events in their own time, there existed a social unconscious that was more important, scientifically speaking, than the events streaming past. The procedure was to break through superficial observations to reach the zone of the unconscious, and then to reduce experience to elements that could be precisely analysed. This would allow for construction of models, characterized by time and space, which could be applied to other social environments similar to those observed.[6] During the 1960s and 1970s, the *Annales* school appeared to focus exclusively on topics that lent themselves to quantification, and even less suitable problems. In their enthusiasm for scientific history, they took quantification to absurd lengths ('using a cyclotron to crack a nut' as one critic put it).[7]

The influence of *Annales* scholarship on crime history has been indirect, having to do mostly with normalizing the use of social science methods for the study of history. But it is interesting to think about Braudel's contribution to crime history from what can be gleaned from his study of the Mediterranean. He built his understanding of the Mediterranean and its peoples from the revelation that human experience moves at more than one speed. There were three historical speeds or kinds of time. Geographical time moved so slowly it appeared to stand still. He referred to the 'almost imperceptible history' of people in relation to the natural environment, the slow, constant repetition of seasonal activities. The mountains, deserts and the sea, operated as the source of constraints on behaviour that persist across generations. Social time moved faster, visible from one generation to the next; it referred to the 'slow but perceptible rhythms' of 'groups and groupings', shaped by long-term trends in trade, transport, empire and forms of war. Then there was individual time, the 'history of brief, rapid, nervous fluctuations' brought about by political and military leaders. It appeared the most real, but this was an illusion. Individual time contained 'the dimensions of anger, dreams or illusions'.[8]

Braudel situated banditry and piracy in social time. In the sixteenth century, outbreaks of brigandage – cutting trees, robberies, etc. – occurred at different places and signalled something outside the limits of ordinary crime. These acts were, first of all, an act of revenge against the state. Bandits tended to operate in areas with weak state authority: Catalonia, Calabria and Albania. In Calabria, they were aided by circumstances and terrain, as well as by the ambitions of certain nobility. Banditry increased towards the end of the sixteenth century, with the coming economic crisis of the seventeenth century. It appeared along with a rise in vagrancy, proof that both sprung from poverty. It was a sign of Mediterranean society splitting into rich and poor.[9] Braudel thought of piracy as a substitute for a declared war. Pirate ships appeared, often with the sponsorship of cities attached to weak states. Like banditry, there was a correlation between piracy and the economic health of the region.[10] Both banditry and piracy belong to social time; bandits and pirates rose and fell with the economic tide. But, both were governed by geo-determinism – not by politics or even economics, but by landscape and seasons. Peace treaties were signed in winter; 'with summer's coming, war sprang to life in all its forms: land warfare, galley warfare, pirate attacks at sea, and brigand raids in the countryside'.[11]

By the 1970s, when historians gained access to mainframe computers, the quantitative approach to crime became a substantive area of historical research. Douglas Greenberg gathered available statistics for his study of criminals and criminal justice in colonial New York. He constructed a sample of 5,297 cases, all that survived between 1691 and 1776, to learn the social characteristics of defendants, and what happened to them as they moved through the legal system. Crime, as captured in court records, was particularly suited to counting, and much of the evidence could be expressed in numbers. But as an exercise in quantitative history, it was limited by missing information. Further, the material suitable for a 'computer assisted' analysis could only be assayed with reference to 'more impressionistic' sources. Calculating crime rates required good population estimates, and while these were available for New York City, this was not possible for the remainder of the counties.[12]

Lawrence Friedman and Robert Percival looked at Alameda County, California, from 1870 to 1910. Friedman pioneered a kind of legal history that avoided the celebrated cases in the law library for the records of ordinary people in criminal courts found 'in the cellar'.[13] To build up a portrait of the criminal justice system, they collected information about individuals known to multiple institutions: the Oakland Police, the Superior Court and San Quentin prison. They compiled statistics from arrest blotters, court registers, felony case files, appellate court records, prison log books and newspapers. From arrest blotters for the city of Oakland, they drew a random sample of 1,555 persons; from the register of the Superior Court, they identified a sample of 696 cases. 'Whenever we could, as often as we could, we used numbers, tables, simple statistics.'[14] They also looked at anecdotes from newspapers and case files to 'get behind' the records and 'get a feel' for what was going on at the time. While Friedman and Percival have no doubts about the value of the numbers as historical evidence, they realized that their findings were limited. How far they can be generalized to other places and times is not a statistical question but a wider question of interpretation.

In methodological terms, the research by Greenberg and Friedman and Percival involves case studies. They use statistics to sketch a portrait of crime and criminal justice at a particular place for a limited period of time. More complex quantitative approaches construct trend data to explore sources of change over time, or cross-sectional designs, which draw comparisons at a point in time across two or more sites. These have been carried out by researchers who see themselves as engaged more in social scientific analysis than writing history. They tend to be framed around present concerns and bring social theory to the past. Ted Robert Gurr, Peter Grabosky and Richard Hula conducted one of the more ambitious studies to appear in the 1970s when they welded the longitudinal approach to comparative methodology. Gurr, a political scientist, had been appointed to serve on the National Commission on the Causes and Prevention of Violence.

Gurr and his colleagues started in the present. They wanted to detect what was behind the apparent decline of public order within large cities in the Western world. They assembled statistics about crime and disorder for London, Stockholm, Sydney and Calcutta for the nineteenth and twentieth centuries. Their research explored the proposition that crime and disorder declined from the nineteenth century, and then increased after 1945, and they wanted to know if this was connected to political institutions (which is what the government wanted to know). Had crime and disorder actually increased? If so, was this partly due to changing policies for public order? They constructed trends of crimes known to the police, arrests, accused/ committed to trial, convictions for indictable crimes, and strikes. They re-categorized the statistics to yield four categories of criminal behaviour: aggression, acquisition, morality and public order. They found that governmental policies to shore up public order worked in some cities, but not in others. Similarly, changing social and economic conditions were contradictory; the same factors could not be said to have produced consistent correlations across all locations. By covering so much terrain, over an extended period of time, they realized that the final product was 'superficial by historians' standards'. It was better described as 'comparative political science'.[15]

By the 1980s, Eric Monkkonen said, there were enough studies to clearly demonstrate the value of quantification. Monkkonen, professor of history and policy studies at the University of California-Los Angeles, brought computers, statistics and social theory to crime in cities. 'Counting is the major means of understanding crime and criminal justice in the present as a part of the sweep of history,' he wrote. 'The point of which I wish to remind is simple. Almost as soon as we begin to conceptualize about crime and the criminal justice system, questions of quantity come to the forefront.'[16] Quantitative research addressed problems, identified major sources of data, raised significant questions and made use of measures, models and techniques from social science. He urged historians to build on what had been accomplished: to clarify models, to apply more appropriate statistical techniques, to analyse sources in greater depth.

There was a great deal of optimism about how far historians, powered by social science, could travel. Social science historians, Monkkonen told a colleague, were the great explorers of the age, privileged to see things no one had seen before because they now possessed the tools, technology and theory.[17] The National Institute of Justice decided to sponsor a workshop on historical contributions to crime and justice. The organizers hoped that history would provide some perspectives on current problems and suggest further topics worthy of investigation. The workshop took place in Virginia in 1979 with presentations about theory and methods, history and policy, and crime, police and prisons. The participants included Europeans as well as Americans. In 1985, the Council of Europe sponsored a criminological colloquium to explore the potential of historical research to inform criminal justice policy. Historians from across Europe discussed conceptual and methodological problems in the study of crime. They resolved that social history makes an important contribution to the study of criminal justice and urged the European Committee on Crime Problems to encourage member states to promote historical research.[18]

Modelling long-term trends

In 1983, Lawrence Stone started a conversation about trends in violence. Stone, professor of history at Princeton, was known for his application of social science to history, and in particular, for his quantitative approach to family history. He challenged the idea that there had once been peaceful English towns and that these had been ruined by the intrusion of modern life. Criminal violence had not increased with industrialization and urbanization, but rather, there had been a long-term trend towards decreasing violence from the late medieval period. Stone saw a decline of violent crimes over the past five centuries brought about by the 'shift from the values of a feudal to those of a bourgeois society'.[19]

Stone said that medieval English society was twice as saturated in violence as early modern English society, and early modern English society was five times awash in violence as contemporary English society. 'The notion that there was once upon a time a peace-loving, conflict free, golden age of the village, whether located in the middle ages or in the early modern period, is shown up to be a myth.'[20] Historians had reached the wrong conclusions, in part, because they had selected the wrong unit of analysis. The English village had too small a population on which to build long-term crime trends. County-level records would have been more suitable. For evidence that violence is lower now than in the past, Stone relied on work by Ted Robert Gurr. Gurr proposed that homicide offered an index of crime more generally because it was the most difficult crime to conceal and most likely to be recorded. Between 1200 and 1400, there were changes in definitions of manslaughter and murder, but there is not sufficient reason to suspect that these changes had a pivotal effect on coroners' decisions. Homicide rates may also have changed artificially due to improvement in medical care. But, taking these sorts of arguments into account, it could still be concluded that from the fourteenth century to the twentieth century, the trend in homicide has been downward. Homicide rates in the thirteenth century were about twice as high as those in the sixteenth century and seventeenth century, and those in the sixteenth century and seventeenth century were some five to ten times higher than those of the twentieth century.[21]

It was a rather surprising move for Stone because only a few years earlier, he seemed to have changed his mind about the value of quantification in history. Historians had turned to a new kind of narrative history, a 'new old history', because they had become disillusioned with quantification. The quantification movement had led to 'the most sophisticated techniques either to prove the obvious or to claim to prove the implausible'.[22] Quantification had sharpened analysis of generalizing claims about what most people were doing based on knowledge of a few, but this tended to leave unanswered the questions in history most worth asking. 'Quantification has told us a lot about the *what* questions of historical demography, but relatively little so far about the *why*.'[23]

It was also surprising, because to supply the 'why', Stone revived modernization theory. Essentially, modernization theory held that all nations proceed through similar stages of development. It originated in the writings of sociologists in the late nineteenth century, chiefly Emile Durkheim, who sought to account for changes occurring in the transition from pre-modern or traditional society to modern society (or feudal to bourgeois as Stone put it). Durkheim imagined a process of evolution taking place in national histories similar to biological organisms in which social order graduated from simple to complex. The theory remained popular with sociologists, anthropologists and political scientists into the twentieth century who associated modernization with industrialization, urbanization and often democratization. However, by the time of Stone's article, modernization theory had been thoroughly criticized for blurring regional differences, trying to account for too much, and insisting on a single path to economic development. That said, it had its defenders. Peter Stearns, the founding editor of the *Journal of Social History*, championed modernization theory in social history because it offered a unifying explanation grounded in social science for multiple trends, including markets, government, family, leisure and education, not to mention crime. In fact, Stearns appreciated Stone's use of modernization because it encouraged the view that crime history was seen as a part of social history rather than a separate field of history.[24]

James Sharpe, a specialist in seventeenth-century English history at the University of York, took exception to Stone's theoretical interpretation of Gurr's material.[25] Estimating crime trends over time was far more problematic than Stone made out. As a new arrival to the study of crime, Stone overlooked the complexities of using court records for crime trends. It was wrong to assume that there were no changes in how coroners classified murders over the centuries. There was also the matter of whether crime rates should be built up from convictions or accusations. So, as far as Sharpe was concerned, 'it is difficult to see the decline of the homicide rate as a sign of "modernization" in quite the way he does'.[26] Sharpe denied that changing patterns of crime could be attributed to the growth of bourgeois society or to the break-up of the English village. The argument about the 'rise of the middle classes' could be used to account for just about anything, and Stone had stirred together a variety of contradictory ingredients to make his claim about the 'opening up within the village'. 'Those who know the most about the problems and sources involved in studying the pre-industrial English village', Sharpe said, 'have been the most likely to disagree with Stone's interpretation'.[27] Homicide rates suggest that early modern England was a more violent society than the twentieth century, but there were qualitative differences as well: to say that early modern society *experienced* violence is not the same thing as saying that it was *characterized* by violence. It was a fine point to put on it, Sharpe acknowledged, but he insisted that 'early modern England was not fundamentally a violent or affectionless society'.[28]

Nothing Sharpe said, however, shook Stone's faith in the 'great decline'.[29] Both he and Sharpe agreed on the basic trends: the rate of recorded homicide was roughly ten times higher in the medieval period compared to the modern era, five times the level in the sixteenth and seventeenth centuries, and then fell to its modern low level between 1660 and 1800. He was well aware of the problem of building a trend in 'real crime' from indictments, which is why he said that one should use the most reliable data available, that for homicide. The difference between his interpretation and Sharpe's should be understood as a 'broad philosophical disagreement' about the practice of 'our craft as historians'. Specifically, there is a difference in the philosophy of how best to deal with gaps in the historical record. 'Given the existential fog in which we exist, what are we to do?'[30] There was a difference between serious criticism of a proposal and nagging about defects in details which, even if true, would not dismiss the overall conclusions. 'The decline in the level of recorded violence – notably homicide – I still believe can plausibly be attributed to a cultural softening of manners, a greater sensitivity to cruelty and violence, and to the rise of a middle-class culture and a more market-oriented society.'[31] Stone then raised the ante with evidence of a shift in societal values, drawn from the response of middle-class husbands to their wives' adultery and the fall in all types of civil litigation.

James Cockburn added his study of homicide in Kent in 1560–1985 to the discussion, a contribution he compared to purveying gunpowder in support of the artillery fire.[32] Stone had suggested the importance of county-wide data, and Kent could supply this across four centuries. There was 'almost certainly' an overall decline in the overall incidence of homicide in England, Cockburn said, but this structure was built on the 'shifting sands' of unreliable estimates of population size and growth. There was also the untraceable impact of improvements in medicine. On balance, this and other factors meant that the difference between early modern and modern levels was less, mainly by deflating the twentieth-century rate. There were a range of factors to explain the pattern of homicide: jurisdictional and legal change, peace and war, dearth, technological advances and custom. The alleged superiority of overarching causal models, such as Stone had claimed, 'conceal the essentially piecemeal and untidy nature of social and cultural change'.[33] The controversy over the world we have lost rests on impressionistic statistics. In setting aside the myth of a conflict-free golden age of village life, we risk exaggerating the tensions in early modern society and overlook those in our own.

Historians from the Nordic countries provided further ammunition, most of which supported Stone's claim of the 'great decline' in violence. Eva Österberg gathered court records for Stockholm and other towns and cities in Sweden from 1452 to 1970. She calculated murder and manslaughter, minor crimes and violence, and thefts per year for 1,000 residents. Although it was difficult to discern a clear trend from the figures, there would appear to be a decline, particularly in murder and manslaughter. Viewed the other way around, there was nothing in the figures to overturn the conclusion that murder and manslaughter became less common over the long term. The timing in Sweden appears to have differed from England: in Sweden, the decline occurred from the mid-seventeenth to the mid-eighteenth century at the latest.[34] Heikki Ylikangas reported that Finland's experience was like that of Sweden's. In Sweden, the level of violence was high from the Middle Ages until the seventeenth century. In a period when the state could not offer protection, people relied on family networks to intimidate those around them. Not until the seventeenth century did the state reign in popular violence. The same was true for Finland. Nicknames given to people are one reflection of this: *Härkä* (ox), *Karhu* (bear), *Pässi* (ram) and *Rotta* (rat). In the Finnish countryside in the mid-sixteenth century, a constant power struggle between families fuelled violence. Judicial control tightened up at the same time in Finland. The reasons for the high rate of violent crime before the sixteenth century and seventeenth century and subsequent decline were much the same across Europe.[35]

For Monkkonen, however, the argument for the 'great decline' had to remain speculative. Was it safe to conclude that a 'violent past, peaceful present' shapes our world? Should we move on to other questions? 'I believe not.'[36] He reviewed the problems in drawing valid conclusions from long-term synthesis and called for new international standards, specifically, upgrading the quality of data collection. Although researchers had done pioneering work, the research was still not good enough to declare that violence had diminished over time, as if the matter had been settled and it was safe to move on to other questions. It was premature to draw a general conclusion from the relatively few sites that had been excavated, particularly, from sites with small populations. The 'inadvertent selection of atypical study sites' remained a possibility. He pointed to difficulties in establishing accurate counts of homicides, as well as population estimates needed for rates. He returned to the point that had been made about the impact of medical care on homicide, emphasizing the dramatically lower numbers of homicides that would have occurred in earlier centuries until modern medical interventions became available. 'Until we have used these higher standards, we must be cautious in the long run.'[37]

For Randolph Roth, the impact of medicine clinches it. All the explanations of long-term trends – growth of states, intervention of courts, improvement of manners – are wrong because there was no overall downward trend to explain. The 'great decline' never happened. Once the impact of medicine is taken into account, the apparent overall decline in violence from the medieval period to the modern era vanishes. Homicide rates in Europe were no higher through much of the medieval and early modern period than in the United States during the interwar period of the twentieth century or even the beginning of the twenty-first century. Given the medical interventions available today, such as care of wounds, antisepsis, antibiotics, anaesthesia, fluid replacement and trauma surgery, some 75 per cent of homicide victims before 1850 would have survived. 'Modern people are more successful at saving lives, but they are not less violent.'[38]

Another conversation, related to that of the decline in violence, is whether it coincided with a great increase in property crime. The 'violence to theft' thesis is also referred to as *de la violence au vol* because it originated with French historians in the 1960s and 1970s. Those associated with Pierre Channu and the *Annales* school observed that in eighteenth-century Normandy, violence declined and theft increased. To explain this, they proposed a shift in aggressiveness from persons to their property. The economic take-off, industrialization, migration to cities and refinement of manners transformed a rural, poor and violent era into a rich, urban and property crime era. Channu's work implied that a social setting, rough, rowdy and fired by emotions in the sixteenth and seventeenth centuries, would have generated a relatively high degree of violence. In the eighteenth century, a more pacified and commercialized society emerged, and this would have generated a greater portion of property offences. The shift from violent crimes to crimes of theft took place in the second half of the eighteenth century.[39]

Howard Zehr brought the violence-to-theft thesis to English-speaking historians with his study of crime trends in Germany and France.[40] He marshalled statistics for homicide, assault and theft for 1830 to 1914. These included court statistics across the two countries at the end of the nineteenth century, court and police records for several large cities in Bavaria and Prussia, annual reports from the French Ministry of Justice from 1831 to 1910 and local police statistics for certain urban centres and rural areas of Germany. While he agreed that statistics showing crimes known to police would have been preferred, he decided that 'comparisons of court and police data suggest that for some purposes court records may not be as bad a source as might be expected'.[41] Zehr concluded that crime rates in general increased throughout the nineteenth century; there was more crime in 1913 than in 1830. Within this overall trend, a change occurred in the ratio of theft to violence: while property crime rates climbed, rates of violent crime, especially serious violence, fell. Zehr explained these changing patterns as part of the 'transition from pre-modern to modern forms of criminal behaviour, reflecting the eventual abandonment of rural traditions, rising standards of living and thus expectations, and in general adjustment to life in an urban, industrial society'.[42]

Zehr's analysis gave him pole position on the modernization of crime circuit. As he explained, patterns of crime reflect changing values and social systems, but not *anomie* or social disorganization as suggested by Durkheim's sociology. Rather, rising rates of theft indicated rising expectations and the diffusion of modern economic values, and were a characteristic of modern, urban society. Theft amounts to forward-looking adaptation to modern social goals, and violence a backward-looking, traditional form of behaviour. His analysis served as an 'important and incomplete beginning, after several impressionistic false starts, for quantitative analysis on the macro level is in many ways a precondition for such close approaches'.[43] But, quantitative analyses at the national level, or even at the regional level, could not map these changes with precision. He advocated further studies of offenders themselves, their circumstances and motivations, and the response of social groups to broader social and economic forces. Studies focused on elements of workers, on limited areas of cities, on criminal records and case histories. Zehr regarded his graphing of 'gross statistical patterns of crime for rather large geographic areas over long periods of time' as a 'necessary first step to an understanding of the crime phenomena'.[44]

Louise Shelley gave modernization theory an enthusiastic 'yes'.[45] In her view, crime patterns over the past 200 years reveal a consistent response to developments encompassed in modernization. Societies characterized by violent crimes came to be dominated by crimes against property. The period of industrialization and urbanization was the period crucial to this process. Violence surged with industrialization and urbanization, then receded as new 'institutional controls' appeared. The rising standard of living pushed up property crime, resulting in crime from relative deprivation rather than poverty. 'Modern patterns of criminal behaviour appear after an agrarian society characterized by violent criminality is replaced by an urban society where the theft of material goods becomes the pervasive form of crime,' she says, and Zehr has offered 'one of the most distinctive and convincing explanations of the impact of nineteenth century developmental process on crime'.[46]

Monkkonen doubted whether the statistical evidence was really as good as it seemed. He wondered whether modernization theory would hold up to more sophisticated statistical testing.[47] Had Zehr's graphs taken into account the amount of more portable personal property and the more pervasive criminal justice system, it would likely have altered the relationships he found. Further, the use of prosecution and trial rates as an index of crime contradicts the idea of modernization. The theory would predict that law enforcement would be the first element of justice affected by modernization processes. So, the machinery would act on the values of modernizing society, thus emphasizing and rationalizing property relations in advance of these values affecting society as a whole. 'I suspect that the clear modernization of crime which Zehr found would disappear in a properly specified multivariate analysis, and a much more complex, less intuitive set of relationships would emerge.'[48]

Monkkonen's wish came true several years later in the form of a German study targeted at statistical trends.[49] The German version of modernization theory, associated with Hans-Ulrich Wehler and Jürgen Kocka, drew more on Weber than on Durkheim. The researcher had gained access to unpublished material from the Prussian Ministry of Justice and was able to carry out analyses in more detail than the printed material on which Zehr had relied. This research pointed to an increase in theft in the early nineteenth century that coincided with a rise in the population of paupers, and a general increase of both theft and violence in the mid-nineteenth century. From 1852 to 1866, theft declined and violence increased, which was inconsistent with Zehr's thesis but for a different period. As Richard Evans explained, 'The real problem with all these figures is that the evidence for "modernization" in the form of a rising incidence of theft compared with violence is located only in a brief period from about the turn of the century to the First World War.'[50] The most obvious trend in Germany is a rise in crimes of violence across the second half of the nineteenth century; this merits explanation more than the reversal of this trend from 1895 on.

The violence-to-theft thesis received extensive treatment in *The Civilization of Crime* (1996), a collection of essays edited by Eric Johnson and Eric Monkkonen.[51] In his chapter, James Sharpe put the figures for England under a magnifying glass. He concluded that while the numbers revealed a decline in the level of violence, the pattern was not clear for the rise in theft. Pieter Spierenburg, in his analysis of homicide in the Netherlands, pointed out that the thesis has to with the relative portion of these crimes in courts. It seeks to explain changes in caseloads over time, but has less to say about the incidence of the types of crime taken separately. In other words, the thesis offers a better representation of judicial policy than of patterns of criminal behaviour. Jan Sundin found nothing to corroborate the violence-to-theft theory in Sweden. Crimes of violence did vary over time in pre-industrial Sweden, but did not suggest a linear pattern. Nor did the data suggest a rising line in theft. Rather, the rates can be seen to fluctuate with the economic situation in pre-industrial Sweden. In a subsequent study of Swedish trends, Dag Lindström concluded that *de la violence au vol* has some relevance to the long-term transition from medieval to modern society. However, violent crime began to decrease centuries before the decrease in theft. Rather than characterizing this long-term transition as being from violence to theft, he favoured a general transition from personal conflicts (violence, slander and defamation) towards impersonal property disputes (debts, inheritance, property). This transition may have started in the seventeenth century or earlier.[52]

Johnson and Monkkonen themselves turned to the 'process sociology' of Norbert Elias, which could be seen as another version of modernization theory. The theory of the civilizing process has been at the centre of explanations for long-term trends, a favourite of social science historians and historian social scientists (as we will see in Chapter 3).[53]

Counting crimes

By the 1980s, it seemed that no one was left sifting through written documents in the archives. The appeal of numbers, availability of personal computers and wider access to public records led more historians to data analysis than archival research. It was not so much quantification as a technique, but social science as replacement for historicism as the basis for historical inquiry that alarmed traditional historians. Jacques Barzun, Gertrude Himmelfarb and Geoffrey Elton wrote down their concerns about what the enthusiasm for social science was doing to history. The struggle for the soul of the profession was on. The moment had arrived when historians stood at the crossroads: Should they run with the new social scientific history or cling to the old traditional history?[54]

Among historians writing about crime, this struggle took place over crime statistics. The debate about the long-term decline in violence had to do with court statistics, that is, with the processing of individual cases. Beginning in the nineteenth century, governments in Europe began issuing crime statistics, that is, the amount of crimes known to police (whether or not a suspect had been identified or anyone had been convicted). In the United Kingdom, the Judicial Statistics series commenced in 1856; each annual volume consists of three parts. The first, known as police statistics, shows indictable offences known to police. The second part, the criminal statistics, gives details of criminal proceedings for judicial districts and the third part, the prison statistics, provides information about commitments to gaols, prisons, reformatories and industrial schools. These statistics were valued by criminologists since the early decades of the twentieth century, especially in the United States, where nothing like it was available. National crime statistics were not published in the United States until the FBI's Uniform Crime Reports series began in the 1930s.

In his 1967 study of crime in Victorian England, John J. Tobias pronounced British crime statistics available for this period to be worthless.[55] Although they purport to be national crime statistics, they are nothing of the sort. A composite is only as strong as its weakest component, and there was wild variation in the contribution of police districts. In the case of national totals, the weakest component was very weak indeed. It was only in 1856 that establishment of a police force became obligatory in all districts, so before this the figures are completely unreliable as they would reflect the entry of new forces. But even after this year, the figures display disturbing patterns. He pointed to the figures for Leeds from 1857 to 1875. There was only one reasonable explanation for the fluctuations observed: the ups and downs in the total corresponded with changing chief constables. Home Office statisticians were bedevilled by differing practices across forces. Some counted events, some counted people, and some invented their own rules for counting so that one prisoner with two offences became two prisoners. 'Thus', Tobias said, 'any national totals may be made up of figures which mean very different things.'[56]

It was clear which road to the past Tobias travelled. He believed in traditional methods of historicism and harboured serious doubts about what the new social science historians were up to. He affirmed written sources and archival materials as the best route to what people at the time thought. Indictable offences known to the police offer a better means of determining the extent of crime in society and changes over the decades than arrests, convictions or other measures from court records. The problem with this, Tobias said, is that at the time, people interested in explaining crime did not think the statistics were worth very much. They knew that many crimes went undetected and unrecorded. They knew that changes in the law or in police practice made comparisons pointless. As early as 1820 it was said that crime had received more fanfare than had been the case decades earlier: offences which in former times would have been ignored or dealt with on the spot now made it into the figures. He issued clear guidance: no attempt should be made to reconstruct the level of crime in Victorian society from Judicial Statistics.[57]

Vic Gatrell and Tom Hadden argued that a statistical reading of the nineteenth century could be made. Despite the drawbacks Tobias had found, they insisted that quantitative analysis was worth pursuing.[58] The position taken by Tobias, for preferring literary sources over crime figures, was misleading. Victorian commentators had little more than anecdotal evidence as an alternative measure, and when they took the statistics on board, they displayed little knowledge of problems in their construction. Further, Tobias's criticism of national statistics as being only as good as their weakest component rather missed the point. Some counties like Dorset would have been susceptible to a newly organized borough force, but this was not true of many counties.

Gatrell and Hadden provided a comprehensive review of sources and methods of tabulating crime in the nineteenth century, including indictable committals to trial, commitments to prison, summary committals and indictable offences known to the police. They concluded that indictable offences known to police, available for 1857–92, represent the best indicator for the actual incidence of criminal activity as they are least vulnerable to variations in local police efficiency, prosecution practice and court procedure. They were satisfied that a decrease in crime figures represented a genuine decline in criminal activity during the second half of the nineteenth century. It was due to increasing police efficiency and growing prosperity. They published their work in a collection edited by E. A. Wrigley which is revealing because Wrigley represented the British contribution to demographic history. He had been the first to import French techniques for estimating populations and founded the Cambridge Group for the History of Population and Social Structure.

Gatrell then found reason for even greater confidence in nineteenth-century crime trends using what he called the 'convergence principle'.[59] In Victorian England, there was an unknown, but theoretically measurable, amount of criminal activity. There were statistics of crime that failed to provide an accurate tally. However, he theorized that there was a consistent relationship between the two, and because of this, some inferences could be made about the 'real' level of crime. He proposed to ignore small fluctuations up or down over the years and concentrate on overall patterns which would be least vulnerable to distortions. Over the long term, the numbers reflected national trends which made them less vulnerable to being blown off course by events. There were two trends: (1) police and court activity were increasing in efficiency and (2) the public were increasingly more willing to cooperate with the law, making prosecutions more likely. This ensured that the actual gap between the statistical trend and the real trend narrowed at a constant rate, so that by 1900 the gap between the two was much smaller than it was in 1800. As recorded crime declined after 1840, this meant that actual crime must have declined as well. 'Then', Gatrell announced, 'our principle of convergence (i.e. of the narrowing gap) insists that actual crime of the common sort must have declined in incidence as well.'[60]

By the 1990s, post-structuralism raised new doubts about the difference between fact and fiction, and the social scientific approach seemed less credible. Rob Sindall served up a 'third approach'.[61] He agreed with Tobias: the method of definition, collection and presentation made the statistics unreliable at least in certain cases. Even if this unreliability could be countered, the use of the statistics for establishing trends lacked validity because of a number of factors at work bringing out distortions. These included changing definitions of offences, the rise in juvenile offenders, the effectiveness in policing and selective enforcement. 'It is apparent from the evidence', Sindall contended, 'that as a direct measure of criminality the usefulness of the criminal statistics is highly suspect ... they are so riddled with pitfalls and inconsistencies that as a measure of the state of crime they may be useless.'[62] But he also agreed with Gatrell and Hadden: the statistics did measure something. The statistics should be read not as a measure of what was happening, but of what people *believed* was happening. In other words, the statistics capture trends, not in criminal behaviour, but in social attitudes towards criminal behaviour.

While the convergence argument enabled some conclusions to be made about the decline of serious theft and violence in Victorian England, it could not be extended to earlier or later periods in English history. Nor could it apply outside of England. In the United States, Harvey J. Graff suggested the use of jail registers to compensate for the lack of national police figures.[63] These were widely available for the United States, Canada and at least parts of Britain. Jail registers could not supply information about rates of crime in any place for any period, because they are limited to crimes for which someone was arrested. 'Perhaps it is time for historians to refocus attention from the problem of crime rates, which has thus far proved insolvable, to those directly accused of having committed a punishable offense, for whom much material in the form of jail registers is available.'[64] The registers furnish information about thoughts and fears and about the experiences of different groups of people related to crime.

Graff's proposal inspired Eric Monkkonen to think through the possibilities for American crime statistics.[65] He wrote a mini-manifesto for statistical analysis in crime history styled as a critique of Graff. Monkkonen said that Graff underplayed the role of social theory and statistical methods. He cautioned against scaling up models developed from local situations; local crime patterns should not be mistaken for regional or national trends. He pointed out that statistics measured behaviour, but not criminal behaviour. The numbers measured the organizational behaviour of the criminal justice system.[66] To construct information about criminality, it was necessary to understand the processes by which these statistics were constructed. Given the lack of national statistics, there were two options. (1) To imagine the available statistical information as a biased sample of all criminal behaviour and try to compensate for this bias through logical analysis. Although all biases could never be precisely estimated, it was possible to make some informed guesses. (2) Rather than imagine the statistics available as a sample, regard it as a universe of formal interactions between the criminal justice system and the larger society. This approach avoided the epistemological problems associated with the attempt to measure the 'real' amount of crime 'out there'. As a universe, comparison could be made to other cities, counties, states and regions.

Douglas Hay observed that Monkkonen had arrived by a different route at a place quite similar to Tobias.[67] Although Monkkonen regarded Tobias's pessimism as both 'naïve and irresponsible', he shared the same negative attitude. Hay found Monkkonen's view problematic. To regard nineteenth-century statistics as indicators of organizational processes rather than social behaviour overlooked interesting questions about the place of crime in popular culture. While it was true that the organizational process of prosecution 'created' criminals, there was a simultaneous and real change in the kinds of behaviour susceptible to prosecution. It was not obvious that making comparisons across jurisdictions was any easier than making assessments between official and real crime. Further, 'real crime' amounted to another way of referring to the 'culture of the poor', and historians should not abandon efforts to understand this.[68]

Meanwhile, back in Britain, Howard Taylor undermined the confidence in national statistics with a provocative critique. He observed that the homicide statistics for England and Wales followed a curious pattern from the mid-nineteenth century. Crimes known to police never varied more than 20 per cent from the mean. From 1880 until 1966, the average number of murders remained at about 150 per year, rising above 179 or falling below 120 on only five occasions.[69] This strange continuity did not reflect the actual number of homicides, but rather, organizational goals driven by financial pressures. The central government had passed the prosecution costs onto local authorities, and they responded by diverting crimes into the lower courts. Further, the police had incentive not to register murders as declining crime figures were taken as a measure of their effectiveness. The statistics reflected a conscious political effort to pare down the crime problem to fit the amount of government resources assigned to contain it. Crime statistics remained artificially low until the 1930s, when the authorities admitted, for the first time, that crime was increasing. Even then, the gradual increase from year after year into the 1960s was not simply a matter of natural fluctuations in an upward tendency. Criminal statistics followed an 'astonishingly uniform' rate of increase for nearly eighty years. The 'police establishment' at the local and national levels 'closely coordinated' crime statistics; the number of crimes fluctuated in relation to the number of serving officers. 'Direct control of the statistics', Taylor concluded, 'provides a far more likely explanation than simple coincidence.'[70]

Taylor raised new doubts about the interpretation of crime statistics as a measure of real crime. He not only unsettled the trust that had been established by Gatrell's convergence principle, but also the convention of relying on the murder rate as the most accurate of English statistics. It was as if Taylor had seen the ghost of Tobias, and quantitative historians needed to provide a rational explanation for this strange apparition. Monkkonen agreed that Taylor had a 'powerful argument' with serious implications for historical homicide research. But rather than challenge the argument for a conspiracy in the production of statistics, he advocated 'capture–recapture'. A straightforward test could be made by comparing the police count of homicide with a count obtained from other sources, such as newspaper and coroners' records. It was a matter of finding the bodies – those of murder victims but not counted by the police as such – if there were bodies to be found.[71]

John Archer took up the suggestion and unearthed some justification for Taylor's misgivings. Archer observed that Taylor's 'supply-side' argument was cast in broad terms. He wondered whether it would hold up to a deeper analysis. Regional and local analysis would likely find that the number of murders would have varied outside the 20 per cent margin. The suggestion that there were only 150 murders a year because the government only had the cash to process this many implies that the cost of prosecution was more or less the same. The costs of murders would have varied from simple to more complex trials. Archer investigated situations in Manchester and Liverpool where there would have been some question about whether to regard it as a crime: babies 'found dead', corpses fished from rivers, wives beaten to death. He came across suspicious deaths that were never investigated, which indicated that Taylor was definitely on to something. But, the police had other reasons not to have pursued the matter, reasons other than financial limitations.[72]

The trouble with statistics

By the 1990s, social scientific analyses had become a familiar part of historical writing. Quantification was no longer as exotic, revolutionary or threatening as it first appeared, and crime historians did their part to normalize the practice. Statistical techniques for data analysis became routine, another gadget in the kitchen drawer available as the need arises. Crime history absorbed quantification, without resolving the issues that had been raised since the new social history had emerged.

One issue is the extent to which historians *can* rely on social science as a guide to research. This was a subject Stone had raised: Do the kinds of evidence available to historians support the application of statistical techniques? James Sharpe observed that borrowing the newest techniques, and arguing about the results, seemed a natural thing for crime historians to do. But, what, really, was to be gained? He proposed that given the limited nature of sources for English crime – indictments – counting was one of the things that could be done with them. Some of the more interesting questions, such as the use of informal controls and sanctions against offenders, defied quantification and could only be glimpsed in the isolated anecdote. Crime, particularly when defined broadly, involved many different courts. To argue that a column of figures from the archives of a particular court reflected the actual level of criminality in society was a delusion. In the absence of national statistics, historians for periods before the nineteenth century had to create their statistics from court archives. That such archives exist for a limited number of counties was bad enough, but even where they did exist, they were fragmentary and incomplete.[73]

A prerequisite to any quantitative analysis is a choice about what is to be counted as crime. Court records available for the eighteenth century and earlier offer cases, offences, persons accused or persons indicted. For the nineteenth century and later, national criminal statistics are available in Europe. But, there is still the matter of what is to be counted: offences, cases, arrests or convictions. Further, these statistics present different series of figures that do not always use the same unit at the same period of time, nor does one series use the same unit over the whole period covered. This creates a trolley full of methodological puzzles that need to be solved and a conceptual confusion that can throw a wrench into the analysis. It is easy to confuse cases with individuals because the same individual might appear more than once in a given period of time. Changes in the population of 'repeat customers' in statistics have technical and conceptual repercussions that need to be taken into account whether using French, German or English statistics.[74]

François Ploux has argued for an anthropological approach. He favours letting go of counting as well as categories. Historians of violence have paid little attention to problems brought up by studying the subject through the 'prism of categories used in judicial thought'.[75] The problem with approaching crime in this way is combining a range of behaviour (homicide, pilfering, sexual violence), as if it had a singular motivation or explanation. It gives criminality a single meaning, separate from the multiple forms that it can take. Use of judicial series for quantitative analysis decontextualizes crimes, robbing the historian of cultural meanings crucial to the explanation.

Ploux emphasizes the replacement of the court series approach with a social approach, a work which contains no figures. The historian does not prepare graphs, statistics, charts or averages. The historian does not seek to reduce criminal acts to quantifiable values. Rather, the task is to reconstruct the social, cultural and normative environment of the crime. The aim is to grasp the meaning of the crime by making connections with social categories: family relationships, violence to avenge honour, etc. Categories need to be thoughtfully 'constructed by the researcher', not thoughtlessly reproduce the 'categories of judicial taxonomy'.[76]

Another issue is the extent to which historians *should* apply modern techniques to past evidence. A good example of this is crime rate. Sharpe has pointed to several problems with calculating crime rates. (1) The basic issue of definition – what is included and what is not in 'crime' of a particular period. (2) The problem of reliable population data, which for most periods before 1800 is uncertain. (3) The smallness of the sample of offences tends to produce very high homicide rates. Massive variations in medieval homicide rates have more to do with the combination of a small sample and unreliable population data. Any conclusions remain tentative. Rather than see statistics as a route to measuring real levels of unlawful behaviour, they could be taken as an indication of conclusions about the activities of the state. Quantification did provide at least an outline of the main lines of the relationship between crime and punishment between 1550 and 1800.[77]

Some historians, such as Randolph Roth, construct rates in the same way contemporary criminologists do. Others question use of rates meaningful for the twenty-first century for historical analysis, despite statistical adjustments. Does it really make sense to regard as equivalent two observations separated by time and place simply because the ratios calculated for the populations give the same result? In what sense do the troublemakers in a town in the early modern period, with 1,000 inhabitants, compare to those in a city of the modern era with 1,000,000? To avoid comparing apples to bananas, it is necessary to construct the reference population as the most likely to contribute to the criminal statistics. It is not enough to know the population, but the characteristics of the population (age, gender and class for a start). This information is not easy to discover, even for the nineteenth century, and even more difficult for earlier centuries. Add to this that in statistical sets, people are not really divided into criminals or non-criminals, as the method of calculating rates assumes, which raises a question about whether there is a genuine 'scientific basis' for the rates, or whether the use of rates amounts to an 'agreement of convenience' among scientists.[78]

These issues relate to a big question about social science and history. That is, whether social science furnishes any techniques that would allow historians to overcome the limitations built into historical knowledge. For some, history is social science, so historians should use available techniques on data sets of interest. For others, history is different from social science, and retrofitting contemporary techniques leads to anachronism. Basically, this is what is at stake in an exchange between Robert Dykstra and Randolph Roth over the American 'Wild West'.

Beginning in the 1960s, Robert Dykstra challenged the myth of frontier violence as presented in western films.[79] Although Dodge City, Kansas, had become notorious for its indifference to violence, this was more cinema than reality. Actually, gunfights, saloon brawls and the like were bad for business, so the town maintained a large police force, enforced regulations on firearms, and kept fist fights and shoot-outs in check. Dodge City was the most violent of the frontier cattle towns in terms of body count (fifteen homicides), but the average of 1.5 per year was no different than the others. He challenged other historians, particularly Roger McGrath, who had reported a high homicide rate for Bodie and Aurora, two California mining camps. Using the method of calculating rates in the FBI's Uniform Crime Reports (the number of homicides per 100,000 population), McGrath had produced an artificially high rate as a consequence of the 'fallacy of small numbers'. The smallness of the population makes the annual number of homicides seem high, and ignoring it amounts to a 'display of statistical illiteracy'.[80]

Dykstra's comments about measuring homicide attracted Randolph Roth.[81] Dykstra, he said, was right about Dodge City. It was a mistake to infer that the frontier was violent from statistics of a few cattle towns and mining camps known for their violence. But he was wrong to discount calculations from studies in Oregon and California for which population statistics were reliable. Peterson Del Mar identified 114 homicides in Oregon from 1850 to 1865, a rate of 30 per 100,000 a year. Clare McKanna found 682 homicides in seven California counties during 1850–65 in indictment records and coroner's inquests, amounting to a homicide rate of 73 per year. The statistics produced by Del Mar and McKanna showed that Dykstra, in attempting to avoid one myth had been taken in by another. There was no such thing as a 'fallacy of small numbers'. Roth said that 'the laws of probability made it possible to predict the character of a large population from a sample of surprisingly modest size, as long as that sample is representative of the population as a whole'.[82] Thanks to the laws of probability, historians possessed the power to make meaningful comparisons across time and place.

Dykstra continued to question the comparison of small frontier places to modern cities.[83] Using the FBI's method of 'computing the ratio of corpses to inhabitants at risk' as the basis for comparing tiny populations with small body counts in the late nineteenth century with Miami, New York or another city of the late twentieth century was not legitimate.[84] True, the homicide rate for Dodge City in 1880 was 100.4, dramatically higher than that of Miami in 1980, at 32.7. But the Miami rate was based on more than 500 killings in a city of 1.5 million, and the Dodge City rate came from a single murder in a town of less than 1,000. The 'fallacy of small numbers' was 'a statistical fact'.[85] There was no getting past the methodological barrier of small venues because the essential information, body counts and overall inhabitants were 'organically entangled' in homicide rate computations. He disagreed with Roth's techniques. To invoke the laws of probability, the rate had to be conceptualized not as a numerical calculation but as an estimate obtained from a random sample. Roth's calculations for California counties in 1850–65 achieved no more than a demonstration of the obvious fact that large populations tend to have small homicide rates, and small towns display large rates. Dykstra had no doubt that 'the larger the population of a place, the lower its homicide rate will tend to be'.[86]

Roth responded by insisting even more strongly that Dykstra's arguments resulted from an insufficient grasp of social scientific methods.[87] Historians could use the same techniques as criminologists and epidemiologists, and when the evidence was analysed, it showed that the American West of the nineteenth century did have extremely high rates of homicide. Dykstra's 'fallacy of small numbers' rested on a misunderstanding of the 'law of small numbers'. Small numbers were not beyond the reach of statisticians, although they need to be handled with care. Many populations he assumed to be too small for analysis were only so if taken year by year; reliable rates could be obtained if calculated for a sufficient number of years. By examining the average number of homicides for a cluster of years, it was possible to make reasonable inferences about homicide rates for small locations or social groups. Dykstra not only misread the evidence for California and Oregon, he even misread the evidence from Dodge City. Contrary to Dykstra's conclusion, the statistics in his own book, *The Cattle Towns*, actually proved that Kansas towns had 'exceptionally high homicide rates'.[88]

Conclusion

Since the nineteenth century, quantification has offered historians of crime a major method for exploring the past. It would be hard to find historians who identify themselves as positivists along the lines of Buckle, or would share the commitment to statistical analysis of the *Annales* school. But the social science history of the 1970s certainly has had a tremendous influence. Quantitative history, guided by probability theory and powered by the latest technology, remains a vital and productive part of writing the history of crime.

The models of crime trends built from court records by Ted Gurr and Howard Zehr enabled bold statements about the overall level of criminal violence and shifts in the form of criminality over the centuries. Work on crime statistics, by Vic Gatrell and Tom Hadden in Britain, and Eric Monkkonen and Randolph Roth in the United States, brought a new understanding of crime in the past, whether Victorian criminality or violence in the American West. Debates about sources, techniques and interpretation continue. The practitioners of quantitative crime history dismiss the scepticism of J. J. Tobias, and although they acknowledge difficulties of the sort James Sharpe pointed out, they would not see this as a reason not to try. So, while there are no positivists of the really old school around, there are modern positivists who believe in the power of social science for historical understanding. For non-believers, the fact that historical 'data' is fragmentary and incomplete means that statistical analysis has limited application. But for believers – Stone, Monkkonen, Roth – historians can overcome limitations in the historical record through the use of statistical techniques.

What was really exciting about quantitative history in the 1970s was not so much the mainframe computer, magnetic tape and automated data processing as the promise that these would enable historians to advise the government on current policy. Traditional historians are reluctant to do this, wary even of analogy as a form of historical argument. But quantitative historians, engaged in the sort of work Gurr was doing, raised expectations about putting historians on an equal footing with social scientists in the role of policy advisors. Since then, there has been some realization that quantitative history had been oversold. The large-scale projects funded in this period did not yield results as clear or convincing as policy research required. But large-scale projects continue to attract support, and the cross-over between social science and history has become less unusual. So the promise remains.

Notes

1 Mary Pickering, 'Auguste Comte', in George Ritzer, ed., *The Blackwell Companion to Major Classical Social Theorists* (Oxford: Blackwell, 2003), 13–39.

2 Henry T. Buckle, *History of Civilization in England*, vol. 1 (London: John W. Parker, 1858), 19.

3 Buckle, *History of Civilization in England*, 6.

4 Buckle, *History of Civilization in England*, 22.

5 H. R. Trevor-Roper, 'Fernand Braudel, the *Annales*, and the *Mediterranean*', *Journal of Modern History* 44 (1972): 466–71.

6 Fernand Braudel, *On History* (Chicago: University of Chicago Press, 1980), 25–54.

7 George Huppert, 'The *Annales* experiment', in Michael Bently, ed., *Companion to Historiography* (London: Routledge, 1997), 880–1, 873–88.

8 Fernand Braudel, *The Mediterranean and the Mediterranean World in the Age of Phillip II*, vol. 1 (London: Collins, 1972), 17–21.

9 Braudel, *The Mediterranean*, vol. 1, 737–52.

10 Braudel, *The Mediterranean*, vol. 1, 865–87.

11 Braudel, *The Mediterranean*, vol. 2, 257, 266.

12 Douglas Greenberg, *Crime and Law Enforcement in the Colony of New York 1691-1776* (Ithaca and New York: Cornell University Press, 1974), 13–14.

13 George Fisher, 'Historian in the cellar', in Robert W. Gordon and Morton
    J. Horwitz, eds, *Law, Society and History: Themes in the Legal Sociology and
    Legal History of Lawrence M Friedman* (Cambridge: Cambridge University
    Press, 2011), 273–92.

14 Lawrence Friedman and Robert Percival, *The Roots of Justice: Crime and
    Punishment in Alameda County, California, 1870-1910* (Chapel Hill, NC:
    University of North Carolina Press, 1981), 311.

15 Ted Robert Gurr, Peter N. Grabosky and Richard C. Hula, *The Politics of
    Crime and Conflict: A Comparative History of Four Cities* (Beverly Hills, CA:
    Sage, 1977), ix.

16 Eric Monkkonen, 'The quantitative historical study of crime and criminal
    justice', in James A. Inciardi and Charles E. Faupel, eds, *History and Crime:
    Implications for Criminal Justice Policy* (Beverly Hills, CA: Sage, 1980), 53.

17 Randolph Roth, 'Eric Monkkonen', *Crime, History and Societies* 9 (2005): 157–8.

18 European Committee on Crime Problems, *Historical Research on Crime and
    Criminal Justice* (Strasbourg: Council of Europe, 1985).

19 Lawrence Stone, 'Interpersonal violence in English society 1300-1980', *Past
    and Present* 101 (1983): 30.

20 Stone, 'Interpersonal violence', 32.

21 T. R. Gurr, 'Historical trends in violent crime: A critical review of the evidence',
    Crime and Justice: An Annual Review of Research 3 (1981): 295–353.

22 Lawrence Stone, 'The revival of narrative: Reflections on a new old history',
    Past and Present 85 (1979): 11.

23 Stone, 'The revival', 22.

24 Peter Stearns, 'Modernization and social history: Some suggestions, and a
    muted cheer', *Journal of Social History* 14 (1980): 189–209.

25 J. A. Sharpe, 'The history of violence in England: Some observations', *Past &
    Present* 108 (1985): 206–15.

26 Sharpe, 'Debate: The history of violence', 211.

27 Sharpe, 'Debate: The history of violence', 214.

28 Sharpe, 'Debate: The history of violence', 215.

29 Lawrence Stone, 'A rejoinder', *Past & Present* 108 (1985): 216–24.

30 Stone, 'A rejoinder', 217.

31 Stone, 'A rejoinder', 217.

32 J. S. Cockburn, 'Patterns of violence in English society: Homicide in Kent
    1560-1985', *Past & Present* 130 (1991): 70–106.

33 Cockburn, 'Patterns of violence', 103.

34 Eva Österberg, 'Criminality, social control, and the early modern state:
    Evidence and interpretations in Scandinavia historiography', *Social Science
    History* 16 (1992): 82.

35 Heikki Ylikangas, 'What happened to violence?', in Heikki Ylikangas, Petri
    Karonen and Martti Lehti, eds, *Five Centuries of Violence in Finland and the
    Baltic Area* (Helsinki: Academy of Finland, 1998), 7–128.

36 Eric Monkkonen, 'New standards for historical homicide research', *Crime, History & Societies* 5 (2001): 5–26.

37 Monkkonen, 'New standards', 19.

38 Randolph Roth, *American Homicide* (Cambridge, MA: Belknap Press, 2009), 12.

39 Xavier Rousseaux, 'From medieval cities to national states, 1350-1850: The historiography of crime and criminal justice in Europe', in Clive Emsley and Louis A. Knafla, eds, *Crime History and Histories of Crime: Studies in the Historiography of Crime and Criminal Justice in Modern History* (Westport, CT: Greenwood Press, 1996), 14–16.

40 Howard Zehr, *Crime and the Development of Modern Society: Patterns of Criminality in Nineteenth Century Germany and France* (London: Croom Helm, 1976).

41 Zehr, *Crime and the Development*, 15.

42 Zehr, *Crime and the Development*, 139.

43 Zehr, *Crime and the Development*, 141–2.

44 Zehr, *Crime and the Development*, 10.

45 Louise I. Shelley, *Crime and Modernization: The Impact of Industrialization and Urbanization on Crime* (Carbondale: Southern Illinois University Press, 1981).

46 Shelley, *Crime and Modernization*, 31.

47 Eric Monkkonen, 'The quantitative historical study of crime and criminal justice', in James A. Inciardi and Charles E. Faupel, eds, *History and Crime: Implications for Criminal Justice Policy* (Beverly Hills, CA: Sage, 1980), 53–73.

48 Monkkonen, 'The quantitative historical', 66.

49 Richard J. Evans, *Rethinking German History: Nineteenth Century Germany and the Origins of the Third Reich* (London: Unwin Hyman, 1987), 175.

50 Evans, *Rethinking German History*, 175.

51 Eric A. Johnson and Eric H. Monkkonen, *The Civilization of Crime: Violence in Town and Country since the Middle Ages* (Urbana: University of Illinois Press, 1996).

52 Dag Lindström, 'Homicide in Scandinavia: Long-term trends and their implications', in Sophie Body-Gendrot and Pieter Spierenburg, eds, *Violence in Europe: Historical and Contemporary Perspectives* (New York: Springer, 2008), 55.

53 Manuel Eisner, 'Modernisation, self-control and lethal violence: The long-term dynamics of European homicide rates in theoretical perspective', *British Journal of Criminology* 41 (2001): 618–38; Helmut Thome, 'Explaining long-term trends in violent crime', *Crime, History and Societies* 5 (2001): 69–86.

54 Robert William Fogel and G. R. Elton, *Which Road to the Past? Two Views of History* (New Haven, CT: Yale University Press, 1983).

55 J. J. Tobias, *Crime and Industrial Society in the Nineteenth Century* (London: B. T. Batsford, 1967).

56 Tobias, *Crime and Industrial*, 20.

57 Tobias, *Crime and Industrial*, 16–17.

58 V. A. C. Gatrell and T. B. Hadden, 'Nineteenth century criminal statistics and their interpretation', in E. A. Wrigley, ed., *Nineteenth Century Society: Essays on the Use of Quantitative Methods for the Study of Social Data* (Cambridge: Cambridge University Press, 1972), 336–95.

59 V. A. C. Gatrell, 'The decline of theft and violence in Victorian and Edwardian England', in V. A. C. Gatrell, Bruce Lenman and Geoffrey Parker, eds, *Crime and the Law: The Social History of Crime in Western Europe since 1500* (London: Europa, 1980), 238–370.

60 Gatrell, 'The decline of theft', 251.

61 Rob Sindall, *Street Violence in the Nineteenth Century: Media Panic or Real Danger?* (Leicester: Leicester University Press, 1990), 16–28.

62 Sindall, *Street Violence*, 23.

63 Harvey J. Graff, 'Crime and punishment in the nineteenth century: A new look at the criminal', *Journal of Interdisciplinary History* 7 (1977): 477–91.

64 Graff, 'Crime and punishment', 479.

65 Eric Monkkonen, 'Systematic criminal justice history: Some suggestions', *Journal of Interdisciplinary History* 9 (1979): 451–64.

66 Monkkonen, 'Systematic criminal justice', 456.

67 Douglas Hay, 'Crime and justice in eighteenth and nineteenth-century England', *Crime and Justice: A International Annual* 2 (1980): 66–7.

68 Hay, 'Crime and justice', 67.

69 Howard Taylor, 'Rationing crime: The political economy of criminal statistics since the 1850s', *Economic History Review* 3 (1998): 569–90; Howard Taylor, 'The politics of rising crime statistics of England and Wales, 1914-1960', *Crime, History & Societies* 2 (1998): 5–28.

70 Taylor, 'The politics of rising', 25.

71 Eric Monkkonen, 'New standards for historical homicide research', *Crime, History & Societies* 5 (2001): 11–12.

72 John E. Archer, '"The violence we have lost"? Body counts, historians and interpersonal violence in England', *Memoria y Civilización* 2 (1999): 171–90; John E. Archer, 'Mysterious and suspicious deaths: Missing homicides in North-West England 1850-1900', *Crime, History & Societies* 12 (2008): 2–17.

73 J. A. Sharpe, 'Quantification and the history of crime in early modern England: Problems and results', *Historical Social Research* 15 (1990): 17–32.

74 Bruno Aubusson de Cavarlay, 'Can criminal statistics still be of scientific use? The French criminal justice system, 1831-1980', *Historical Methods* 26 (1993): 69–84.

75 François Ploux, 'Violence in France's past: An anthropological approach', in Sophie Body-Gendrot and Pieter Spierenburg, eds, *Violence in Europe: Historical and Contemporary Perspectives* (New York: Springer, 2008), 66, 65–78.

76 Ploux, 'Violence in France's past', 66–7.

77 Sharpe, 'Quantification', 27–9.

78 de Cavarlay, 'Can criminal statistics', 77.

79 Robert R. Dykstra, 'Field notes: Overdosing on Dodge City', *Western Historical Quarterly* 27 (1996): 505–14.

80 Dykstra, 'Field notes', 510.

81 Randolph Roth, 'Guns, murder, and probability: How can we decide which figures to trust?', *Reviews in History* 35 (2007): 165–75.

82 Roth, 'Guns, murder and history', 172.

83 Robert R. Dykstra, 'Quantifying the Wild West: The problematic statistics of frontier violence', *Western Historical Quarterly* 40 (2009): 321–47.

84 Dykstra, 'Quantifying the Wild West', 331.

85 Dykstra, 'Quantifying the Wild West', 342.

86 Dykstra, 'Quantifying the Wild West', 334.

87 Randolph Roth, Michael D. Maltz and Douglas L. Eckberg, 'Homicide rates in the Old West', *Western Historical Quarterly* 42 (2011): 173–95.

88 Roth and others, 'Homicide rates', 176.

Further reading

Aebi, Marcelo and Antonia Linde. 'Long-term trends in crime: Continuity and change', in Paul Knepper and Anja Johansen, eds, *The Oxford Handbook of the History of Crime and Criminal Justice*. New York: Oxford University Press, 2015.

Eisner, Manuel. 'Long-term historical trends in violent crime'. *Crime and Justice: An International Annual* 30 (2003): 83–142.

Friedman, Lawrence and Robert Percival. *The Roots of Justice: Crime and Punishment in Alameda County, California, 1870-1910*. Chapel Hill: University of North Carolina Press, 1981.

King, Peter. *Crime, Justice and Discretion in England 1740-1820*. Oxford: Oxford University Press, 2000.

Monkkonen, Eric. 'The quantitative historical study of crime and criminal justice', in James A. Inciardi and Charles E. Faupel, eds, *History and Crime: Implications for Criminal Justice Policy*. Beverly Hills, CA: Sage, 1980, 53–73.

Monkkonen, Eric. *Crime, Justice, History*. Columbus: Ohio State University Press, 2002.

Roth, Randolph. *American Homicide*. Cambridge, MA: Belknap Press, 2009.

Sharpe, James. 'Quantification and the history of crime in early modern England: Problems and results'. *Historical Social Research* 15 (1990): 17–32.

Von Hofer, Hanns and Tapio Lappi-Seppälä. 'The development of crime in light of Finnish and Swedish criminal justice statistics 1750-2010'. *European Journal of Criminology* 11 (2014): 169–94.

CHAPTER THREE

Evolution and psychoanalysis

Writing the history of crime has always been an exercise in interdisciplinary history. Crime historians have been ready to borrow ideas from other fields of knowledge and bring them to the study of the criminal past. Many of the theories and techniques have come from conventional social sciences, but there have also been some from further afield.

Attempts to develop a philosophy of history from evolutionary theory have been around since the nineteenth century. This effort has included scholars from a range of backgrounds and several with criminal tendencies. Lawyer-historians Luke Pike and O. W. Holmes Jr wrote about evolution, crime and history, as did the Italian physician-criminologist Cesare Lombroso. In recent years, James Q. Wilson, David Courtwright, Jeffrey Adler and Martin Wiener have also experimented with biology, crime and history. They draw on evolution, or 'evolutionary psychology', for their theoretical architecture, but do not build on the earlier work. Instead they begin with recent scientific findings in genetics, physiology and the like and imagine how these would have played out in the past. This strategy avoids incorporating outdated or discredited scientific concepts. It also avoids the troubled history of efforts to formulate a theory of history from natural science.

Historians have also borrowed from psychoanalysis. In the early twentieth century, Freud considered the social implications of what he had learnt from his clients on the couch and proposed a theory about the formation of conscience through time. During the past few decades, historians have pursued his theory of the mind and developed 'psychohistory', an examination of the psychological motivations behind historical events. But the primary use of Freud in writing in the history of crime has relied on Freud's theory of history, and it has travelled via the work of Norbert Elias. The theory of the 'civilizing process' has become increasingly popular in the histories of punishment and analyses of long-term trends in criminal violence (Chapter 2). Pieter Spierenburg has devoted some forty years of his professional career to exploring the implications of the civilizing process on the response to crime. Others, including Eric Johnson and John Pratt, have written about the civilizing process, crime and punishment as well.

The first half of this chapter covers the application of evolutionary theory to the history of crime. Part 1 reviews efforts in the late nineteenth century and interwar period, including Pike, Holmes, Lombroso and Barnes. Part 2 examines recent efforts to apply evolutionary psychology or other biological ideas; it includes work by Wilson, Courtwright, Adler, Wiener and more. The second half covers theories associated with civilization, beginning with, in Part 3, Freud's work in the early twentieth century. Part 4 reviews the work of Norbert Elias and Spierenburg on the civilizing process and punishment and Part 5 analyses the work of Eric Johnson and Eric Monkkonen, and others, on the civilizing process and trends in violence.

The natural history of crime

During the second half of the nineteenth century, evolution, understood as the progressive unfolding of a cosmic teleology, was an intoxicating idea. Darwin presented his theory of evolution by natural selection, but he did not have much, if anything, to say about progress in human affairs. Others, such as Lamarck and Spencer, offered their own theories of incremental progression and seemed more than willing to speculate. Anthropologists, philosophers, journalists and novelists found inspiration in the idea of evolutionary progression, as did biologists, physicists and botanists. There were historians, too, such as John Fiske, who brought Spencer to American readers. Fiske popularized evolution as a grand, progressive process that embraced all aspects of the natural and human worlds. The appearance of humanity, he taught, opened a new epoch in the history of the universe in which the evolution of the mind took over from evolution of the body. He envisioned harmony between human history and natural history with all things working together towards a common destiny: the fulfilment of the highest spiritual qualities in human character.[1]

The effort to connect evolution, history and crime has been troubled. Luke O. Pike, an English lawyer, produced *A History of Crime in England* (1873) which also drew on biological development to interpret crime through the ages. 'The history of crime', he wrote, 'taken in connexion with the history of criminal law, is a history of the ever-increasing restraint placed upon savage impulses, and the ever-increasing encouragement to the wider play of sympathy.'[2] While inherited tendency was not the only source of criminal motivation, it had to be considered in accounting for the antecedents of criminality. The origin of criminal acts, against the person and also against property, was found, not in the growth of towns and development of civilization, but in the 'propensities of the savage, which had been handed down from generation to generation'. It was, Pike thought, a simple and direct relationship: 'The more violent the robbery, the more is the past to blame for it.'[3]

Pike was convinced that the naturalists were on to something big. They had identified a class of primitive organisms that still survived in their original form, even though new species had developed out of them. 'In the same manner there are savages still living in our midst, of the same blood and origin as ourselves, and yet unlike us in all except our common ancestry.'[4] This could be seen not only in the development of the human population on the whole, but in the growth and development of individuals over the life course. The young male, in the course of attaining the full range of 'animal powers' had a strong tendency to display lawlessness and cruelty characteristic of his 'savage ancestors'. Statistics of crime confirmed it. Whether for England, France, Germany or Belgium, the numbers revealed an association with age: the tendency to commit the great majority of acts, now commonly described as crimes, and especially crimes of violence, was at its greatest strength when the human being attained the peak of physical power. Pike regarded habitual criminals as a population with the attitudes and behaviour of the uncivilized, tendencies inherited from the remote past. Their misfortune was to be born into an age which could not appreciate their actions as brave and skilful behaviour, but saw them as violent misconduct worthy of the gallows.[5]

The idea of law as development, progressing from simple to complex, has appealed to legal historians. Oliver Wendell Holmes Jr, an associate justice of the United States Supreme Court, found the idea of evolution an appealing way of understanding legal history. Holmes rejected the view of the law as a moral philosophy worked out according to mathematical principles. As he put it in *The Common Law* (1881), 'The life of the law has not been logic; it has been experience.'[6] Holmes became a lawyer in a period when Darwin's ideas stirred intellectuals in many fields, and he applied the principle of natural selection to society. He joined the Metaphysical Club, whose members thought through the implications of the new science, including how evolution produced the consciousness of the self. Holmes viewed the law as an adaptive mechanism that groups of people used to advance their interest in the struggle for existence. He covered areas of law – criminal, torts, contracts, inheritance – and showed how seemingly unrelated legal rules resulted from a common origin in vengeance. The primitive impulse of revenge was transformed into the rational aim of socially defined harms.[7]

The Common Law, which began as a series of lectures, paints the development of law on a canvas of evolutionary theory. Evolutionary change seldom appears in the foreground, but can be glimpsed in the language of metamorphosis from barbarism to civilization. Through various examples from ancient times to the nineteenth century, Holmes argues that the law is always changing, moving closer to consistency but never achieving it. It incorporates new principles from current experience, and always retains old ones from the past, which have yet to be absorbed or sloughed off. He thought up some fabulous analogies such as that of the cat's clavicle in the opening chapter: 'Just as the clavicle in the cat only tells of the existence of some earlier creature to which a collarbone was useful, precedents survive in the law long after the use they once served is at the end and the reason for them has been forgotten.'[8] For Holmes, biological development was more than a metaphor but a guide to public policy in the form of eugenics. He wrote the majority decision in *Buck v Bell* (1927), which authorized sterilization as a means of crime prevention, a decision that contains 'the highest ratio of injustice per word ever signed on to by eight Supreme Court Justices'.[9]

The Italian Cesare Lombroso formulated an elaborate two-volume history of crime on the scale of Pike. Lombroso produced many articles and books, which built his reputation as a criminologist, but his book on the history of political crime and revolution, *Il Delitto Politico e la Rivoluzione* (1890), Political Crime and Revolution, has never been translated into English. The analysis starts from the premise that most people are committed to 'misoneism', a physiological characteristic that makes them reluctant to accept change.[10] This accounts for the persistence of culture, religion and literary convention within advanced civilization. A few individuals, who represent a physiological aberration, challenge the inertia of the majority in the form of political crime. It is essential for political crime to exist, because without it, civilization would never move forward. However, political crime takes two forms, revolution and rebellion. Revolutions, led by individuals of true genius, are not criminal but are only viewed as such at the time. They are essential for civilization to progress, and are ultimately successful, regardless of how slowly they proceed, because they are in harmony with evolutionary adaptation. Alternatively, rebellions are apt to be sudden, energetic bursts that dissolve without lasting impact. They are led by criminals, and are often fuelled by alcohol or climate, and cease with the death of their leaders. Looking forward, it is impossible to tell the difference, Lombroso taught, because even true revolutions involve some amount of violence. Rebellions can only be distinguished from revolutions by looking backward – only historians were in a position to grasp their long-term legacy.[11]

Lombroso wrote a great deal in criminology, and much has been written about him. Much of it is a denunciation of his idea that the behaviour of some criminals could be explained by atavism, a reversion to an earlier evolutionary stage. This led Lombroso to conclude that gypsies and prostitutes were less fully evolved than European men. When the Lombroso Museum opened in Turin, which housed his collection of skulls and other human artefacts, protestors gathered outside shouting 'Lombroso razzista, Mazzini terrorista' (Lombroso was a racist, Mazzini a terrorist). According to the protestors, Lombroso had used his science to legitimize murder, oppression and violence against Southern Italians.

Harry Elmer Barnes, who taught history at Columbia University in the 1920s, offered one of the most thorough elaborations of evolution in history in his historical penology. *The Evolution of Penology in Pennsylvania* (1927) presents Pennsylvania as the foremost example of a modern, advanced system of punishment, the culmination of reform movements to have occurred over more than a century. 'Herbert Spencer's formula of evolution as a passage from a crude and undifferentiated homogeneity to a differentiated and specialized heterogeneity', Barnes declared, 'admirably describes and summarizes the course of development of the penal, reformatory and correctional institutions of Pennsylvania, as well as those in the country as a whole.'[12] Barnes regarded the establishment of a state prison in 1789 within Walnut Street Jail as the first step in a 'differentiated treatment of criminals'; the second step was a house of refuge for delinquents opened in Philadelphia in 1828. Further advances occurred in the creation of the hospital for the insane at Harrisburg, the training school for 'feeble-minded children' at Elwyn, and in the 1920s, the implementation of non-institutional supervision through probation. Barnes concluded by saying that more progress had been made in the 'real scientific basis of criminology' in the past forty years than had been achieved since the dawn of history, but that it could be successfully applied only after a 'persistent campaign of public education'.[13]

A prolific writer, Barnes produced books of history, criminology and other topics. During the interwar period, he became enamoured with scientific criminology. Every form of human conduct, he decided, was determined by biological heredity and the social environment. Crime was not a legal issue but a socio-medical problem to be dealt with through a comprehensive prevention scheme, founded on biological and eugenic provisions to ensure that future generations would contain more 'well born' and fewer 'defective' individuals. His views put him in ideological kinship with the eugenics programme of the National Socialists in Germany, and after the war, he became the American leader of Holocaust denial. Among his many misstatements, Barnes stated that the allied devastation of Germany was more painful than 'the alleged extermination [of Jews] in the gas chambers'.[14]

Evolutionary psychology and violence

In the 1970s, several books appeared about how evolutionary origins could explain present conditions and problems. These included academic work by Edward O. Wilson, *Sociobiology*, which pointed to biology as an explanation for behaviour, as well as that of writer Arthur Koestler, *The Ghost in the Machine*, in which he supposed that something had gone wrong in the human brain in the course of evolutionary formation, leaving us hardwired for hierarchical social organization. The starting point for evolutionary theorizing is that animal species have evolved from one another and therefore share a common physiology, so for humans to think of themselves as different from animals because of their consciousness or volition is an illusion. Human behaviour is subject to the same scientific laws as all animal behaviour. The moral of the story, however, is that humans have in some way upset the evolutionary order of things and are posed to destroy themselves and the planet unless they make some changes.

Austrian scientist Konrad Lorenz received a Nobel Prize for his work on ethology, the study of animal behaviour. He offered a theory of aggression that explained human problems as a form of behaviour in animal species and that stems from innate aggressive tendencies. To explain the existence of any behaviour begins with looking for its survival value within the species. To explain aggression, and specifically, intra-species aggression, seems challenging. What would be the survival value of fighting and threats between the same species? He speculated that it may have to do with making efficient use of territory, preserving the strength of family/herd, or establishing a hierarchy within groups. He observed that it is rare for animals in the wild to kill or injure each other, so that what is going on is the 'ritualisation' of fighting. An activity that yielded biological advances for the species without damage to individuals along the way. Human beings on the other hand are the only animals to engage in mass slaughter of their own species. The technology of weapons had óutpaced restraints on their use. Now that human beings had progressed from sticks and stones, to arrows and swords, to bullets and bombs, to chemical and nuclear weapons, they have created a dangerous situation.[15]

In *Crime and Human Nature* (1985), James Q. Wilson, a political scientist, and Richard J. Herrnstein, a psychologist, asserted that a comprehensive explanation for criminal behaviour had to take into account 'individual predispositions and their biological roots'.[16] This implied that wide-scale, long-term social changes associated with criminal behaviour originated in human nature. Although legal sanctions and social institutions were important, levels of crime fluctuated in synchronization with demography, and specifically, the proportion of young males in the population (who were more likely to be aggressive). Wilson developed the argument further in his book on morality; moral judgement was not a matter of culture or social convention but had a biological basis as well. The 'moral sense' evolved because it had adaptive value. The evolutionary process built in sympathy, self-control and fairness into human nature because it contributed to survival. But mutual interdependence was not inevitable because these traits could be overwhelmed by predation, immediate gratification and self-centredness. Wilson said that he offered his argument about a biological basis for morality as a hedge against arguments about morality as a matter of cultural relativism (of the sort advocated by Foucault and postmodernists – Chapter 6).[17]

David T. Courtwright brought these ideas to his interpretation of violence in American society. Why were violence and disorder so prevalent in a land of freedom and abundance? His explanation 'emphasizes the interplay of large biological, demographic, cultural, social, and economic forces'.[18] To understand violence in American society, Courtwright says, we must recognize that it has always centred within a particular population of historical actors, that is, young, unmarried men. Men have always been more aggressive than women, and young men are more aggressive than older men. This is due to 'reproductive asymmetry': men want many sexual partners, and women have a limited reproductive capacity, so men compete for women. As part of this competition, women are attracted to displays of prowess and risk-taking. This was as true in nineteenth-century America as in tribal societies in prehistoric times and the animal kingdom (successful hunters have more opportunities to mate than their less successful rivals). Young men are fuelled by an elevated level of testosterone, and as levels diminish during the ageing process, the appetite for prowess and aggression weakens. Courtwright insists that his explanation is not a 'reductive exercise in historical sociobiology'. Rather, he argues for the braiding of biological and sociological explanations to provide a more comprehensive explanation of historical trends.[19]

Like Courtwright, Martin Wiener begins his study of violence with the biological difference between men and women. Wiener examines the culture surrounding criminal justice practices in England during the Victorian period. Although he is interested in crime in general, he focuses on homicide and rape cases. Drawing on a range of records, he reviewed thousands of criminal cases, including virtually every case of spousal murder. He concludes that men's violence, particularly against women, became in this period a matter of great significance, and for all the remaining contradiction, it was viewed with even greater disapproval and treated with greater severity than ever before.[20] He deals with culture and 'discourses of male violence', the ways in which men's violence evoked strong and conflicted sentiments and legal actions.

Wiener's book could be read as a cultural history except for his suggestion, at the beginning, that the problem of male violence originates in the scientific fact 'that from birth, males on the average tend to be more aggressive, restless, and risk-taking than females, and in general, less amendable to socialization'.[21] 'Masculine criminality' is a cultural construct that originates in biological propensity – a propensity that appeared in early stages of the evolutionary process, but 'has if anything, grown in modern times'. This trait has lost most of its former functionality, but because of its long gestation, it is one that is not easy to banish.[22] Wiener argues that the 'self-isolation of cultural history' should be broken. Cultural historians should pursue connections to sociology and psychology, and evolutionary psychology is well-suited to this task.[23] To evolutionary psychologists, behaviour is the product of an open-ended interaction between gene-based natural potentialities and external circumstances. Human evolution is a never-ending process of adaptation, a continuous effort to adjust to circumstances which are always in flux. Culture itself fits within a Darwinian perspective, perhaps best seen as a 'meta-adaptation' that enables an endless number of specific adaptations to new circumstances within years rather than generations.[24]

The current version of evolutionary thinking about history, John Carter Wood says, is different from the determinist, reductionist view of Lombroso.[25] Evolution should 'not be seen as a machine for general universal, reductionist and deterministic laws but rather as a subtle framework for analysing the legacy of the evolutionary past with which individuals, societies, and cultures continue to contend'.[26] As Wood explains it, the brain is a collection of 'regulatory circuits' that organize the way people interpret experiences. In this way, it gives culture a physical location, specifically, situated in the human mind (assuming that the mind is contained within the brain). It offers a different kind of analytical tool for historians. Historians tend to look for the proximate causes of historical events, the conscious motivations that explain why people acted as they did in particular circumstances. Evolutionary psychology furnishes an argument for ultimate causes, the underlying reasons why particular kinds of proximate causes have come to exist. That is to say, historians examine outcomes of the human psyche; evolutionary psychology offers a reason for why the human psyche exists.[27]

For Wood, evolutionary psychology offers a perspective for understanding the meaning of violence: it is not pathological, or an aberration, or localized within few psychopathic individuals. Rather, it is part of the human condition. People possess complex psychophysiological machinery for the production and regulation of violence. Some domains of human behaviour may be more susceptible to social change than others.[28] At the same time, the evolutionary psychology perspective is more useful in some investigations than others. It does not provide a satisfactory explanation of specific violent acts, nor of the emotions or motivations that generate them: anger, jealously or impulsivity.[29] Wiener points out that while evolutionary psychology can account for the behaviour of the masses of ordinary people, and long-term developments or trends in societies, it is not useful for understanding the actions of elites or individuals. Nor is it useful for understanding historical events which involve accident, miscalculation and mistaken assumptions.[30]

Randolph Roth left biology out of his *American Homicide* (2009). He analysed trends in murder statistics for Europe and the United States over a period of 400 years. If human beings possess 'roughly the same capacity for violence', he asked, why do homicide rates vary so widely from one society to another, from one time to another? To find out why homicide rates rise and fall over time, it is necessary to get beyond 'generalizations based on proximate causes to discover the ultimate causes of murder'. For Roth, there is a 'predisposition' to violence, but this is culturally conditioned. The 'predisposition to violence is rooted in feelings and beliefs', and the key to explaining it is found in charting statistical fluctuations over time.[31] However, Roth has also suggested the possibility of a 'deep history of homicide'. He has been impressed by research into neurological and endrocrinological bases of behaviour, and although this would take years to develop, he believes that it can contribute to a social science history. To understand why rates of violence against children and between adults have varied so widely over time, it would be useful to map the social or environmental circumstances triggering aggression and violence alongside the physiological causes of violence.[32]

Jeffrey Adler has experimented with biological concepts. In his study of homicide in New Orleans during the interwar period, he suggests that brain functioning offers part of the explanation for interracial murder. Half of the interracial homicides involved a White police officer and a Black suspect, and in virtually all of these cases, the killers claimed to have acted in self-defence. The Black suspect had a weapon, even though no weapon was found at the crime scene. It could be because the White police were simply lying, or, Adler surmises, because they had actually 'seen' a weapon. Within the brain, there is a small almond-shaped structure that processes emotional reactions, that is, fear and anxiety. It operates as a 'survival mechanism' that signals the brain of the need for a split-second fight-or-flight response. This portion of the brain registers African-Americans as a threat. 'The combination of fear-conditioned racial bias and the need to act quickly may also help account for the disproportionate rate at which police officers continue to shoot African-American suspects making furtive movements or seeming to reach for a weapon.' Adler acknowledges that he is relying on the latest advances in brain research, which raises a question of the legitimacy of this as historical interpretation: Does it make sense to explain activity from the early twentieth century using a theory from the twenty-first century? He concludes that since brain activity has not changed since 1945, 'any methodological insights that might help explain individual and collective behavior are useful'.[33]

Adler appears to be less impressed with evolutionary psychology, which he tried out in a study of bar brawls and other forms of violence in late-nineteenth-century Chicago.[34] Evolutionary psychologists explain violence as a legacy of 'adaptive mechanisms' shaped over thousands of years of evolutionary development. These adaptive processes appeared in prehistoric environments but contribute to history because they remain part of the physiological and psychological make-up of human beings even though they no longer serve the purpose to which they evolved.[35]

For his test drive, Adler examined 5,600 Chicago homicide cases from 1875 to 1920, compiled from police files, health department records, prison registers and newspaper sources. The rate of homicide increased during these decades, but this, he suggests, is less interesting than the basic model which remains consistent. The typical case, involving men killing other men, most often in drunken brawls, remains paradigmatic. This represents the leading source of homicide throughout this period, in which men far outnumber women. The sources of change, whether culture, geography, time or technology, in these decades do not alter the basic pattern. The perspective of evolutionary psychology can accommodate this pattern of consistency and change. Acts of violence reflect the 'evolved mechanisms of male competition': men are involved in violence compared to women (consistency) and the level fluctuates (competition). Men respond to common impulses, but changing conditions shape or direct the expression of these impulses. However, Adler acknowledges that the ready explanation has its drawbacks. Continuity supports the theory, and change supports the theory, making it as hard to disprove as to prove, and because of this, evolutionary psychology offers historians very little. Perhaps the primary lesson of the exercise is a reminder that historians ought to pay attention to continuity as well as change.[36]

Foucault may have accepted evolution as a source of explanation. He used the term *genealogy* to express his notion of historical notion of change, a term which suggests a biological sequence. Further, his conception of power invokes 'strategies without strategists', a process in history operating outside the consciousness of historical actors. This suggests an evolutionary process, or something much like it, at work. Foucault denied that genealogy referred to the evolution of a species or destiny of a people, although Foucault made many claims about his work which must be critically assessed rather than accepted as true because he said so.[37]

One historian that definitely does not accept evolution as historical explanation is John Lukacs. He insists on the importance of the mind in history, that is, the 'remembered past'. What Darwin found out about natural selection does not apply to human beings, because unlike plants and animals, human beings possess a mind. The acquisition of human characteristics is not merely an unconscious, mechanical or chemical process, but also a mental process that involves personality, aspirations and imagination. The basic human factor is personal, not environmental, since people transcend all kinds of tendencies, including heredity.[38] For Lukacs, the only kind of evolution important for history is the 'evolution of consciousness'. In thinking about human characteristics as a scientific category, historians interested in evolution perceive the relationship between mind and brain as constant throughout history. But the mind has expanded much faster than the brain, which makes evolution rather weak as an explanation for history. There is an essential difference between *evolution* and *history*. If evolution means something like development of untapped potential, it operates within the human realm. But what is really happening, and will happen in the future, is not decided by evolution, but by the field of history, that is, by what is brought into existence by thought.[39]

Civilization

Just as some form of evolution was on the minds of many biologists and philosophers in the late nineteenth century, the unconsciousness, too, had exciting prospects. The idea appears in work of poets and philosophers before then, but it became associated with Freud following publication of his work on hysteria (produced along with Josef Breuer) in 1895. Since then, much of the vocabulary of psychoanalysis has migrated from therapeutic psychiatry to cultural analysis.

Freud built his reputation from clinical work. In his treatment of individual clients, he worked out an understanding of the mind based on levels of consciousness: conscious, unconscious and preconscious. Later, he organized these into a theory of personality: the ego, or sense of self; the superego, or conscience; and the id, the primitive biological expression of the unconsciousness. He described a series of stages that individuals pass through in the course of personality development: oral, anal, phallic and genital. He also worked out techniques for studying the unconscious, the interpretation of dreams, jokes and slips-of-the-tongue. These techniques were important in treatment of personality disorders, including repression, in which people keep painful memories locked away in their unconscious, and projection, in which people transfer anxiety and guilt on to others. Freud, like Agatha Christie, was intrigued by archaeology. In his case histories and her mystery novels, we see the importance of digging. The past must be unearthed and revealed for what it is if we are to know the truth.[40]

After the First World War, Freud thought deeply about social issues. He decided that the evolution of civilization could be compared to the growth of the individual, and he turned the concepts developed for clinical analysis towards the study of history. In 1929, he completed a book, *Civilisation and its Discontents* (1930), which became one of his best-selling titles.[41] He described the endless clash between human desires and modern civility. The individual could never be perfectly happy since all people could not avoid permanent sources of suffering: knowledge that the human body was destined to decay, fear of an external world capable of destruction, and the demands of living alongside others. We realize that 'civilization itself is to blame' for the greater part of our misery and that we would be happier if we returned to primitive conditions. Rather than creating space for freedom, external authorities make demands on individuals that thwart the natural desire for immediate and unrestrained gratification. Because civilization is built up on the 'renunciation of instinctual gratifications', it can never escape the threat of disintegration and individuals turning primary aggression towards each other. In order to hold together, civilized society reserves for itself the right to employ violence against criminals, but this is not sufficient. Instead, civilization relies on culture to internalize the aggressive instinct and form a conscience capable of punishment through guilt. Freud offered a powerful metaphor for this: 'Civilization therefore obtains the mastery over the dangerous love of aggression in individuals by enfeebling and disarming it and setting up an institution within their minds to keep watch over it, like a garrison in a conquered city.'[42]

The 'most interesting' aspects of Freudian analysis for history – noted one of Freud's contemporary interpreters, Peter Gay – are 'defence mechanisms', the psychological adjustments individuals make in response to collective external realties. These act to minimize the anxieties aroused by others, situations that provoke deep passions, enervate hidden desires and fantasies. But these defences generate more problems than they resolve: overreacting to normal desires led to phobias, obsessions and inhibitions. These could be the source of behaviours that fall outside the criminal law. Further, another task of cultural defences was to work out reasonable compromises. To this end, the individual's war with culture results in social institutions, legal codes, moral injunctions and police forces.[43] The idea that defence mechanisms change over time offers a model for history. Looking back, it is possible to detect a shift in cultural defence between the seventeenth and nineteenth centuries. The once regular practice of torturing animals for sport (bear-baiting, cock-fighting, fox hunting, etc.) declined with the growing impulses towards humanitarianism, an outlook that saw reductions in suffering imposed on the poor, children and prisoners.[44]

Joy Jackson offered a psychoanalytic view in her history of crime in New Orleans.[45] During the final decades of the nineteenth century, a period of general lawlessness and extraordinary violence characterized the city. While this took place to some extent in other cities, it was more intense in New Orleans owing to contempt for police and authority cultivated by experience of military government in the aftermath of the Civil War years. Criminality escalated until 1891, with the murder of the chief of police, David Hennessy. His assassination in 1890, and the lynching of those accused of his murder, dramatically exposed the problem of crime. The violent episode stunned a public supposedly indifferent to violent death. Vigilantes had targeted criminals but did not attempt to pre-empt justice. It was the moment when the conscience of the city took control of its instinct. As Jackson puts it, 'The terrible cathartic effect of this incident scoured the conscience of the city and set it back upon a path of more civilized justice.'[46]

In the United States, Freud's ideas have made psychohistory into a substantial and recognized branch of historical research. Much of this involves applying concepts from Freud's clinical methods to historical personalities (political leaders supplying the most frequent targets). There is the large question about the wisdom of applying a theory of the early twentieth century to other centuries. To some extent, we can only understand the past in the language of our own time, but unless this explanation can be modified (and discarded), the past becomes nothing more than a reservoir of examples of what we think we already know. It seems counter to historical inquiry to maintain that levels of consciousness can be treated as universal and constant for purposes of understanding events. Another question concerns the notion of causality in history. The complexity of motivation should invite a problematic or shared understanding, based on a multi-levelled explanation. But in practice, the adherents of particular approaches to history, such as psychoanalysis, reveal a preference for explanation at a single level. The psychoanalytic basis becomes the definitive or real explanation for actions.[47]

Heikki Ylikangas could not see the usefulness of Freudian theory in the history of crime in Finland. In the sixteenth century, when the records first become available, there was a great deal of lawlessness, including murders in western provinces. From the sixteenth century to the end of the nineteenth century, there was a period of decline. Violence was low except for southern Ostrobothnia which experienced the *pukkojunkkat*, the 'knife-fighters', between 1790 and 1880. At the peak of the violence, there were 50–60 murders per 100,000 in some parishes in this region at a time when the rate for the whole country averaged 2–3. During the twentieth century, violence increased in Finland; there was a surge before 1913, and again, after 1945. For Ylikangas, the fluctuations in the level and type of crime in Finnish history demonstrate the inadequacy of psychoanalysis. Even if it were possible to demonstrate at the peak of the violence a weak superego or mis-specified sexual roles compared to periods of decline in violence, this would still not explain where these personality defects originated or why this deterioration took place so suddenly. Such an explanation would stray outside the parameters of psychoanalysis.[48]

For David Garland, this is not the case.[49] He focuses on the array of criminal justice policies in the United States and United Kingdom in the final decades of the twentieth century, including policing, punishment, private security, crime prevention and the response to victims. Garland's sources are government documents, research reports, and books and articles by criminologists. He describes his approach as a 'history of the present' and makes specific reference to Foucault. His study examines the shift in penal policies that began in 1970, from rehabilitation as part of the welfare state, to a more diffused system of security as part of a system of control. Although Garland refers to 'underlying social forces' as the primary reasons for these changes in the structure of criminal justice, 'the most important changes have been in the cultural assumptions that animate them'.[50] He explains the shift in the emotional language of policies from references to decency and humanity to fear and insecurity. The confident management of welfare administrators has been replaced by a sense of crisis and the need to shift responsibility for crime control from the government to community, and even commercial, organizations.

Garland brings psychoanalysis to his subject, revealed through language and occasionally footnotes. In examining the language of punishment, he regularly invokes Freudian terms, such as catharsis, denial, repression and sublimation. His approach can be taken as an application of psychoanalysis to culture, as Freud suggested in his commentary on civilization. The sovereign state becomes the ego who fails to realize the ego-ideal, that of a crime-free society. In order to cope with this failure, it employs adaptive strategies, such as acting out, meaning or expressive punitive behaviour. These punitive attitudes involve the transference or projection of anxieties onto criminal others. This last point draws on the Freudian concept of becoming criminal from a sense of guilt. Garland supposes that revulsion shown in punitive attitudes towards crimes against children might be rooted in the public's own antisocial desires.[51]

The civilizing process

Much of what qualifies as Freudian analysis in the history of crime has not been taken from the source, but filtered through the work of Norbert Elias. Elias arrived in London in the 1930s, a refugee from Hitler's Germany. He spent his time browsing in the library of the British Museum and came across books on etiquette. He found them quite intriguing because they revealed how much standards of appropriate conduct had changed over the centuries. The entire sensibility of Europeans with regard to eating, sleeping, sex and violence had changed since the medieval period. Further, the whole process had taken place so slowly as to be hidden from view.[52] By 1939, Elias published his own book on manners, *The Civilizing Process*, in which he set out to understand how the civilizing of the West came about, what it involved, and what were its causes or motives.[53] Originally written in German, it was neglected, due to the circumstances of the war, until the 1970s when it reappeared. Since then, it has become a popular guide to the history of crime, particularly to the history of punishment and the response to crime.

The Civilizing Process has been described as a fusion of history, social theory and psychoanalysis.[54] Elias explored the behaviour of people who believed themselves to be civilized, with a focus on France, Germany and England. He did not portray this as a level or stage which societies passed through, but rather as continuous change. He saw the formation of manners as a psychic process extending over many centuries, a process that could be glimpsed from examples of everyday life: eating at the table, activities in the bedroom, attitudes towards bodily functions. He wanted to show how violations of the rules for these activities generated feelings of shame and repugnance. In explaining how this change came about, Elias referred to how elites launched offensives or missions intended to establish cultural superiority. And he described the formation of the state and the monopoly of force. This monopolization of violence brought about an array of social demands and prohibitions, which drilled down into how people felt about themselves, and altered the make-up of individual personality. While Elias is often taken for a sociologist, he was definitely interested in history, and his key insight, the civilizing process, was a historical process inspired by Freud.

Elias himself referred to *Civilisation and its Discontents*, and psychoanalytical concepts form the centre of his theoretical history.[55] Elias agreed with Freud that the human soul has not remained the same through time. It has undergone a development in which external restrictions became increasingly internalized. But he disagreed about the method of inquiry. Freud was engaged in theoretical history of the sort in which historical events serve to illustrate concepts. Elias elaborated theory from empirical work. From the details of ordinary people, and the trivialities of everyday existence, he built a story of a great transformation. Freud identified the formation of the superego over time. Elias went further by explaining the structures that led to the formation of the superego.[56] It may be that 'the idea of a psychical process extending over many generations appears hazardous and dubious', Elias said. It could not be decided in a theoretical or speculative way as Freud had done. 'Only a scrutiny of documents of historical experience can show what is correct and what is incorrect in such theories.'[57]

Elias did not write about crime or criminal justice. Except for some comments about punishment of servants during the life of a medieval knight, there is nothing about crime in *The Civilizing Process*. His impact on the history of crime has been achieved through the efforts of champions and none more so than Pieter Spierenburg. Spierenburg recalls that he met Elias in 1969, while he was a history student in Amsterdam and Elias lectured there. A month or so into Elias's history seminar, Spierenburg began reading *The Civilizing Process*, which had been published in a new German-language edition the year before. He found it fascinating and continued to attend Elias's lectures at the Historical Institute. Spierenburg decided to write a PhD dissertation on the topic of violence and judicial sanctions in the conceptual vocabulary that Elias had formulated. Spierenburg had occasion to speak with Elias about his plans, and at some point in thinking about the usefulness of Elias's developmental framework, decided to become a historian of crime and punishment.[58]

Spierenburg's dissertation, *The Spectacle of Suffering* (1984), covers the rise and fall of public executions. He develops an explanation for the transformation of punishment: from pre-industrial Europe, where whipping, maiming and hanging were public events, to the twentieth century, in which the death sentence all but disappeared (and where it remains, takes place in secret). Spierenburg drew on court records from Amsterdam, supplemented with material from Germany, the Netherlands, France and England. He covers the work of executioners, the aims of the authorities, the crowd of spectators and characteristics of the condemned. He provides details about the working lives of executioners: the income they received, the knowledge and skills they possessed, the pressure they felt to deliver a good performance. Executioners occupied an ambivalent place in society. People tried to avoid social contact with hangmen and their family members. People insulted them, and they had to live outside the city or just inside city wall. At the same time, people turned to hangmen for surgery. They sought them out to purchase items used in executions because these were believed to possess magical powers.[59]

As Spierenburg explained, an original punitive attitude towards the suffering of convicts slowly gave way to a rising sensitivity, which reached a critical threshold in the nineteenth century, when executions disappeared from public life. These aspects of 'conscience formation' took place together with the rise of a network of states, and more specifically, the transformation from the early modern state to the modern nation state. Elias's theory had the advantage over Foucault's because it was 'truly historical'. Elias saw the 'evolution of repression' as part of processes involving changing sensibilities of the upper classes in relation to the rise of states.[60] Initially, Spierenburg regarded Elias's perspective as a counter-paradigm to that of Foucault, but later decided that the two theories shared key aspects. Foucault had a tendency to see 'abrupt change' or discontinuities in the history of punishment and tended to project France as a paradigm. Elias emphasized that societies change continuously and historians should trace the interdependence of long-term developments. Elias shared with Foucault a belief that power is everywhere, a preference for ambitious historical explanations, and a habit of working at a high level of generalization.[61]

For Erling Sandmo, *power* is precisely what is wrong with Elias. He researched violence in the Nordic countries in the seventeenth and eighteenth centuries, and concluded that Elias's model has an 'obvious weakness'.[62] It fails to capture essential aspects of power in the development of medieval society. Cases of violence in court records decrease from the seventeenth century relative to sexual and economic offences. Sandmo proposes that a new concept of violence emerged that was distinguished as either power or violence. Power became associated with the formal, public, legitimate use of force, and violence was stigmatized as the illegitimate private use of physical force. What Elias called the state monopoly on violence would be more accurately labelled as the transformation of violence into power. Violence changed from part of people's everyday lives and culture into the dark opposite, a strange and infrequent interruption of social conventions. This understanding explains how the frequency of violent crimes fell quickly from the 1620s onwards.[63]

John Pratt, who learnt of Elias from Spierenburg's book, found more and more to appreciate. Pratt's history of punishment in New Zealand develops methods and strategies from Foucault; he 'uses his method of discourse analysis to present a genealogy of the New Zealand punishment system'.[64] But Pratt noted Spierenburg's work on the civilizing process. The decline of punishments of the body did not suddenly disappear at the beginning of the nineteenth century with the introduction of the prison, but was much more gradual. Pratt saw the civilizing process at work from 1850 to 1950.

In later work, Pratt took full advantage of Elias's theory. He relies on civilizing as an organizing concept for his history of punishment from the early nineteenth century to the end of the twentieth century in 'England and parts of the civilized world'.[65] He discusses aspects of prison administration, drawing on official reports, commentaries and memoirs, the equivalent, he suggests, of the 'manners books' Elias relied on because they reveal the standards and values of administrators. Pratt aims to reveal how the system of 'civilized' punishment was established in the nineteenth century and continued for much of the twentieth century. Pratt suggested that the overall pace has accelerated during the past two centuries, affecting wider application across the social fabric and deeper into the middle and lower classes. He devotes much more of the discussion to ideas from Elias, including 'decivilizing forces', an idea not developed in Elias's 1939 work but suggested later. The civilizing process, Pratt concludes, should be seen as taking a very general form, subject to different, local manifestations. It was interrupted by war or other sudden social changes. At such times, it was 'put into reverse' and decivilizing forces guided cultural development. Decivilizing does not mean turning the clock backward in a wholesale, but it makes possible the reintroduction of sanctions from previous eras. It explains the slower pace of change in certain places.

Decivilizing processes are one way of accounting for the exceptions. Greg T. Smith examined the decline of public physical punishments in London from 1760 to 1840.[66] During these decades, there was a remarkable change in the techniques of punishment in England; physical punishments delivered in public, such as the pillory and whipping, were eliminated. To explain this change, it is necessary to look at 'cultural dispositions', specifically the 'complexity and frequent contradictions embedded within culture'.[67] However, while the changing attitudes towards violence and physical punishment transformed punishments in London beginning in the eighteenth century, informed Victorian punishment and continued to shape attitudes in the late twentieth century, this did not amount to any single mechanism, which Smith would dismiss as a 'contrived determinism'. He emphasized the persistence of some cultural attitudes that seem out of place in the twentieth century. Celebrations surrounding executions in the United States (some university students organized barbeques) and the continued use of violence by animal rights activists in Europe (who disrupted fox hunts and set fire to research laboratories) revealed that the civilizing processes did not pursue a 'steady progressive growth'. Rather, the willingness of activists to use violence to promote so-called humanitarianism amounted to evidence of the 'ebb and flow' of Elias's civilizing processes.[68]

Carolyn Strange points out that whipping and execution continued in liberal states after they embraced the welfarist notion of punishment.[69] Resolving this contradiction requires more than a footnote. As she explains, physical punishment remained in the penal repertoire for more than 100 years after it was hidden from view. She examined the debates in Canada during the 1930s and 1950s over the use of corporal and capital punishment. Although cultural certainties about official use of pain and death had eroded, Canadian authorities continued to inflict physical forms of punishment until well into the twentieth century. Elias stressed that the civilizing process did not mean progress because interruptions occurred from time to time; countervailing forces of barbarism did occur. But in his 1939 work, he presented civilizing as a 'zero sum game, in which more civility equals less barbarity'.[70] In later work, he acknowledged what he called the 'civilized barbarism' of the twentieth century, which was helpful in grasping the retention of corporal and capital punishment in liberal-democratic governments. The debates in Canada reveal how refined sensibilities about pain and suffering coexist with rationales for punishment. In the 1950s, Canadians found paddles, whips and the noose to be clearly old-fashioned and worried even about pictures of them appearing. But given the persistence of beliefs about the purpose of punishment, it seems clear that officials sought more modern mechanical or medical methods of punishing the body. 'Only by probing the meanings that historical actors attribute to different forms of and rationales for punishment can we chart the changing currents of penal culture.'[71]

Randall McGowen develops a similar line in his examination of debates in the House of Commons between 1840 and 1869.[72] He reports that even nineteenth-century discussions of the death penalty in England reveal some ambiguity. Consistent with what Elias would predict, abolitionists advanced the argument that society was being swept along by a powerful current which held great promise for humanity. There was a new sensitivity for suffering and a new appreciation for human life, and the transformation of penal practices provided a clear measure of this change. But statements in parliamentary debates and prominent journals between those arguing for abolition of the death sentence and those conservatives in favour of retaining it were not expressed in terms of civilization versus barbarism. Both sides claimed to be true advocates of the principle that human life was sacred. The conservatives took the view that capital punishment was necessary for the realization of modern civilization. Both sides argued that the intentional taking of life presented the greatest threat to society and that the state had a unique responsibility for protecting life. The mid-nineteenth-century debate ended without a clear victory for the abolitionists; Britain did not abolish the gallows until 1969, a century later. 'The ambiguous outcome of the debate points to the paradoxical conclusions that could flow from the notion of civility. Although the narrative of increasing civilization seemed to imply only one outcome, in fact it was open to different interpretations.'[73]

There is also the question about how far the civilizing process can be recognized outside the few states Elias studied. 'For any analysis of the European "civilizing process" to be complete', John McGuire argues, 'the colonial settler states that comprised its margins should be taken into account.'[74] McGuire examines the transition from public to private executions in colonial Australia. In Queensland, Western Australia and South Australia, the authorities found it expedient to preserve the public spectacle of execution in cases where Aborigines were to be executed. To preserve the 'didactic function' of execution, which sought to communicate different messages to European settlers and non-European peoples, the colonial government maintained a practice of semi-public execution even after the introduction of private punishment. In the 1860s and 1870s, the authorities arranged for Aborigines to be hanged before a selected audience, including Aborigine spectators. The transition from public to private reflected less changing sensibilities than frontier violence and racial conflicts. In the settler colonies, racial conflict remained a continuing barrier to a total transition to the civilized methods of death penalty.

Stacey Hynd looks into the tension between violence and humanitarianism in British East Africa between 1900 and 1947, specifically, the case files of 800 capital trials. The length of time – fifty years – is hardly long enough to constitute a model of the civilizing process. But the colonial context does raise an interesting point about precisely what is being modelled. As Hynd points out, it is one thing to explain punishment as a legal activity and the civilizing process as a source of legal reform. The reluctance to use capital punishment appears as a gradual trend and any setbacks in this effort can be categorized as decivilizing processes. The law became the site of forces and counter-forces for reform. It is another thing to understand it as a political aspect of governance, to extend or withdraw it based on the larger trend of colonial governance. As she points out, capital punishment was as much a political penalty as much as a legal punishment. The extension of mercy in Nyasaland was decided not only on the facts of the cases, but on British conceptions of justice, order, criminality and 'African behaviour' within the colonial context. In colonial government, violence was subject to different forms of discipline and legitimation. Most judges in Nyasaland saw the necessity of adapting law to fit local circumstances and of reconciling it with 'native custom'. Many avoided death sentences, less in opposition to capital punishment or paternalism towards Africans than as a matter of the particular character of justice and the ideological landscape of colonial governance.[75]

The decline of violence

By the 1990s, Eric Johnson and Eric Monkkonen had seen enough to convince them that Elias provided *the* explanation for long-term trends in violence.[76] The founders of sociology – Durkheim, Simmel, Tönnies, the Chicago School – imagined that with the breakdown of the family and community; the declining significance of religion, and the rising forces of modernity – urbanization, industrialization, class division – crime had, and would continue, to increase. But historians of trends in Europe and North America found that discernible trends over the centuries do not fit with these traditional social theories. Violence has decreased, not increased (as discussed in Chapter 4). As traditional explanations failed, historians turned to Elias. He offered a coherent explanation at a general level, with sufficient parts, on which could be built explanation for specific situations. 'Elias's significance has come to be recognized in part because his descriptions of the "civilizing process" match so well what crime historians have been finding.'[77]

The theory of the civilizing process has proved to be a popular accompaniment to statistical analyses of crime trends. Elias's work provides a coherent explanation for an array of wide-scale changes taking place over the centuries. It offers assumptions for further study: (1) that control of violent behaviour originated in judicial practices, (2) that cities became more, rather than less, civilized, (3) that areas where state systems had not yet reached were more violent and (4) that over time, the overall trend in criminal violence was downward.[78] In addition, as other historians would point out, Elias's ideas can be adjusted to fit shorter time frames in specific places. The civilizing process has been used to explain crime trends over several decades, in regions or cities.

Maria Kaspersson looked at crime trends in Stockholm over 400 years, from the sixteenth century to the twentieth century. Specifically, she looked at homicide and infanticide during three time periods from records of the city's district courts.[79] She found that people continued to kill each other in the same way, in the same places and for the same motives. But there was a change in the frequency of homicide, particularly from the sixteenth century to the eighteenth century. The level of crime fell markedly in the seventeenth century and reached its lowest point in the early twentieth century. 'The one theory that does appear to have the greatest explanatory potential would be the theory of the civilizing process,' Kaspersson concluded.[80] As proposed by Elias and elaborated by Spierenburg, the theory specifies the internal and external conditions that would account for a decrease in use of lethal violence. However, crime figures showed the greatest decrease in the 1600s, which would indicate the need for more specific explanation rather than a theory of overall decline. But, simply because the civilizing process is less well-suited for explaining the rather sudden decline in homicide in the seventeenth century, it does not mean that the theory is 'fatally compromised'. Rather, it means that it would benefit from further elaboration.

Jeffrey Adler brought Elias to late-nineteenth-century Chicago.[81] Between 1875 and 1924, the homicide rate increased from 3.21 to 13.70, which amounts to an increase of more than 426 per cent. Apparently, Chicago did not participate in the civilizing process. Adler acknowledges that the Chicago case is not a fair test; it is stretching the theory too far to expect cultural changes at the level Elias had in mind to operate within a few decades. Nevertheless, the Chicago story makes a nice chapter in Elias's book. Adler suggests that the rising tide of violence in Chicago does not refute the importance of the civilizing process because it was a city of immigrants. The city absorbed immigrants, meaning, it was not the same people, but new groups of people, and the cultural absorption would not be expected to happen so fast. So a portion of the increase is explained by the effect of demography, not the absence of civilizing process. In fact, the city saw major campaigns against violence, what Elias termed 'civilizing offensives'. The police and other city authorities tried desperately to enlist schools and workplaces to reduce violence in all its forms, whether brawls in bars, drunken fathers in homes or careless drivers of new automobiles. This led to the criminalization of a greater range of behaviour, and the inflation overall of figures for homicide, rather than reduction. 'The soaring homicide rate in early twentieth-century Chicago did not reflect the failure of the civilizing process, but rather it reflected the success of the civilizing process.'[82]

The theory also fits rural Illinois, according to Susan S. Rugh, who examined murder in Hancock County in the nineteenth century. The changes experienced in the western part of the state, bordering the Mississippi River, were typical of the Midwestern United States: the rapid transformation from agricultural production characterized by agrarian capitalism to an industrial framework controlled by corporate capitalism. Despite fears and anxiety about crime expressed by residents, the murder rate fell from the 1840s to 1870s. And to the extent that homicide represents the most accurate measure of crime trends, it is suggestive of a wider decline in crime. The ideas of Elias have been influential in explaining the civilizing process that occurred in cities, that is, the way in which industrial discipline tamed impulsive behaviour. Men turned to courts instead of settling matters in tavern fights. The situation in rural Illinois revealed the civilizing process at work, including a shift that resulted from communal to state authority. The rural middle class, particularly women, struggled to maintain order through temperance and appealed to civil authority to replace the diminishing power of community controls. The traditional world of communal control gave way to civil authority which delivered justice according to the law.[83]

Ian O'Donnell thinks Elias can explain trends of murder in Ireland, at least in some ways.[84] O'Donnell collected statistics during the late nineteenth century and early twentieth century: judicial statistics, the national police for the Republic of Ireland, mortality statistics, and the Royal Ulster Constabulary (which after partition became Northern Ireland). He looked at characteristics of offenders and victims, situations in which these killings occurred (work or family), including kinds of weapons, and fights and brawls. Overall, trends for murder in Ireland confirmed the importance of the civilizing process and the emergence of stronger internal controls contributing to a decline in impulsive outbursts of violence. That said, the role of the monopolization of violence was less straightforward. Policing and prosecution were centralized and professionalized early in the nineteenth century, but the cultural idea of a 'fair fight' persisted into the twentieth century. The conflict was seen as between the private parties rather than between a private party and the state. 'Attempts by the state to define what constituted acceptable interpersonal conduct and to seize control, the mechanisms for dealing with it had to compete against strong cultural interpretations of what violence actually *meant* and when a contretemps was *really* criminal.'[85]

While the theory of the civilizing process has enjoyed support in Britain and the United States, German historians of crime have almost completely rejected it. German sceptics, led by Martin Dinges and Gerd Schwerhoff, have questioned claims of a long-term decline in violence, the suggestion of a medieval society devoid of personal control, the significance of ritual and honour in the meaning of violence, the role of the state in the monopolization of violence, and the implications of the theory for the twentieth century. Spierenburg has continued to promote and defend Elias.[86] He responded to the German challenge by saying that while a few of the claims in the 1939 book have proved wrong, these amount to details and do not add up to a falsification of theory. The 'explanatory potential, for violence and other social phenomena, of the theory of civilization remains strong'.[87] Research during the past two decades on the long-term trends in homicide has provided 'impressive new evidence for the theory of civilization'.[88] Most of the criticisms, Spierenburg has insisted, are based on a misunderstanding of concepts. Elias never intended for his approach to be read as a linear and universal theory of evolution from violence to less violent society. It is a curious argument because the subtitle of *The Spectacle of Suffering* contains the word 'evolution'. Nevertheless, Spierenburg insists Elias should not be taken as thinking along these lines: 'The theory of civilization is of course based on past trends and has no room for evolution. Future generations may witness social integration at even higher levels than the state or they may not.'[89]

The Germans remain unmoved.[90] Schwerhoff takes issue with Spierenburg's assessment, beginning with the idea that long-term decline in violence supports Elias. While the evidence for some centuries does suggest a downward trend, the available evidence from the medieval period is not there. There is a danger in 'tailoring these data to fit Elias' paradigm' and a danger that the 'Elias' paradigm is about to become the Elias' bias'.[91] Interpreting one or more of the concepts is not really the problem Spierenburg makes it out to be; it is not a matter of misunderstanding but of applying the concepts which allow them to be disproved. Spierenburg, Schwerhoff suggests, insists on a version of Elias that is immune to falsification. Further, for Spierenburg to suggest that there is no better alternative theory than Elias is to insist on a particular definition of theory. This is true of theory if it only refers to an explanation of trends parallel to the theory of civilization. Schwerhoff concludes that the theory of the civilizing process has instigated research into changing levels of crime over time, but does not offer a convincing explanation for the ultimate causes of this change. 'As inspiring as singular ideas of Elias may be, his whole model for the discussion of violence is restricting.'[92]

In the United States, Steven Pinker brought new attention to Elias. A Harvard psychologist and popular science writer, Pinker examined the evidence and explanations for the decline of violence since the medieval period. As far as he is concerned, the evidence about what happened – the decline in violence – is clear enough, and what really needs explaining is why this occurred. To explain the decline in violence, Pinker assembled a large multidisciplinary theory combining political, intellectual, economic and social trends with psychological aspects leading to or away from violent behaviour. His 'better angels' (empathy, self-control, moral sense, reason) follow James Q. Wilson. To explain the line graphs produced by Gurr and Eisner, Pinker turns to Elias and the civilizing process. Elias had rightly theorized that a major part of the explanation for the decline of violence in Europe was a psychological change. Elias, Pinker says, offers the only credible theory, although it requires some alteration. Pinker removes the Freudian basis from Elias's theory and replaces it with evolutionary psychology. Pinker also embellished the theory by extending it into the twentieth century, and explaining the surge of the crime in the United States in the 1960s as 'decivilizing' and decline of crime in the 1990s as 'recivilizing'. Generally, he contends that the psychological mindset associated with lesser violence took hold in the middle classes, and only gradually trickled down to those in the lower socio-economic status (so rates of violence among African-Americans remained high).[93]

Conclusion

The impact of evolution on writing the history of crime has been rather modest. Despite the efforts of Martin Wiener, John Carter Wood and others, who propose that evolutionary psychology should be available with the regular stock on the shelves, it remains a fairly specialized product. One reason for this is that it operates at a high level of abstraction, somewhere above or outside the world in which people live, interact with one another, and generate the activities historians are most interested in explaining.

The scholars who propose evolutionary psychology as a theory for crime history represent a diverse lot. There are professional historians, like Adler, Courtwright and Wiener, but others from social sciences: Wilson, political science, and Pinker, psychology. One thing they share is a refusal to engage the earlier work by Pike, Holmes and Lombroso (a diverse lot as well). Pursuing a 'modern' approach allows them to avoid confronting the problematic aspects of nineteenth-century conceptualizations, such as determinism, reductionism and reification. It also allows them to avoid the history of attempts to mix biology, crime and history, which has in the past, involved racism, eugenics and anti-Semitism. This does not mean that recent attempts will end the same way. But it does mean that this legacy of evolutionary thinking about crime requires an explanation; it cannot be passed over with the claim that the newer version has nothing to do with the older version. The science is new, but the political, social and moral implications of applying science to history are not.

Unlike evolutionary psychology, the civilizing process has become a popular approach to crime history. It has attracted determined advocates, chiefly Pieter Spierenburg, who has done more than anyone else to develop and extend Elias's work in the history of crime. The civilizing process has also proved to be especially suitable for those engaged in statistical analyses such as Eric Johnson and Eric Monkkonen. As a number of historians have shown, it works well as an explanation for crime trends. It can fit various time periods and geographic settings, and when supplemented by ideas such as 'decivilizing processes', it can account for contradictory findings. The civilizing process can explain crime within a generation or several centuries, a city or a continent; it can explain falling trends, it can explain rising trends.

Like evolutionary psychologists, however, historians interested in the civilizing process have been less interested in revealing its intellectual footings. The concept of conscience formation through time has been used, even while its Freudian provenance has been repressed. Elias said he was offering a different version than Freud, a version that was more substantive and less fanciful, and historians have taken him at his word. But this merits investigation. Thinking through Elias and Freud would expose the civilizing process to critiques levelled at psychoanalysis, but it would also make available a deeper philosophical base and wider set of concepts.

Notes

1   Bernard Lightman, 'Darwin and the popularization of evolution', *Notes and Records of the Royal Society* 64 (2010): 12–14.

2   L. Owen Pike, *A History of Crime in England*, vol. 2 (London: Smith, Elder, 1876), 510.

3   Pike, *A History of Crime*, vol. 2, 509.

4   Pike, *A History of Crime*, vol. 2, 512.

5   Pike, *A History of Crime*, vol. 2, 509–13.

6   O. W. Holmes Jr, *The Common Law* (Boston: Little, Brown and Co, 1881), 1.

7   Jan Vetter, 'The evolution of Holmes, Holmes and evolution', *California Law Review* 72 (1984): 343–68.

8   Holmes, *The Common Law*, 31.

9   Victoria Nourse, '*Buck v Bell*: A constitutional tragedy from a lost world', *Pepperdine Law Review* 101 (2011): 101.

10 Cesare Lombroso, *Il Delitto Politico e la Rivoluzione* (Turin: Fratelli Boca, 1890).

11 Trevor Calafato, '*Gli Anarchici* and Lombroso's theory of political crime', in Paul Knepper and Per J. Ystehede, eds, *The Cesare Lombroso Handbook* (Oxford: Routledge, 2013), 45–71.

12 Harry Elmer Barnes, *The Evolution of Penology in Pennsylvania* (Indianapolis: Bobbs-Merrill, 1927), 3.

13 Barnes, *The Evolution of Penology*, 406.

14 Deborah Lipstadt, *Denying the Holocaust: The Growing Assault on Truth and Memory* (London: Penguin, 1993), 22, 32.

15 Konrad Lorenz, *On Aggression* (London: Methuen, 1966).

16 James Q. Wilson and Richard J. Herrnstein, *Crime and Human Nature* (New York: Simon and Schuster, 1985), 103.

17 James Q. Wilson, *The Moral Sense* (New York: Free Press, 1993).

18 David T. Courtwright, *Violent Land: Single Men and Social Disorder from the Frontier to the Inner City* (Cambridge, MA: Harvard University Press, 1996), 7.

19 Courtwright, *Violent Land*, 7.

20 Martin J. Wiener, *Men of Blood: Violence, Manliness and Criminal Justice in Victorian England* (Cambridge: Cambridge University Press, 2004), xii.

21 Wiener, *Men of Blood*, 1.

22 Wiener, *Men of Blood*, 2.

23 Martin J. Wiener, 'Evolution and history writing', *Cultural and Social History* 4 (2007): 545–51.

24 Wiener, 'Evolution and history', 546.

25 John Carter Wood, 'The limits of culture? Society, evolutionary psychology and the history of violence', *Cultural and Social History* 4 (2007): 95–114.

26 Wood, 'The limits of culture', 109–10.

27 Wood, 'The limits of culture', 102.

28 Wood, 'The limits of culture', 107.

29 Wood, 'A change of perspective', 482.

30 Wiener, 'Evolution and history', 547.

31 Randolph Roth, *American Homicide* (Cambridge, MA: Belknap Press, 2009), 3.

32 Randolph Roth, 'Biology and the deep history of homicide', *British Journal of Criminology* 51 (2011): 535–55.

33 Jeffrey S. Adler, 'Cognitive bias: Interracial homicide in New Orleans, 1921-1945', *Journal of Interdisciplinary History* 43 (2012): 59–60.

34 Jeffrey S. Adler, '"On the border of snakeland": Evolutionary psychology and plebian violence in industrial Chicago, 1875-1920', *Journal of Social History* 36 (2003): 541–60.

35 Adler, 'On the border', 542.

36 Adler, 'On the border', 553.

37 Peter Atterton, 'Power's blind struggle for existence: Foucault, genealogy and Darwinism', *History of the Human Sciences* 7 (1994): 1–20.

38 John Lukacs, *Historical Consciousness, or The Remembered Past* (New Brunswick, NJ: Transaction Publishers, 1994), 256–7.

39 Lukacs, *Historical Consciousness*, 346–7.

40 Cornelius Holtorf, 'Doing archaeology in popular culture', in Hans Bolin, ed., *The Interplay of Past and Present* (Stockholm: Södertörns högskola, 2004), 42–9.

41 Sigmund Freud, *Civilisation and its Discontents* (London: Hogarth Press, 1930).

42 Freud, *Civilisation and Its Discontents*, 105.

43 Peter Gay, *Freud for Historians* (Oxford: Oxford University Press, 1985), 163–5.

44 Gay, *Freud for Historians*, 167–8.

45 Joy Jackson, 'Crime and the conscience of a city', *Louisiana History* 9 (1968): 229–44.

46 Jackson, 'Crime and the conscience', 230.

47 T. G. Ashplant, 'Psychoanalysis in historical writing', *History Workshop Journal* 26 (1988): 103–19.

48 Heikki Ylikangas, 'Major fluctuations in crimes of violence in Finland', *Scandinavian Journal of History* 1 (1976): 81–103.

49 David Garland, *The Culture of Control: Crime and Social Order in Contemporary Society* (Oxford: Oxford University Press, 2001).

50 Garland, *The Culture of Control*, xi.

51 Amanda Matravers and Shadd Maruna, 'Contemporary penality and psychoanalysis', in Matt Matravers, ed., *Managing Modernity: Politics and the Culture of Control* (Oxford: Routledge, 2005), 129, 118–44.

52 Norbert Elias, *Reflections on a Life* (Cambridge: Polity Press, 1994), 54–5.

53 Norbert Elias, *über den Prozess der Zivilisation: Soziogenetische und Psychogenetische Untersuchungen*, vol. 2 (Bern: Haus zum Falcken, 1939).

54 Rod Aya, 'Norbert Elias and "The civilizing process"', *Theory and Society* 5 (1978): 220.

55 Robert Van Krieken, *Norbert Elias* (London: Routledge, 1998), 19–20.

56 Wolf Lepenies, 'Norbert Elias: An outsider full of unprejudiced insight', *New German Critique* 15 (1978): 61–2 (57–64).

57 Norbert Elias, *The Civilizing Process: The History of Manners* (New York: Urizen Books, 1978), xii.

58 Pieter Spierenburg, 'A personal recollection of Norbert Elias and how I became a crime historian', in Pieter Spierenburg, *Violence and Punishment: Civilizing the Body Through Time* (Cambridge: Polity Press, 2013), 174–80.

59 Pieter Spierenburg, *The Spectacle of Suffering: Executions and the Evolution of Repression: From a Preindustrial Metropolis to the European Experience* (Cambridge: Cambridge University Press, 1984), 13–42.

60 Spierenburg, *The Spectacle of Suffering*, x.

61 Pieter Spierenburg, 'Punishment, power, and history', *Social Science History* 28 (2004): 607–36.

62 Erling Sandmo, 'The history of violence in the Nordic countries: A case study', *Scandinavian Journal of History* 25 (2000): 53–68.

63 Sandmo, 'The history of violence', 65.

64 John Pratt, *Punishment in a Perfect Society: The New Zealand Penal System 1840-1939* (Wellington: Victoria University Press, 1992), 10.

65 John Pratt, *Punishment and Civilization: Penal Tolerance and Intolerance in Modern Society* (London: Sage, 2002), 6–9.

66 Greg T. Smith, 'Civilized people don't want to see that kind of thing: The decline of public physical punishment in London', in Carolyn Strange, ed., *Qualities of Mercy: Justice, Punishment and Discretion* (Vancouver: University of British Columbia, 1996), 21–51.

67 Smith, 'Civilized people', 22.

68 Smith, 'Civilized people', 47.

69 Carolyn Strange, 'The undercurrents of penal culture: Punishment of the body in mid-twentieth century Canada', *Law and History Review* 19 (2001): 343–85.

70 Strange, 'The undercurrents of penal', 347.

71 Strange, 'The undercurrents of penal', 384.

72 Randall McGowen, 'History, culture and the death penalty: The British debates, 1840-70', *Historical Reflections/Réflexions Historiques* 29 (2003): 229–49; Randall McGowen, 'Civilizing punishment: The end of public execution in England', *Journal of British Studies* 33 (1994): 257–82.

73 McGowen, 'History, culture', 247.

74 John McGuire, 'Judicial violence and the "civilizing process": Race and the transition from public to private executions in colonial Australia', *Australian Historical Studies* 29 (1998): 190.

75 Stacey Hynd, '"The extreme penalty of the law": Mercy and the death penalty as aspects of state power in colonial Nyasaland, c. 1903-47', *Journal of Eastern Africa Studies* 4 (2010): 542–59.

76 Eric A. Johnson and Eric H. Monkkonen, 'Introduction', in Eric A. Johnson and Eric H. Monkkonen, eds, *The Civilization of Crime: Violence in Town and Country since the Middle Ages* (Urbana: University of Illinois Press, 1996), 4–5.

77 Johnson and Monkkonen, 'Introduction', 4.

78 Johnson and Monkkonen, 'Introduction', 4–5.

79 Maria Kaspersson, '"The great murder mystery" or explaining declining homicide rates', in Barry Godfrey, Clive Emsley and Graeme Dunstall, eds, *Comparative Histories of Crime* (Devon: Willan, 2003), 72–88.

80 Kaspersson, 'The great murder mystery', 82–3.

81 Jeffrey S. Adler, '"Halting the slaughter of the innocents": The civilizing process and the surge in violence in turn-of-the-century Chicago', *Social Science History* 25 (2001): 29–52.

82 Adler, 'Halting the slaughter', 48.

83 Susan Sessions Rugh, 'Civilizing the countryside: Class, gender and crime in nineteenth-century rural Illinois', *Agricultural History* 76 (2002): 58–81.

84 Ian O'Donnell, 'Killing in Ireland at the turn of the centuries', *Irish Economic and Social History* 37 (2010): 53–74.

85 O'Donnell, 'Killing in Ireland', 73.

86 Pieter Spierenburg, 'Violence and the civilizing process: Does it work?', *Crime, History & Societies* 5 (2001): 87–105.

87 Spierenburg, 'Violence and the civilizing', 102.

88 Spierenburg, 'Violence and the civilizing', 103.

89 Spierenburg, 'Violence and the civilizing', 100.

90   Gerd Schwerhoff, 'Criminalized violence and the process of civilization: A reappraisal', *Crime, History & Societies* 6 (2002): 1–21.

91   Schwerhoff, 'Criminalized violence', 6–8.

92   Schwerhoff, 'Criminalized violence', 9.

93   Steven Pinker, *The Better Angels of Our Nature: The Decline of Violence in History and its Causes* (London: Allen Lane 2011).

Further reading

John Pratt. 'Norbert Elias, the civilizing process and penal development in modern society'. *Sociological Review* 59 (2011): 220–40.

Matravers, Amanda and Shadd Maruna. 'Contemporary penality and psychoanalysis', in Matt Matravers, ed., *Managing Modernity: Politics and the Culture of Control*. Oxford: Routledge, 2005, 118–43.

Pinker, Steven. *The Better Angels of Our Nature: The Decline of Violence in History and its Causes*. London: Allen Lane, 2011.

Spierenburg, Pieter. 'A personal recollection of Norbert Elias and how I became a crime historian', in Pieter Spierenburg, *Violence and Punishment: Civilizing the Body Through Time*. Cambridge: Polity Press, 2013, 310–17.

Spierenburg, Pieter. 'Democracy came too early: A tentative explanation for the problem of American homicide'. *American Historical Review* 111 (2006): 104–14.

Wilson, James Q. *The Moral Sense*. New York: Free Press, 1985.

Wood, John Carter. 'A change of perspective: Integrating evolutionary psychology into the historiography of violence'. *British Journal of Criminology* 51 (2011): 479–98.

CHAPTER FOUR

The British Marxist Historians

The British Marxist Historians infused the history of crime with themes of class, authority, hierarchy, ideology and control. Their approach originated in the Communist Party Historians Group, which had been active after the Second World War, and talked about writing a 'people's history' of England. Cambridge historian George M. Trevelyan had published his *English Social History* in 1942 which he described as 'the history of a people with the politics left out'. What the historians from the Communist group had in mind was a social history with the politics very much left in.

In 1972, several of them met in London at the University of Westminster (then known as the Polytechnic of Central London) for a meeting of the Society for the Study of Labour History. Eric Hobsbawm, E. P. Thompson, Douglas Hay and Peter Linebaugh read papers on bandits, poachers and smugglers, the 'bloody code' and hangings. The British Marxist Historians not only invented the theme of 'social crime' but produced a surge of energy that propelled the history of crime for decades. In focusing on the lives of ordinary people, and criminals in relation to law, they shifted crime outside the province of legal history. By pursuing a 'history from below', and drawing on Marxist social theory, they introduced the history of crime not only to social history but also to social sciences.

This chapter covers Marxist approaches to the history of crime with a focus on the work of the British Marxists. Part 1 introduces work by the Webbs and the Frankfurt School as early examples of histories of crime inspired by Marx. Part 2 reviews research on Hobsbawm's social banditry, followed by Part 3 on rural protest and the Swing riots. Part 4 considers social crime as developed by Hay, Linebaugh and others, and Part 5 considers Thompson's work on poachers and the administration of the Black Act. Part 6 examines the history from below as a leitmotif for the history of crime.

Marx, history and crime

Although Marx has inspired a great deal of historical writing, he himself did not write history. Most of his work would be characterized as political analysis or journalistic commentary. He devoted most of his energy to a critique of capitalism, and from this, attempted to offer a complete account of human history.

At the centre of Marx's view of history is the mode of production. Any society will be characterized by its technology or industry (the means of production) and the way in which labour is deployed in relation to this (the social relations of production). Marx devoted most of his time to exposing the false promise of industrial capitalism as it existed in Europe. He saw its class structure: the industrialists (capitalists), who owned the factories and machines, and workers (proletariat), who had nothing to trade on the market except for their own labour. The relations between these were never static, because the means of production were always changing, bringing new demands on labour and new tensions between labour and capital. Once the situation reached the point at which the social relations were no longer compatible with capitalist demands, revolution would be inevitable. Marx imagined that history emerged from the progression through these modes of production, although he realized that this did not follow a single process throughout the world but took place in particular societies at different speeds.[1]

Marx's concepts are poorly defined in his writings, and he had difficulty finishing his literary projects. The closest he came to constructing a working model was the 1859 preface to *A Critique of Political Economy*. This passage contains what has been called the base–superstructure metaphor, that of a determining base and a determined superstructure. The base refers to the economy and the superstructure to ideas. Historical change originates in the base and plays out in the superstructure. This model provides a philosophy of history, a way of understanding changes in Europe over the centuries. The base–superstructure metaphor is, however, less a lens through which Marx interpreted the past than a steel for sharpening his critique of capitalism. In other words, to conduct a Marxist analysis of history involves 'working backwards': the process of understanding a legal reform or political action begins with looking at a shift in the economy.

Marx's own comments suggest that he attributed crime to a *lumpenproletariat*, the riff-raff, scum or degenerates of society. Marx viewed them with disdain, but not for the same reasons as other Victorian gentlemen. The *lumpen* were thieves, prostitutes and drunkards, who extracted their survival by victimizing the proletariat, and became tools of the ruling class. But Marx never really set out to offer an explanation of criminal behaviour, and there are differing views of what might be called Marx's 'theory of crime'.[2] Rather, he saw crime in the context of class struggle: one class possessing the power to criminalize the actions of another. Hobsbawm suggested that Marx provided the theoretical basis for a social history of crime. Although the concepts that have enjoyed the most influence in Marx's approach to the history of crime are less his (or Engels's) specific comments than more general concepts from his wider approach to history. Marxist social theory offers an interpretative framework that can be applied to a wide variety of historical activities. Taken as a starting point for analysis, Marxist concepts have been extended in a variety of ways, all compatible within the borders of social history.[3]

Sidney and Beatrice Webb believed that Marx would have approved of their history of prisons, although they differed in their view of historical change. They were members of a distinctively English society, the Fabians, who set out to win educated, middle-class professionals to socialism. They shared a belief that socialism could not be achieved through class conflict, but through welfare legislation administered through a civil service. The Webb method of 'analytical history' examined the evolution of particular forms of social organizations and institutional forms. They concentrated on the institutions within the relatively fixed social context of Britain which enabled them to address questions of growth and decay. They tried to understand the development and function of social institutions in society (the analysis) and explain the processes by which social wrongs could be abolished and ideals attained (action). Even before Beatrice met Sidney, she had become convinced of the 'inevitability of gradualness'. Society did not approximate a fixed state, but rather, a process of continuous change. A new society founded on socialist principles would not emerge from revolution, but the gradual metamorphosis of the new order from the old.[4]

English Prisons and Local Government (1922) reflects the Webb's commitment to analysis of social institutions. They describe the stages by which the national prison system emerged from the local prisons (gaols) of the sixteenth, seventeenth and eighteenth centuries. Local prisons had been run as profit-making concerns by gaolers. In the late eighteenth century, the government realized that as long as the keepers were allowed to regard the gaol as a profit-making enterprise, it would be impossible to secure conditions of decency and humanity. The government began a campaign of closing two-thirds of the corrupt and antiquated gaols. New penitentiaries replaced the gaols, which transferred control from local keepers to the Home Office. In Whitehall, a central body of prison administrators was established. The Webbs regarded their history as an objective marshalling of the facts, and avoided, they said, editorializing on the prison system at any particular stage in its development. Nevertheless, they did offer advice to the Home Office of the 1920s. It was clear from history, they said, that 'if we are to have places of confinement at all, and to make them such as the conscience of the nation would approve', they would need to be specialized for prisoners of different sexes, ages and sentences.[5]

A rather different history of prisons, also inspired by Marx, appeared in the 1930s. This one was associated with what became known as the

Frankfurt School of critical social theory. The Frankfurt School was established in connection with the Institute of Social Research in Frankfurt, Germany. The Institute commissioned Georg Rusche to write a study of punishment and the labour market. Before he could deliver the final manuscript, Hitler assumed power in Germany, and the National Socialist government forced the closure of the Institute. The scholars escaped with their library to New York City and reopened the Institute in connection with Columbia University. They asked Otto Kirchheimer to extend Rusche's study, which resulted in *Punishment and Social Structure* (1939). It was the first of the Institute's books to be published in English. Rusche had written the part up to 1900; Kirchheimer translated Rusche's work and added the twentieth century.[6]

Punishment and Social Structure analysed the relationship between methods of punishment in societies in Europe from the late medieval period to the early twentieth century.[7] As Rusche explained, previous histories of punishment focused on the idea of punishment rather than the experience of punishment. The legal connection between punishment and crime was not a sufficient guide. Punishment should be examined historically not merely as a 'juristic concept' but also for its 'social ends'. They examined changes in systems of punishment – fines, galleys, transportation, confinement – across specific historical periods. 'Every system of production tends to discover punishments which correspond to its productive relationships.'[8] The changes in legal principles that guide punishment are themselves the product of social conditions, and above all, economic forces. The twentieth century, Kirchheimer said, illustrated the limits of prison reform. Prison conditions were determined less by legal ideals (or as the Webbs put it, the 'conscience of the nation'), than by the labour market. The harshness of penalties depends, not on the conception of prisoners as rights-bearing individuals, but as human machines of uncertain value apart from their labour. Penalties, and specifically prison conditions, must generate worse conditions than the living standard of free workers (the 'less eligibility' principle).

Social bandits

In his books on primitive rebels and bandits, Hobsbawm opened up a new area of social history. Following the Twentieth Congress of the Communist Party in 1956 (at which Kruschev denounced Stalin's purges and the Soviet invasion of Hungary), he became interested in peasant revolts. The events led to a re-evaluation of the 'bases of revolutionary activity', as Hobsbawm put it, and he came up with his theory of 'primitive rebellions' through visits to the Mediterranean and conversations with Italian communists over coffee and cigarettes.[9]

Social banditry studies grew out of a chapter in *Primitive Rebels* (1959). Originally, Hobsbawm described social banditry as the most primitive form of social protest. In peasant societies, bandits offered protection. The peasants regarded them as their champions and turned them into a myth. Robin Hood is the archetype, although Spain and Italy produced more social bandits than England. Ordinary bandits became 'social bandits' because they did something which was not regarded as criminal by local conventions, but was held as such by the state or local rulers. Social bandits appeared in rural conditions, in pre-political and pre-capitalist societies, especially when the equilibrium was upset and the normal level of hardship was intensified by famines or wars.[10] Hobsbawm followed with a wider survey, *Bandits* (1969), and examples from Bulgaria, Greece, Hungary, Russia and Turkey, using primarily poems and ballads. He supposed that there were always some real characters behind the legends, who lived up to their image, at least in some ways at some times. Bandits grew out of societies based on agriculture, and more specifically, rural societies divided into landless peasants who were exploited by lords, towns or banks. There were three exemplary forms: the 'noble robber', the 'primitive resistance fighter' and the 'terror-bringing avenger'.[11]

The idea of an 'archaic' form of social protest comes into view when taking a Marxist perspective on history. The persistence of this form of protest constitutes a curiosity, something that belongs to a previous stage of economic history. Social banditry, Hobsbawm said, did not constitute a social movement or revolutionary activity; rather, its participants looked back to a traditional peasant society and an order they regarded as just. Social bandits did not pursue a dream of social justice but promoted resistance towards excessive levels of injustice. He believed that social banditry took place throughout the world, although it was limited to societies in a particular period of socio-economic development. It occurred in societies in the period of transition from tribal or kinship organization to modern capitalist, industrial society. In Europe, this meant that the high tide of social banditry had taken place between the sixteenth and eighteenth centuries. In other parts of the globe, this high point occurred in the nineteenth and even twentieth centuries. By the 1950s, social banditry was 'extinct, except in a few areas'.

Anthropologist Anton Blok became the first to see a black crow hovering over Hobsbawm's bandits. There was more to brigandage than the fact that it may have contained an element of social protest. Drawing on his research in Sicily, he insisted that bandits were not champions of the poor and weak, but more often terrorized those from the very ranks out of which they had emerged. Bandits did not represent effective agents to transform the organization of peasants into a politically conscious or effective force.[12]

To understand the social dimensions of banditry, it was necessary, Blok insisted, to look beyond their activities to the organization of peasant societies of which they were part. To be sure, bandits were 'social', but less in the sense of protest than in the sense of various ties to other people. To succeed as outlaws, bandits had to have the protection of powerful politicians. Without this, they would have been cut down by the landlord's retainers, police or other peasants. The more bandits took on this political character, the more their activities assumed an 'anti-social character'. The first loyalty of bandits, including many of those Hobsbawm cited, was not to the peasants. When they sided with political protectors, they served to thwart and prevent peasant mobilization. In understanding the myths and legends of Robin Hood-type bandits, it was crucial to distinguish between impressions of those who did not experience bandits, such as city populations, and those in contact with real bandits. It was easy to idealize things with which people were not acquainted – actual bandit life was not heroic or aesthetic but unpleasant and grim.[13]

Pat O'Malley also offered criticism early on. Hobsbawm had said that social bandits sprouted up among traditional peasantry but neglected to say what he meant by 'peasantry'. He complicated matters by saying that social bandits appeared when 'traditional peasant society' gave way to 'the modern economy'. Whatever he meant by modern economy, he could not have meant 'modern industrial era' because he also said social bandits were 'unlikely to be found in the modern industrial era'. O'Malley pointed to the activities of Ned Kelly and the struggle for land in Australia from 1878 to 1880. The Kelly gang conforms closely to Hobsbawm's concept of social bandits. They deliberately pursued a Robin Hood style, preying on enemies of the poor and championing the cause of the disinherited. In these respects, Ned Kelly appears as the archetypal social bandit. Yet there existed neither traditional peasants nor pre-capitalist economy, but rather, a capitalist economy, with highly developed police and communication systems. Hobsbawm's 'rather vague ideas' left room for finding bandits in modern, urban, capitalist and industrial conditions.[14]

Hobsbawm responded to Blok by suggesting that they had no disagreement about the facts of the bandits' existence, but only about the historical meaning of banditry. There was one type of bandit that was not completely divorced from the Robin Hood myth, and the strongest evidence for this was the fact that people made a distinction between bandits who did and did not play the role of Robin Hood. While some bandits attempted to play the role, even the most social of bandits were never conscious social protestors. Hobsbawm said that he never set out to provide a comprehensive history of banditry in general, but only to write about one kind of bandits: those not regarded as criminals by public opinion. He did yield to Blok's criticism in one respect. He should have made a clearer separation between versions of the myth and myth-makers at more or less social distance from them.[15]

Hobsbawm appreciated O'Malley's class analysis. 'Clearly, O'Malley and I agree, as he acknowledges, that social banditry wanes as modern organized and collective modes of representing class interests becomes available.'[16] Where they were not available, banditry remained attractive, even into the twentieth century, at least in those societies with a tradition of banditry.

Hobsbawm said he was more interested in the demise of banditry rather than specific conditions that encouraged its survival. The banditry of the Kelly gang, despite its immediate milieu, displayed 'an organic connection to a pre-capitalist or even pre-industrial economy'.[17] In shoring up his view of Australian bandits, Hobsbawm drew on work dealing with American bandits, from Jesse James to John Dillinger. The Depression era gangsters in the United States showed that the social banditry tradition had persisted at least until the 1930s. 'In its final stages … the role of the rural social bandits is transformed, insofar as it played out on a new stage, that of modern capitalist/industrial society, amid new social, economic and technological scenery, and possibly by new actors, who can no longer be adequately described as traditional peasants.'[18]

The fact that Hobsbawm was only ever interested in one kind of bandits reveals a great deal about his motivations, and particularly his effort to pursue historical research consistent with his political commitments. Hobsbawm, Gertrude Himmelfarb pointed out, admitted that as a Marxist he was 'inclined to avoid arguments and facts that he knows to be true lest they undermine the orthodox doctrine or divert him from his polemical task'.[19] Nevertheless, the attractiveness of the concept, combined with the ambiguity of the original formulation, led to banditry studies throughout the world. Historians have found social bandits across Europe, the Americas, Asia and the Mediterranean. They have collected the ingredients for understanding social banditry as an international phenomenon, although few can resist the temptation to refine Hobsbawm's original recipe.

Richard White observed that some outlaws in the American 'Wild West' enjoyed substantial amounts of local support and 'must be taken seriously as social bandits'. The peculiar social conditions of western Missouri in the 1860s and 1870s, and Oklahoma in the 1890s, in which belief in the honesty and competency of public law enforcement eroded, gave rise to outlaw gangs such as that of Frank and Jesse James. These gangs enjoyed assistance from kinship networks, active supporters and passive sympathizers. While social bandits did exist in the American West, their social impact was minor, limited as it was to extreme conditions. But their impact on American culture has been immense. They rode out of Missouri and Oklahoma to a prominent place as cultural heroes accessible to the nation as a whole.[20] William Van De Burg found social bandits among Black populations before the Civil War. African-Americans regarded some troublemakers in their communities as social bandits because of the difficulties they raised for common enemies: illegitimate and corrupt authorities. Although the boldness of 'Black social bandits' sometimes drifted into excess, they could be regarded as actual criminals only by those who feared a just social order. 'Truly bad Blacks' were never confused with noble robbers, resistance fighters and avengers of European folk tradition. Unconcerned about the community mores, they preyed on the weak as well as the strong, with no agenda beyond self-aggrandizement.[21]

Drawing on the stories surrounding Jaime el Barburo in nineteenth-century Spain, Ben Dodds proposed a category of 'literary bandits' alongside social bandits.[22] While social bandits embody the grievances and aspirations of oppressed populations in the countryside, literary bandits appear in the reading material consumed by wealthier groups, often in towns. Literary bandits, as the heroes of wealthier populations, merit historical investigation, not merely for what they reveal about social banditry and the poor, but for what they indicate about the role of crime in popular culture. Literary bandits do not occupy the same role in class conflict as Hobsbawm wished for them; rather, their mythology reflected a wider variety of political and social agendas. This was possible because 'bandits live alongside and not within society'; their society can be held up as a mirror to real society.[23]

Charles van Onselen located social banditry among Irish settlers in South Africa. In the last decades of the nineteenth century, Irish settlers contributed a disproportionate share of brigands. The remoteness of the Kimberley mines and the absence of railway links attracted bandits who robbed migrant workers of their earnings or plundered gold and diamonds from coaches en route to coastal cities. The Irish bandits sought out targets for their economic rather than political significance; they made no distinctions between privately and publicly held property. But in an environment where banks, mine owners and the state moved to consolidate their holdings, and thousands of ordinary working men lost their livelihoods, the activities of the Irish brigands took on political significance. The association of the Irish brigands with heroic criminals, outlaw legends and social bandits crystallized during the depression of 1890–2. In the popular view, anyone who selected the rich and powerful as their targets could not be wholly criminal. In the newspaper columns and pub conversations, men such as the McKeone brothers and 'One armed Jack' McLaughlin lost their Irish identities and became English folk heroes in the mould of Robin Hood and Dick Turpin.[24]

At some point, historians interested in bandits no longer argued with Hobsbawm; they argued with each other about what he had said. *Bandidos* (1990), a collection edited by Richard Slatta, brought together a range of scholars with an interest in South America to make a comprehensive examination of Hobsbawm's model. They agreed with Blok about the importance of 'distinguishing myth from reality'. They added two more types, 'guerrilla bandit' and 'political bandit', to Hobsbawm's typology, but stressed that bandits never amounted to a political force in the nineteenth century. Generally, they concluded that Hobsbawm overplayed the relationship between bandits and peasant communities, that the examples he offered to support social banditry did not meet his own criteria, and that his linear depiction of banditry giving way to more organized political protest was flawed. Slatta concluded that although he and his colleagues had 'galloped in hot pursuit of bandits across several Latin American countries and through two centuries', the only bandits they had been able to track down in the archives had 'visages different from the ideal type postulated by Hobsbawm'.[25]

In a review of Slatta's conclusion, Gilbert M. Joseph argued that histories of Latin American banditry had been too narrowly focused on Hobsbawm's model. Hobsbawm had made a great contribution in describing social banditry as an archaic or pre-political activity in peasant societies on the verge of transformation by capitalist market and nation state. But neither Hobsbawm nor his followers had done the difficult job of matching the bandit types in the folklore and literature with those in police, judicial and other records. Working with 'official' records had become a standard means of research in banditry since 1969 when Hobsbawm's book appeared. But, as Joseph conceded, Hobsbawm's model continued to have a magnetic appeal. 'Few historical actors have generated more excitement, intrigue and mythology over the long term than bandits.' Joseph agreed with much of what Slatta and his colleagues argued, but did not see the value of their new bandit types. To insist on 'guerrilla bandit' over 'haiduk' amounted to a distinction without a difference.[26]

Bandits remain as important a subject as ever. In a recent study, Amy Robinson, observes that the figure of Chucho el Roto has often been held up as an example of the social bandit in Mexico. But an examination of the literary sources favoured by Hobsbawm reveals a biography that does not fit his model or at the very least takes his model in a new direction. Using reports in the newspapers, a play and a novel, Robinson explores Chucho's criminal career before, during and after the Mexican Revolution. While social banditry was seen as a symbol of resistance against elites in peasant societies, Chucho was an urban bandit who generated an intense reaction among the poor and the privileged in Mexico City during the period of modernization. He gained notoriety not as an impoverished rebel in the shanty towns but as a literate and skilled carpenter living, working and thieving among the city's affluent citizens. The relationship between social bandits, the city and a growing middle class challenged the class-bound understanding of social banditry.[27]

Rural crime and Captain Swing

In the 1960s, Hobsbawm carried out research with George Rudé into the Swing disorders. During 1830–1, various disturbances occurred throughout the south of England, including arson, mobs, food riots, threatening letters and damage to threshing machines. Rumours circulated about the appearance of a mysterious stranger at the scene of fires and wrecked machinery. Some claimed to have glimpsed a well-dressed gentleman in the shadows. Almost certainly there was no real person named Captain Swing, although many of the threatening letters bore 'his' signature. Possibly, the name was a reference to a tool familiar to people in the agrarian countryside: the *swing* or *swingel* was the part of the flail that struck the corn. Many of the riots had been touched off by the threat of machine-threshing to the men's winter employment of threshing by hand with a flail.[28]

Hobsbawm and Rudé examined the causes of the disorders, the extent of the movement and characteristics of those involved. *Captain Swing* (1969) was an inquiry into 'history from below', an attempt to reconstruct the mental world of an anonymous and undocumented people.[29] Although the response from the authorities was severe – many Swing rioters were transported to the Australian colonies for their actions – they were not common criminals. Hobsbawm and Rudé claimed that few had anything close to previous convictions. Most, in fact, had good reputations. They were labourers who believed in the right to work and earn a living wage, who refused to accept that machines, who robbed them of this right, should enjoy the protection of law. The Swing rioters were 'primitive rebels'. They invoked the authority of justice, government, the King and the Heavens to justify their actions. The rising of the 1830s was the greatest episode of machine-breaking in English history. Although the methods were 'archaic', it was also the most successful: 'The threshing machines did not return on the old scale. Of all the machine-breaking movements of the nineteenth century that of the helpless and unorganised farm labourers proved to be the most effective.'[30]

Captain Swing was one of the few works of academic history to become a bestseller.[31] It generated continuing academic interest in the Swing events, and further research in local archives indicated that Swing was even bigger than Hobsbawm and Rudé thought. Subsequent evidence for East Kent, where the first Swing event was said to have occurred, suggests that they had not realized the actual level of Swing activity, nor the full geography on which it played out. They had identified 67 incidents of machine-breaking, arson, etc., and further research turned up 124, suggesting that they had undercounted by 85 per cent.[32] For England as a whole, Hobsbawm and Rudé found 1,475 Swing events, but researchers connected with the Family and Community Historical Research Society found 3,283 incidents. This meant that Swing covered a larger geographical area with outbreaks of violence on a far wider scale than previously imagined.[33] This research also suggested that attempting to characterize the events according to a typology of machine-breaking, wage meeting or robbery missed the importance of social process in how the incidents developed. Many Swing actions began as peaceful gatherings of farmers, but took on a different character as local radicals or drink entered in.[34]

Other work has examined the issue of violence. Hobsbawm and Rudé concluded that the Swing disorders were in the main non-violent and that the gains had been achieved without assault, murder and other interpersonal violence. This conclusion has been re-evaluated by Carl Griffin. As he pointed out, the term *Captain Swing* had a double meaning: it contained not only a reference to flail threshing, but at the same time, to the swinging of the corpse in a hanging, a common allusion in the threatening letters (as Thompson had found in 1975). As such, it was not a comment on threshing machines, but a violent threat. The combination of the threatening letters and the fear generated by the gang's successes effectively removed the need for interpersonal violence. Griffin emphasized that Swing participants 'were not pacifists' and that many did have prior convictions for assault. Perpetrating violence does not completely account for the power of the movement; rather, hundreds of acts of aggression and violence, magnified by thousands of gestures, symbols and threats, generated the force of the Swing movement.[35]

Peter Jones has called for 'a fundamental reassessment' of the Swing disturbances in view of accumulating evidence.[36] Virtually all historians who have looked into events in the 1830s refer to Swing as a 'movement', and Hobsbawm and Rudé were clear that it was a movement of farm labourers. But in what sense can Swing be called a 'movement'? Despite the fact that Swing put his name to a number of letters, in many other disturbances there is no reference to Swing at all. More importantly, there is little evidence in the sources that the Swing emblem was invented, or even acknowledged, by those who took part in the events. The figure of Swing was an invention of outsiders, particularly those writing newspapers. *The Times* reported in December 1830 the arrest of Captain Swing, Joseph Saville, said to possess copies of threatening letters and a large amount of cash. But 'the actual and original Swing' arrested turned out to be crackpot.[37] The point, Jones explains, is not really about Saville, but about the need for contemporaries to find some 'organising principle' behind the disturbances of the 1830s and the extent to which historians have gone along with this exercise. Swing was not a national movement of the labouring poor, but an aggregate of many small, local actions comprised of thousands of labourers and their sympathizers. These local events had an organizing principle or theme in the sense that those who participated in them shared a cultural understanding of just, fair and natural relationships.

Katrina Navickas has taken this argument a step further. She carried out research into Swing riots in Carlisle in 1830, a rather unexpected location for a movement of farm labourers in southern England.[38] The incidents are significant, not for what they indicate about the geography of Swing, but for the way contemporaries and historians have characterized the event. In linking a series of events with a variety of motivations with the imaginary leader Captain Swing, magistrates and police commissioners in Carlisle gave much more coherence to the movement than was actually there. The Swing rioters were not agricultural labourers, but disparate groups with various ambitions, including personal motives of revenge. They were seen within the rumour-obsessed imaginations of the time as united by a military leader. Hobsbawm and Rudé played into this characterization because their reading of Marx had told them what they should see. Marxism looked for an agricultural proletariat and a movement to express the rights of labourers. 'The search for class foundered and set back the history of Swing.'[39]

Law, ideology and property

Albion's Fatal Tree (1975) offers a collection of essays concerning the meaning of certain criminal activities in the eighteenth century. Peter Linebaugh spotlighted the conflict over bodies taken down from the Tyburn gallows, Cal Winslow examined the 'war' between smugglers and revenue officers on the Sussex coast and John G. Rule identified those involved in 'wrecking' on the shores of the British Isles. Hay described poachers, keepers and landowners in the countryside near Birmingham, and E. P. Thompson contributed an essay on anonymous letters published in a London newspaper. As the authors explain, the essays present examples of 'good' criminals, those who expressed a form of social protest in their activities. Although, as the authors acknowledged, the evidence did not suggest a neat distinction. There were not mutually exclusive groups of good criminals (rioters, smugglers and poachers) who stood apart from ordinary or common criminals (thieves, highwaymen, forgers, arsonists and murderers). Nevertheless, it became possible to see 'social crime' in the response of the common people, who were more likely to shelter smugglers and poachers than horse-thieves and sheep-stealers.[40]

The volume opens with Hay's essay, 'Property, Authority and the Criminal Law', which explores the meaning of capital statutes. The number of capital offences multiplied throughout the eighteenth century to some 200 by the early nineteenth century, although relatively few executions were actually carried out. Hay examined why the law remained in force during a period in which the number of executions remained low or declined. He argued that the law had much to offer the ruling class. They regarded the introduction of a regular police force as distasteful and preferred to rely on the force of the law. For rulers as much concerned with protecting their authority as their property, courtroom procedures involved spectacle. They were careful to preserve the appearance that the law in England held everyone to account. 'The ideology of the law', Hay said, 'was crucial in sustaining the hegemony of the English ruling class.'[41] The essay proved to be extremely influential. It inspired further studies of discretionary justice, including studies of mercy in the administration of law in Canada and Australia. 'Hay's earlier work on mercy in eighteenth and nineteenth-century England', Carolyn Strange said in 1986, 'still sets the standard for historians (and scholars in a variety of disciplines) who continue to puzzle over the administration of punishment.'[42]

Hay's chapter also ignited a fiery debate. A few years after it appeared, John Langbein published his article 'Albion's Fatal Flaws' in which he questioned not only Hay's conclusions about the contours of law in the eighteenth century, but about where the history of crime should be located within wider history. Drawing on cases from sessions at the Old Bailey between 1754 and 1756, Langbein denied that the law had been administered by the ruling class to suit their interests. It was a mistake to romanticize criminal offences as a challenge to the elite. Most of the 'little crooks' at the Old Bailey (shoplifters, pickpockets and pilferers) were employed, but poor, and most of their victims were hardly better off, typically small shopkeepers, artisans and innkeepers. So, 'social crime' was less a reaction to the rich exploiting the poor than the poor victimizing other poor. Hay had secured his evidence by targeting the game law, although the larger problem was not selective use of the evidence but the interpretation. Hay had offered the 'legitimisation thesis' which interpreted cases in which the courts held the wealthy to account as part of the symbolic process of disguising the ruling-class conspiracy. Absorbing contrary evidence in this way meant that Hay's argument was 'not a thesis about the evidence' or even a 'thesis about history'. Rather, it was an essay about what Marx taught. 'The criminal law', Langbein concluded, 'is simply the wrong place to look for the active hand of the ruling classes.'[43]

Hay found Langbein's critique to be 'mildly annoying'. The presentation in 'Albion's Fatal Flaws' had ignored most of his evidence and misrepresented his argument. He prepared a response, which was meant to appear in a subsequent issue of Past & Present, but never did, owing to a change in editorship.[44] Peter Linebaugh did respond to Langbein. Linebaugh chiselled away at Langbein's various points before sapping the foundations of the legal approach. By pursuing 'his brand of narrow legal scholarship', Langbein had missed the point. Hay and colleagues had turned to legal records because of what they revealed of 'history from below', about the operation of law in a society divided by class. Hay had not pursued the methods of legal history, but brought together legal history and social history to reveal the lives of people who left few written records.[45]

Linebaugh argued that Langbein had visited the wrong archives and mismanaged what he found. He had not bothered to examine evidence from the countryside as Hay had done. Instead, Langbein looked at London, and missed seeing what was going on – 'even the most cursory historical investigation suggests a dynamic of class relations'.[46] The idea that criminal proceedings should be read exclusively within a legal context denied any understanding of their social meaning, and revealed a tendency to approach the law 'ahistorically, suggesting that crime and specific crimes are eternal or inherent in human society'.[47] Langbein had violated two main tenets of the historian's craft: (1) the principle of historical specificity, which requires an examination of everything, even legal ideas, within the context in which they appeared, and (2) the principle of historical periodization, which establishes epochs, periods and phases, and seeks to account for changes among them. Although these tenets leave room for argument, they cannot be appreciated by denying historical particularity and change.

Linebaugh concluded that Langbein's 'narrow view of historical inquiry is incapable of leading him to other subjects of social life'.[48]

Peter King challenged Hay's argument about the 'hegemony of the law'. Using records of quarter sessions relating to property offenders from late-eighteenth-century Essex, King proposed that a number of groups shared discretionary decision-making.[49] This did not invalidate Hay's argument that the law was ultimately a weapon of class warfare. It could be said that the appearance of a wider base of consumers served to legitimize the rule of law within the wider public, and in this way, the ruling class tightened their grip. Hay's argument proved difficult to assess, because when framed in this way, the hegemony concept could 'accommodate almost any form of evidence that is cast upon it'.[50] King's research had led him to conclude that the administration of the law relating to property theft was, however, not merely the prerogative of a small elite. It was a forum in which different groups, each with their own ambitions and views of the law, demonstrated discretionary authority. Among these were 'the middling group' of tradesmen, manufacturers, commercial men and farmers, responsible for more than half of England's wealth in this period. They had great influence at the local level.

In his chapter in *Albion's Fatal Tree*, Peter Linebaugh sought to dispel the notion that the crowds gathered at Tyburn to witness executions amounted to little more than 'raucous spectacle'. He revealed the determination of family members and friends of the condemned to collect the corpse for burial, an act which demonstrated the scorn of the crowd for law and authority. In examining the archival records, he became even more interested in the social background of individuals who died on the Tyburn gallows. And, as the archival record was particularly detailed and hanging was the pinnacle in the range of available punishments, he decided to carry out further study of the ways in which 'the Tyburn hangings were the central event in the urban contention between the classes'.[51] In *The London Hanged* (1981), Linebaugh followed up the point on which his chapter of *Albion's Fatal Tree* had closed: What was the relationship between crime and the working class? The conclusion had been that law was central to ruling-class authority. But by focusing on law, the discussion led to a question of whether hanged men and women were social criminals taking from the rich or anti-social criminals stealing from the poor. By shifting the discussion away from the law and towards the lives of the condemned, it became possible to see more clearly the relationship between labouring people and their rulers. Linebaugh presented hangings over four generations between 1690 and 1800 within a framework of changing economic organization. 'The material exchange between labour and capital', Linebaugh explained, 'is a theme virtually present in every chapter because ... it is essential to understanding the who, when and why of the Tyburn hangings.'[52]

Thomas Laqueur said that he did not recognize the story of executions as dramatized by Linebaugh and Hay.[53] As Laqueur explained, in their view, the state is the primary actor of a drama in which it assigns to itself the leading role and the people are assigned a subsidiary role as the audience meant to absorb the message of power. This, he insisted, was not quite right because there was a wide range of evidence to suggest much less orchestration and much more improvisation in the staging of hangings. The crowd, and in particular, the carnivalesque crowd, was in the starring role. Too many things could, and did, go wrong in the messy, unpredictable business of theatrical dismemberment – the accused refused to die, body parts failed to sever, blood spilled in embarrassing ways. At the centre of the historical stage was the crowd – boisterous women, men, children of all ages, engaged in festival. 'Whatever the proportion of disastrous to decorous executions, there was enough variation within any "hanging fair," enough laughter and comic chaos, to make them unsuitable for the imaginative realm of sublime terror, just reward or tragedy.'[54]

Albion's Fatal Tree inspired further research into crime in the eighteenth century and beyond. John Brewer and John Styles co-edited *An Ungovernable People* (1980), something of a sequel.[55] The collection extended the analysis of the rule of law in the seventeenth and eighteenth centuries with additional case studies: villagers and grain rioters, incarcerated debtors, colliers, counterfeiters and radicals. Some of the essays affirmed earlier conclusions, particularly Hay's observations about the significance of discretion. But others questioned whether the concept of social crime was sustainable. Styles's essay on Yorkshire coiners concludes that while the 'yellow trade' (a combination of practices including counterfeiting and clipping) fit the category of 'social crime', in the sense that it received wide popular support, in another sense, it did not. Unlike poaching and wrecking, it was not justified as an ancient right or customary practice. Nor was there evidence of hostility to laws of coinage. Styles concludes that any clear distinction between social crime and normal crime must be counterbalanced with so many exceptions that the concept of 'social crime' should be shelved. In Yorkshire, popular support for counterfeiting did not express a view of the authority of the law so much as a specific set of social alliances related to economic aspects of the trade.[56]

Crime, Protest and Popular Politics in Southern England 1740-1850 (1997), by John Rule and Roger Wells, includes studies of protest ranging from Chartism to sheep-stealing. The authors aim to show 'that agricultural labourers and other southern working people had a capacity to fight to redress their grievances'.[57] The labourers engaged in mass mobilizations and politically motivated movements. The notion of social crime is useful for making sense of activities regarded by the law as crime, but not by the local people. Activities such as sheep-stealing grew out of the context in which profit-conscious farmers refused to allow the ancient right of gleaning after harvest. Although not all criminal behaviour can be neatly categorized as such, Rule and Wells point to a mix of motivations and participants in rural crime. 'Hungry men rob orchards, poach hares or steal sheep. So do professional dealers or those intending to supply them. So, too, do those who have scores to settle against local farmers.'[58] Further, not all crime in the countryside can be explained by the rural context. Some rural crimes were the work of gangs working from towns.

The perspective advanced by Hobsbawm, Thompson, Hay and others has remained popular. In a sense, it suffers from its own popularity. Two decades after *Albion's Fatal Tree*, Louis Knafla referred to it as the standard account in need of revision. 'The old paradigm', he wrote, 'of crime as an activity of the poor or unemployed against the propertied, and the resulting theory of the criminal law as a tool of the state to maintain class control and the supremacy of the elite, has been allowed to go too far in the historiography of crime.'[59] Knafla called for perspectives that recognized the capacity for criminality as an 'innate element of the human condition', which involved not only crimes of the poor against the wealthy, but crimes of the poor against other poor people and crimes of the wealthy doing the same.

The Black Act

Thompson's chapter in *Albion's Fatal Tree* became *Whigs and Hunters* (1975).[60] It concerns 'The Black Act', enacted during four weeks of 1723, which criminalized forest offences such as hunting deer, poaching of hares and cutting of trees. The law made such offences, more than fifty in all, capital crimes, which made for an extreme and severe criminal code. The Black Act came to the legislature as an emergency act, for three years only, but remained in force until the nineteenth century. Parliament passed it in response to poachers in the forests of Windsor and Hampshire, who hunted deer at night and advertised their activities with blackmail and threatening letters. The name came from the practice of the poachers disguising themselves with blackened faces. Once the act was passed, it was turned to other uses. The authorities did not turn the provisions of the act against the blacks, but common people defending forest rights of grazing, turf-cutting and wood-taking.

The 'emergency' that led to passage of the act, Thompson said, was not the offences themselves. Poaching deer, cutting trees and taking hares did not trouble the authorities. And despite the menacing letters, there was little violence to persons. Rather, the emergency was the threat to the authority: the 'repeated public humiliation of the authorities' and insult to 'royal and private property'. Thompson shows that blacking arose in response to an attempt to reactivate what had been a relaxed forest policy. It represented a mode of resistance by the foresters to the assertion of authority by large estate holders. The blacks had the support of people, and this 'displacement of authority' provoked the government into over-egging the custard when it came to the legislative response. They were, Thompson thought, 'not quite (in E. J. Hobsbawm's sense) social bandits', nor were they 'agrarian rebels', although they shared 'something of both characters'. The blacks were ordinary country people, who in taking deer for venison, defended rights they had come to see as their own.[61]

Thompson rejected the view of the blacks as 'gangsters at large', 'gangs' of criminals or members of a 'criminal subculture'.[62] To see them in this way invoked an anachronistic analysis that pressed a twentieth-century photograph into an eighteenth-century frame. What emerged in 1723 was not a novel form of criminality, but a new definition of crime. 'Crime', as defined in the eighteenth century, was the prerogative of those who owned property, controlled the state and could pass laws in its name, and they made the threat to property the most serious form of criminality. The act registered the long decline of old methods of class control. In place of the whipping post, stocks and harrying of vagabonds, the rulers of eighteenth-century England impressed the discipline of low wages and instilled the threat of execution. The definition of crime was transformed: 'crime' was no longer an offence between persons but a threat to property.[63]

Subsequent research has invited some doubt about the false alarm Thompson thought he saw. He discounted the possibility of a real emergency because there was little evidence at the time of a popular threat. He ruled out links between the blacks and the Jacobites, because, he said, the Jacobites did not appear to be effective at organizing among the common people. But about ten years after *Whigs and Hunters*, researchers uncovered a letter in the Royal Archives at Windsor Castle indicating significant Jacobite activity at the time.[64] The author, Sir Henry Goring, helped organize the Waltham blacks and had played a role in the conspiracy known as the Atterbury plot in 1721. It suggests that popular Jacobitism was a recent phenomenon and enough of a worry that Sir Robert Walpole, Britain's first 'Prime Minister', was informed of it. Thompson acknowledged the letter represented 'the most significant new information to appear' on the origins of the act, and realized what it suggested about the reasons for its passage. If the plans outlined in the letter had reached the government, he admitted, 'it may afford a little excuse for the hasty passage of the Act'.[65]

Alan Howkins and Linda Merrick offer important insight into the practice of disguise, cross-dressing and face-blacking. Although they made the point in reference to Captain Swing, it puts the blacks in different light as well. A simple question: Why bother with disguise? It may be, Howkins and Merrick would allow, that the participants hoped to avoid capture and reprisal. But they believe there is more to it than this. Disguise allowed the participants to break not only the legal rules of highly stratified English society, but also the moral rules of their own communities, families and households. By taking on the identity of someone, but no one in particular, they could challenge the authority without abandoning the rules of conduct important in their own culture.[66] Blacking was never meant to be a literal disguise to resist the law, but a symbolic disguise to avoid moral condemnation within their own communities. If Howkins and Merrick are right about this, they hold the equivalent of a dagger pointed at the heart of social crime.

Thompson concluded *Whigs and Hunters* with an editorial on the rule of law that surprised, annoyed and dismayed his followers. Given what he had said in the earlier chapters, he might have summed up with a statement about legal procedure as the most powerful tool possessed by the wealthy for tightening the screws on the poor. Instead, he talked about the role of law in society as a positive good. Participation in the *Albion's Fatal Tree* project left him with the feeling that too much emphasis had been given to the law as a tool of the ruling class. For many of England's governing elite, the rule of law was a nuisance, to be manipulated in ways they could. But, it was also 'a legacy as substantial as any handed down from the struggles of the seventeenth century to the eighteenth'.[67] It was a bequest too precious to waste. 'If we suppose that law is no more than a mystifying and pompous way in which class power is registered and executed, then we need not waste our labour in studying its history and forms. ... It is because law *matters* that we have bothered with this story at all.'[68]

History from below

Not only did the British Marxist Historians introduce enduring themes into the historical study of crime and criminal justice, they also advanced a wider social history or 'history from below'. The phrase comes from the title of an article Thompson published in 1966 in *The Times Literary Supplement*. The idea of writing history from below, James Sharpe has observed, is an attractive one. It holds out the promise, and challenge, of recovering the lives of ordinary people, lives seen as too unimportant and insignificant to merit attention of historians. But the history from below confronts several difficulties.[69]

Specifically, there are three difficulties, according to Sharpe. (1) Evidence: There is a mass of material that can be consulted for the twentieth century and even for the nineteenth century. Writing history from the bottom up requires a change in interpretation, not research technique. But the further back the historian wishes to go, the more restricted the evidence becomes. Diaries, memoirs and other documents from which it is possible to glean information about the lives of the lower classes are, with a few exceptions, rare before the eighteenth century.[70] (2) Conceptualization: Where, exactly, on the conceptual map is *below*? Although the amount of historical writing that can be categorized as bottom-up history has increased, the analyses have not produced any definition of the bottom other than as a residual category. The people from below are defined by who they are not, rather than who they are. The difficulty is formidable for the reason that 'ordinary people' have been a varied group as far back as the sixteenth century, divided by vocation, language and gender.[71] (3) Significance: What should be done with the history from below once written? Aside from those consciously writing within a theoretical framework mapped by Marx, what meaning should be attached to 'belowness' in history? For the British Marxist Historians, below meant episodes in which the masses engaged in overt political activity or familiar areas of economic development. Court records furnish an important source of evidence about ordinary people, but building up a view of ordinary lives from court records leads to a distorted understanding. Criminal lives should not be taken as representative of ordinary lives.[72]

Each of the difficulties has been the subject of some discussion. John Beattie observed that the evidence for social crime derives from a particular methodology: the case study. In his study of crime in Surrey from 1660 to 1800, he looked for patterns of criminal behaviour in cases processed by courts of quarter sessions and assizes. He zeroed-in on offences against person and property that made up the 'everyday business' of the criminal courts: robbery, burglary, larceny, homicide, infanticide and rape. Although Hay, Linebaugh and Thompson had done 'excellent work' on social crimes, he said, he could not hope to find comparable activities in Surrey owing to the nature of the information. Offences such as smuggling, poaching, coining and riot required case studies to make them intelligible, detailed reconstruction of social, economic and political circumstances in which they occurred. In dealing with a large number of offences over more than 150 years, he could not achieve the level of resolution achieved with the case study technique.[73]

This is not necessarily a bad thing. Even if case study is the required vehicle, it still allows for a significant amount of exploration. Early on, Hay demonstrated that the conclusions from studies of crime and criminal law in eighteenth-century England could be extended by means of comparative studies. The history of crime dealt with interrelationships of property, power and hierarchy as well as ideology and the means of labour discipline and control. These relationships could be seen not only in countries with industrial economies in Europe and North America, but also in developing economies of states in Africa. To the extent scholars were interested in more than legal procedure, aggregate statistics and institutional history, comparative research could yield hypotheses, possible explanations, lines of inquiry, and worthwhile problems for future work. Further, comparative studies could generate inquiry about the role of law in society and avoid the tendency to subordinate 'broad theoretical questions' to the 'demands of analysis'.[74]

However, in limiting themselves to certain crimes, the British Marxist Historians left themselves vulnerable to the allegation of selective use of evidence. At worst, they started with particular political commitments, chose those few activities related to the law that seemed to fit and manufactured support for it. Joanna Innes and John Styles suggested that social crime amounts to a category of activity suggested by Marxist social theory, and that *Albion's Fatal Tree* presented those activities that matched the theory. As an explanation for crime in society, social crime explained very little. The proponents of social crime looked for instances of criminality to confirm the view they had started with, and in the process, overlooked the forms that made up most of the business for the courts: larceny, burglary, robbery and theft.[75] They walked past forests to marvel at a few trees.

The inventory of crimes that appeared in *Albion's Fatal Tree*, it should be said, was not selected according to a plan. It started as a book about eighteenth-century crime and turned into a book about crime as a form of social protest because several planned contributions never came together.[76] Linebaugh's response to the insinuation of selective use of evidence was to charge those interested in the forests with a bias of their own. The real problem, as he saw it, was not searching for evidence of social crime, but the use of ordinary crime as a standard from which social crime could be analysed. The starting position for studying social crime is that the definition of crime in any historical period is ambiguous. To insist on looking at ordinary or mainstream crime as the more revealing activity is to presume that the meaning of crime has remained stable over the centuries. The critique of social crime from the standpoint of ordinary crime exaggerates the clarity of crime and mistakes its historic meaning for its twenty-first-century meaning. What the critical response to social crime gained in 'methodological sophistication' it lost in 'conceptual timidity' and the narrowing of 'historical imagination'. The history of crime became the 'history of the administration of justice'.[77]

Conceptualization of social crime has been difficult. At the 1972 Labour conference, Thompson suggested that it could never really be nailed down firmly.[78] Historians of the eighteenth century had drawn a line between individual crime, as defined by the legislature, and social crime, meaning, social protest movements, backed by strong community feeling. While there was a difference, it was important to 'draw the distinction cautiously and with reservations' and to 'handle the evidence with the great care'.[79] Most of the rioters at Wilkes and Gordon were journeymen, and as such, may well have had an economic motivation. But most of those hanged at Tyburn were also journeymen, who presumably also had an economic motivation. Further, smugglers engaged in protest activity were also involved in blackmail and protection rackets; they beat each other and murdered informants. 'We may have more sympathy for the food-rioter than for the horse-stealer, but the records don't authorize us to see one rather than the other as more typical of labouring people. There is not "nice" social crime here and "nasty" social crime there.'[80]

Timothy Shakesheff has proposed that the definition of social crime should be widened to include the perpetrators of 'mundane criminal acts'. From his research on rural crime in nineteenth-century Herefordshire, he suggests that wood-thieves and sheep-stealers should join poachers, wreckers, smugglers and rioters as social criminals. The large numbers of men and women engaged in theft of wood and crops suggests that no stigma was attached to them within the community of rural poor. The small-scale rural criminal act has been overlooked as a form of protest, yet the pattern of crime in Herefordshire suggests that 'men and women ... reacted to agricultural change and unemployment by the only means open to them: crime, that most primitive form of insurrection'.[81] But the problem with comparing activities such as poaching and smuggling, which are 'clearly' social crimes, with activities such as wood-theft and sheep-stealing, which are 'nearly' social crimes, is the same as comparing social crime with ordinary crime. The discussion takes place as if poaching had the same meaning regardless of when and where it occurred.

Although historians have used the term 'social crime', they do not seem to have the same thing in mind. Some define it as the same as protest crime; for others, it means something closer to collective (as opposed to individual) behaviour.[82] John Rule has tried to sort this out. Reduced to a phrase, social crime refers to 'criminal action legitimized by popular opinion'.[83] He suspects that a good deal of felonies committed in rural areas during the eighteenth century fit this definition, although it is no easy task for the historian to determine when crimes became a form of protest. The meaning of social crime depends on what the perpetrators thought of themselves, and what others thought of them – they did not regard themselves as criminals, neither were they viewed as such by the community. The distinction between social crime and ordinary crime should not be confused with professional and casual crime, with violent and non-violent crime, nor with serious and non-serious crime. Rule also provides a further conceptualization of social crime: (1) Crimes not regarded as crimes by the community because they explicitly represent a form of protest. (2) Actions not regarded as criminal by the community even though the purpose may have been more criminal than protest.[84]

Finally, there is the difficulty of significance. In his analysis of arson, John Archer points out that the meaning of fire-setting changed in the course of the nineteenth century. It had been a feature of social crime in the 1830s but became less so after 1852.[85] Social crime was not a fixed or absolute category, and the British Marxist Historians would readily agree, although from reading their work, it is easy to get the impression that it was. They also revealed the tendency in presenting criminals, who in their actions, or in the actions taken by the authorities in response, to romanticize their violations of the law of the land as revolutionary or insurrectionary activities. But the 'temptation to hail such men as vanguards of the working class should be resisted'.[86] Understanding the motivation of those who maimed animals, poached game and set fires is key to categorization of such activities, whether social crime or ordinary crime. It is an extraordinarily difficult exercise for historical investigation, but it is clear that lawbreakers did not share the same motivation. 'Some of these men were, in short, brutal and wild men who operated under their own laws, not those of the state or their own communities.'[87]

Social crime as a form of protest raises further questions about the idea of 'history from below'. The problem is stated by King.[88] The idea of social crime comes from a conceptual framework that sees the law in the hands of the ruling class. Contrary to the view of the law as a 'multi-use space', the proponents of social crime see it as the province of the ruling elite. The ruling class use it to affirm their hold on institutions in society. If this is the case, and the point is to write a history from below, what other role is there for the middling class and the labourers, other than in the form of resistance to legal authority? By denying a place for labourers in the administration of the law, crime must become 'social' in some sense, because it is the only way in which the labourers can demonstrate that they make history. This implies that a person nearer the bottom of society can make history in only one way, that of the criminal, the smuggler, the poacher, the arsonist. The preoccupation with the power of the elite, and the law as an expression of this power, leads to overlooking the ways other than illegal activity in which poor labourers were participants in the law.

Conclusion

The idea of 'social crime' articulated by the British Marxist Historians had a simple enough message: ordinary people, forced by larger injustices, to break the law. Even if the characters were familiar and the plot rather predictable, it was always an engaging story. Eric Hobsbawm, Edward Thompson, Douglas Hay and the others found fascinating topics of universal and timeless appeal: tales of bandits, poachers, hangings, trials and rioters. Their work inspired countless historians to consider the benefits of crime as a topic of investigation, and inspired many social scientists to reflect on the importance of history in understanding social problems.

The Marxist threat to conventional history, the debates among adherents about what Marx really meant and the excitement of socialist revolution have passed along with fashions of the 1970s. Many of the specific conclusions the British Marxist Historians made about bandits, poachers, etc., have fallen on hard times; John Langbein, John Styles, Peter King and others have challenged their interpretation. Louis Knafla spoke for many crime historians when he said that 'social crime', to the extent it existed at all, was rare and exceptional, and encouraged historians to move on. To understand the significance of crime in the past, it was necessary to get beyond protest and rebellion, and certainly there was much more going on in the way of criminal victimization than the British Marxist Historians allowed. But what makes Hobsbawm, Thompson and Hay still important for writing the history of crime (and merits a full chapter devoted to their work) is their view of history from the bottom up. The idea that ordinary people matter, even those who break the law, remains a significant value in crime history, and many historians who would otherwise reject Marxist theory accept that it is worthwhile to recover the view of those arrested on the street, who stand in the dock, and who wind up in prison.

Notes

1 Eric Hobsbawm, *On History* (London: Abacus, 1998), 207–25.

2 Paul Q. Hirst, 'Marx and Engels on law, crime and morality', *Economy and Society* 1 (1972): 28–56.

3 Hobsbawm, *On History*, 222–5.

4 T. S. Simey, 'The contribution of Sidney and Beatrice Webb to sociology', *British Journal of Sociology* 12 (1961): 106–23 (110–11).

5 Sidney and Beatrice Webb, *English Prisons Under Local Government* (London: Longmans Green, 1922), 234.

6 Martin Jay, *The Dialectical Imagination: A History of the Frankfurt School and the Institute for Social Research* (Boston: Little, Brown, 1973), 149.

7 Georg Rusche and Otto Kirchheimer, *Punishment and Social Structure* (New York: Columbia University Press, 1939).

8 Rusche and Kirchheimer, *Punishment and Social*, 5.

9 Harvey J. Kaye, *The British Marxist Historians* (London: Macmillan, 1995), 145–6.

10 Eric Hobsbawm, *Primitive Rebels: Studies in Archaic Forms of Social Movement in the Nineteenth and Twentieth Centuries* (New York: W. W. Norton, 1959), 13–29.

11 Eric Hobsbawm, *Bandits* (London: Weidenfeld and Nicolson, 1969).

12 Anton Blok, *The Mafia of a Sicilian Village 1860-1960: A Study of Violent Peasant Entrepreneurs* (New York: Harper and Row, 1974), 99–102; Anton Blok, 'The peasant and the brigand: Social banditry reconsidered', *Comparative Studies in Society and History* 14 (1972): 494–503.

13 Blok, 'The peasant', 501.

14 Pat O'Malley, 'Social bandits, modern capitalism and the traditional peasantry: A critique of Hobsbawm', *Journal of Peasant Studies* 6 (1979): 489–501.

15 Eric Hobsbawm, 'Social bandits: Reply', *Comparative Studies in Society and History* 14 (1972): 503–5.

16 Eric Hobsbawm, *Bandits*, rev. edn (New York: Pantheon, 1981), 150–1.

17 Hobsbawm, *Bandits*, 151.

18 Hobsbawm, *Bandits*, 155.

19 Gertrude Himmelfarb, *The New History and the Old: Critical Essays and Reappraisals* (Cambridge, MA: Belknap Press, 1987), 89.

20 Richard White, 'Outlaw gangs of the middle border: American social bandits', *Western Historical Quarterly* 12 (1981): 387–408.

21 William L. Van De Burg, *Hoodlums: Black Villains and Social Bandits in American Life* (Chicago: University of Chicago Press, 2004), 76–7.

22 Ben Dodds, 'Jaime el Barbudo and Robin Hood: Bandit narratives in comparative perspective', *Social History* 36 (2011): 465.

23 Dodds, 'Jaime el Barbudo', 481.

24 Charles Van Onselen, *Masked Raiders: Irish Banditry in Southern Africa, 1880-1899* (Cape Town: Zebra Press, 2010), 5.

25 Richard W. Slatta, 'Conclusion', in Richard W. Slatta, ed., *Bandidos: The Varieties of Latin American Bandits* (New York: Greenwood Press, 1987), 191, 198.

26 Gilbert M. Joseph, 'On the trail of Latin American bandits: Re-examination of peasant resistance', *Latin American Research Review* 25 (1990): 7–53.

27 Amy Robinson, 'Mexican banditry and the discourses of class', *Latin American Research Review* 44 (2009): 5–31.

28 G. E. Mingay, '"Rural war": The life and times of Captain Swing', in G. E. Mingay, ed., *The Unquiet Countryside* (London: Routledge, 1989), 36, 36–51.

29 E. J. Hobsbawm and George Rude, *Captain Swing* (London: Lawrence and Whishart, 1969).

30 Hobsbawm and Rude, *Captain Swing*, 298.

31 Carl Griffin, 'Swing, Swing redivivus, or something after Swing? On the death throes of a protest movement, December 1830-December 1833', *International Review of Social History* 14 (2009): 460.

32 Carl Griffin, '"There was no law to punish that offence": Re-assessing "Captain Swing": Rural Luddism and rebellion in East Kent, 1830-31', *Southern History* 22 (2000): 139–40.

33 Michael Holland, 'The Captain Swing project', in Michael Holland, ed., *Swing Unmasked: The Agricultural Riots of 1830 to 1832 and Their Wider Implications* (Milton Keynes: FACHRS Publications, 2005), 5, 1–25.

34 Adrian Randall, '*Captain Swing*: A retrospect', *International Review of Social History* 54 (2009): 425–6 (419–27).

35 Carl J. Griffin, 'The violent captain Swing?', *Past and Present* 209 (2010): 149–90.

36 Peter Jones, 'Finding Captain Swing: Protest, parish relations, and the state of the public mind in 1830', *International Review of Social History* 54 (2009): 429–58.

37 Jones, 'Finding Captain Swing', 439.

38 Katrina Navickas, 'Captain Swing in the north: The Carlisle riots of 1830', *History Workshop Journal* 71 (2011): 5–28.

39 Navickas, 'Captain Swing', 7.

40 Douglas Hay, Peter Linebaugh, John G. Rule and Cal Winslow, *Albion's Fatal Tree: Crime and Society in Eighteenth Century England* (London: Allen Lane, 1975), 13–14.

41 Douglas Hay, 'Property, authority and the criminal law', in Hay et al., ed., *Albion's Fatal Tree*, p 56.

42 Carolyn Strange, ed., *Qualities of Mercy: Justice, Punishment and Discretion* (Vancouver: University of British Columbia Press, 1986), xi.

43 John H. Langbein, 'Albion's fatal flaws', *Past and Present* 98 (1983): 96–120.

44 Douglas Hay, 'Writing about the death penalty', *Legal History* 35 (2006): 37.

45 Peter Linebaugh, '(Marxist) social history and (conservative) legal history: A reply to Professor Langbein', *New York University Law Review* 60 (1985): 212–43.

46 Linebaugh, '(Marxist) social history', 225.

47 Linebaugh, '(Marxist) social history, 222.

48 Linebaugh, '(Marxist) social history, 238.

49 Peter King, 'Decision-makers and decision-making in the English criminal law, 1750-1800', *The Historical Journal* 27 (1984): 25–58.

50 King, 'Decision-makers', 51.

51 Peter Linebaugh, *The London Hanged* (London: Penguin, 1981), xvii.

52 Linebaugh, *The London Hanged*, xxvi.

53 Thomas W. Laqueur, 'Crowds, Carnival and the state in English executions, 1604-1868', in A. L. Beier, David Cannadine and James M. Rosenheim, eds, *The First Modern Society: Essays in English History in Honour of Lawrence Stone* (Cambridge: Cambridge University Press, 1989), 305–56.

54 Laqueur, 'Crowds, Carnival', 319.

55 John Brewer and John Styles, *An Ungovernable People: The English and their Law in the Seventeenth and Eighteenth Centuries* (New Brunswick, NJ: Rutgers University Press, 1980).

56 John Styles, '"Our traitorous money makers": The Yorkshire coiners and the law', in Brewer and Styles, *An Ungovernable People*, 245–8.

57 John Rule and Roger Wells, *Crime, Protest and Popular Politics in Southern England 1740-1850* (London: Hambledon, 1997), 2.

58 Rule and Wells, *Crime, Protest*, 8.

59 Louis A. Knafla, 'Structure, conjuncture and event in the historiography of modern criminal justice history', in Clive Emsley and Louis A. Knafla, eds, *Crime History and Histories of Crime: Studies in the Historiography of Crime and Criminal Justice in Modern History* (Westport, CT: Greenwood, 1996), 37.

60 E. P. Thompson, *Whigs and Hunters: The Origin of the Black Act* (London: Allen Lane, 1975).

61 Thompson, *Whigs and Hunters*, 64.

62 Pat Rogers, 'The Waltham blacks and the black act', *Historical Journal* 17 (1974): 465–86.

63 Thompson, *Whigs and Hunters*, 207 (Or Rogers 207?).

64 Eveline Cruickshanks and Howard Erskine-Hill, 'The Waltham black act and Jacobitism', *Journal of British Studies* 24 (1985): 358–65.

65 Cruickshanks and Erskine-Hill, 'The Waltham black act', 361.

66 Alun Howkins and Linda Merrick, '"Wee be black as hell": Ritual, disguise and rebellion', *Rural History* 4 (1993): 41–53.

67 Thompson, *Whigs and Hunters*, 265.

68 Thompson, *Whigs and Hunters*, 268–9.

69 Jim Sharpe, 'History from below', in Peter Burke, ed., *New Perspectives on Historical Writing* (Cambridge: Polity Press, 2001), 25–42.

70 Sharpe, 'History from below', 27.

71 Sharpe, 'History from below', 27–8.

72 Sharpe, 'History from below', 27–8.

73 J. M. Beattie, *Crime and the Courts in England 1660-1800* (Oxford: Clarendon Press, 1986), 6–8.

74 Francis Snyder and Douglas Hay, 'Comparisons in the social history of law, labour and crime', in Francis Snyder and Douglas Hay, *Labour, Law and Crime: An Historical Perspective* (London: Tavistock, 1987), 7.

75 Joanna Innes and John Styles, 'The crime wave: Recent writings on crime and criminal justice in eighteenth century England', *Journal of British Studies* 25 (1986): 397.

76 Hay, *Albion's Fatal Tree*, 14.

77 Linebaugh, *The London Hanged*, xviii–xix.

78 E. P. Thompson, 'Eighteenth-century crime, popular movements and social control', *Bulletin of the Society for the Study of Labour History* 25 (1972): 9–11.

79 Thompson, 'Eighteenth-century crime', 9.

80 Thompson, 'Eighteenth-century crime', 10.

81 Timothy Shakesheff, *Rural Conflict, Crime and Protest: Herefordshire, 1800 to 1860* (Woodbridge: Boydell Press, 2003), 6.

82 Innes and Styles, 'Crime wave', 395.

83 John G. Rule, 'Social crime in the rural south in the eighteenth and early nineteenth centuries', *Southern History* 1 (1979): 137.

84 Rule, 'Social crime', 137.

85 John Archer, *By a Flash and a Scare: Incendiarism, Animal Maiming, and Poaching in East Anglia 1815-1870* (Oxford: Clarendon Press, 1990), 7.

86 Archer, *By a Flash*, 9.

87 Archer, *By a Flash*, 9.

88 King, 'Decision-makers', 52.

Further reading

Greenberg, David F., ed. *Crime and Capitalism: Readings in Marxist Criminology.* Philadelphia: Temple University Press, 1993.

Harring, Sidney. *Policing a Class Society: The Experience of American Cities, 1865-1915.* New Brunswick, NJ: Rutgers University Press, 1983.

Hay, Douglas. 'Writing about the death penalty'. *Legal History* 10 (2006): 13–52.

Humphries, Stephen. *Hooligans or Rebels? Oral History of Working Class Childhood and Youth 1889-1939.* Oxford: Blackwell, 1981.

Lea, John. 'Social crime revisited'. *Theoretical Criminology* 3 (1999): 307–25.

O'Brien, Patricia. *The Promise of Punishment: Prisons in Nineteenth Century France.* Princeton: Princeton University Press, 1982.

Rusche, Georg and Otto Kirchheimer. *Punishment and Social Structure*. New Brunswick, NJ: Transaction, 2003.

Thompson, Laura. *A Different Class of Murder: The Story of Lord Lucan*. London: Head of Zeus, 2014.

Yang, Anand A. *Crime and Criminality in British India*. Tucson: University of Arizona Press, 1987.

CHAPTER FIVE

The city and its criminals

Urban history has had an important role in the historiography of crime. Many crime historians focus on the nineteenth and twentieth centuries, when modern cities took shape, and borrow from theories of sociologists writing about how this shape came to be. This roundabout of crime history, urban history and sociology has led historians to think twice about whether the city produced crime and to re-examine claims about the influence of the city on crime and criminal justice.

In the 1950s, few historians specialized in cities. This changed with the arrival of a model of urban history in the 1960s which held that the ultimate aim of writing the history of cities was to grasp complex changes brought about by urbanization and industrialization. To understand these changes, historians relied on social science methods, particularly quantification. The social science model of urban history produced some of the most productive crime historians, none more so than Eric Monkkonen at the University of California-Los Angeles. When he began his career in the 1970s, politicians and editorialists frequently expressed the view that a high rate of crime was a consequence of urban life. The growth of cities brought anonymity, stress and conflict, which inevitably led to crime and disorder. Monkkonen became one of several historians to regard this as a myth encouraged by mistaken sociological theory.

By the 1980s, the social science model of urban history gave way to new methods and perspectives. The 'postmodern turn' and 'new cultural history' encouraged historians to view the city less as a social space than a cultural space. Sociological models of urbanization and industrialization lost their prime shelf position, and urban historians shifted their attention to other products. Timothy J. Gilfoyle, Dominique Kalifa, Pablo Piccato and others did not share the commitment to quantitative models nor the focus on testing sociological theories of urbanization. The new generation of urban historians brought methods of social and cultural history to understanding the meaning of urban crime. They revised conceptions of the 'criminal class' and the 'underworld', and they returned to arguments about delinquency and policing.

This chapter explores the place of cities in crime history. Part 1 reviews the research by Monkkonen and others in response to the arguments of Louis Chevalier on urbanization on criminal behaviour. Part 2 examines the concept of the criminal class defended by J. J. Tobias and reactions to it. Part 3 focuses on the underworld, as defined in work by Mark Haller, and critiques from cultural perspectives. Part 4 looks at the discussion of urban delinquency sparked by Anthony Platt and Part 5 discusses research into urban policing by Robert Storch, Joanne Kein and others.

The urbanization effect

'Criminal', Louis Chevalier said, 'is the key word for Paris in the first half of the nineteenth century.'[1] In his book on the working classes of Paris, published in French in 1958, he described the proliferation of criminal acts across the city. Crime was an everyday worry of the inhabitants, the source of widespread fear and misery. Novelists and journalists wrote about crime; they found plenty of material in the daily police gazette. Fear of crime did not merely have to do with the aggregation of people and the inevitable inclusion of pickpockets, thieves and robbers. It was a very different kind of menace. 'It was not an incidental and exceptional consequence of social existence, but one of the largest consequences of the growth of the city; not something abnormal, but one of the most normal aspects of the city's daily life in this phase of its development.'[2] Chevalier said that unprecedented levels of migration to Paris doubled its population and overwhelmed its infrastructure. Consequently, urban forces of order surrendered to a natural state of affairs beyond human control. Chevalier's earlier work on nineteenth-century Paris had won him the chair of history at the Collège de France, so *Classes laborieuses* became required reading.

The English translation of Chevalier's book appeared in 1973 when the urban history movement was at full throttle in the United States. It was read by historians familiar with the problem-oriented tradition of urban studies established early in the twentieth century. Much of this urban history examined pathological conditions of urban life as a consequence of city growth: social tensions, inadequate services, minority discrimination and political corruption.[3] It had been informed by the anti-urban visions of nineteenth-century sociologists – Durkheim, Tönnies and Simmel – who supplied many reasons for why cities led to criminality. They taught that urbanization contributed to the loss of community, to anonymity and alienation, to congestion and conflict, all of which meant a rise in criminal behaviour. Focusing on crime in the urban environment, and equipped with the quantitative methods of social science, a group of American historians set out to disprove what they regarded as 'the sociology fallacy'. Roger Lane, Charles Tilly and Eric Monkkonen, among others, said that Chevalier and the sociologists had got it wrong. The experience of cities, whether in the United States, Europe or South America, supported the conclusion that urbanization generated *less* crime, not more.

Following the summer of riots in 1967, President Johnson appointed the National Commission on the Causes and Prevention of Violence. The Commission chose Hugh Graham, a historian at Johns Hopkins, and Ted Robert Gurr, a professor of politics at Princeton, to find out what they could about the causes of collective violence. They put together a report that became a popular paperback, *The History of Violence in America* (1969).[4] The publication included a reprint of Roger Lane's study of urbanization and violent crime in nineteenth-century Massachusetts. There was no 'necessary or inevitable connection between the growth of cities and the growth of crime', Lane declared. 'In fact the existing historical evidence suggests the very reverse, that over a long-term urbanization has had a settling, literally a civilizing, effect on the population.'[5]

In his research on late-nineteenth-century Philadelphia, Lane dismissed the 'central fallacy of the older sociological version of the link between growth and violence'.[6] He charted trends for homicide alongside suicide and accidents during the second half of the nineteenth century, and found that the homicide rate had steadily declined. Contrary to the image of disorder and disintegration, urbanization reduced criminality. Cities had a moderating effect on lawlessness and disorder, and the urban environment had become safer as time went by. Certain processes within industrial cities, specifically, the disciplined behaviour required in factories, schools and other social institutions, encouraged nineteenth-century urban order. Social institutions enforced rules that encouraged a new sense of deportment in individuals, and showed people how to resolve conflicts without violence, leading to a steady rise in public order. The increase in populations into courts, jails and almshouses did not reflect a rise in criminality and disorder, but the result of stricter controls and enforcement. With some exceptions, the homicide rate fell. Lane proposed that while the effect of urban-industrial discipline was increasingly felt by White men, the absence of such discipline allowed for violence among the city's Black population. The 1800s were, then, on the whole, fairly successful in imposing demands on the population that came to live in it.

Eric Monkkonen gathered additional evidence to support Lane's thesis in his analysis of public order offences. He collected statistics concerning arrests for drunkenness and disorderly conduct for twenty-three of the largest cities in the United States from 1860 to 1977. Overall, there was a downward trend. 'It seems clear from this trend that, as arrest categories, drunkenness and disorderly conduct continue to diminish and may be destined to disappear.' Although some cities proved exceptions (Buffalo, St Louis, San Francisco and Louisville), the largest cities displayed the national trend: New York,

Philadelphia, Chicago, Cincinnati, Cleveland, Washington and Newark. By aggregating the statistics, it was possible to spot a larger pattern. 'American historians', Monkkonen concludes, 'have a new and interesting phenomenon to explain – the apparent rise of urban order.'[7] He fortified this conclusion with a study of homicide in New York. The history of crime trends in New York City disproved the idea that cities represented cauldrons of murder and violence. Throughout the first half of the twentieth century, the city had a lower homicide rate than the United States on the whole. As the city became bigger, it became safer, and this was true even during the most miserable periods of its history. Despite claims that an influx of soldiers after the Second World War would produce a crime wave, the post-war years were some of the most peaceful of the twentieth century.[8]

Eric Johnson challenged the urbanization effect in his study of crime in Germany.[9] In the decades between 1871 and 1914, Germany set the pace for urbanization and industrialization. Berlin, Cologne, Hamburg, Munich and other industrial cities in the Ruhr doubled or tripled in size, and villages and towns grew into moderate-sized industrial cities. This did not produce soaring crime rates. Neither urban growth nor the urban condition itself had a particularly powerful impact on most German crime rates. There are several possible reasons for this. German workers were among the highest paid in Europe, and social inequality was not as severe in Germany as in other countries. The government delivered a welfare system that attended to the needs of workers and pursued urban planning and regional government. Whatever the reason, Johnson suggests that Germany was not exceptional. German cities were not crime-ridden despite the sociological logic that insisted they should be. Some German cities, such as Cologne and Düsseldorf, did experience soaring crime rates, but other cities, including Munich, Hamburg and Leipzig, did not. These cities also had large migrant populations and rapid urban growth, which makes a straightforward explanation about cities and crime difficult to sustain. 'The notion that urban growth and big cities engender crime is a long-standing and well-articulated myth.'[10]

Julia Blackwelder and Lyman Johnson reported that the trends Lane had found in North America held true for South America as well. Like Boston, Chicago and New York, Buenos Aires experienced a similar pattern of population rise due to immigration and commercial and industrial development during the same time period. They found that political and cultural influences were as important as economic factors in explaining crime and the limited effectiveness of police in securing order. The city followed a familiar cycle: an initial period of perceived disorder followed by a later period of increased social order. Residents did not enjoy the same level of security throughout the twentieth century; there was a rise in property crimes in the decades surrounding the First World War. This was due to the arrival of poor migrants who crowded into commercial areas and gained access to private residences. But overall, crime fell as the city modernized.

Buenos Aires transformed from a rowdy, congested urban space in the nineteenth century to an orderly built environment in the twentieth century, as the influx of immigrants declined and residents created institutions for private space.[11]

Even Chevalier's conclusions about Paris came under attack, not only from American but French historians as well. In the United States, Abdul Q. Lodhi and Charles Tilly subjected the Chevalier thesis to the discipline of statistical analysis. Using population figures from census data, reports of collective violence and annual crime figures, they conducted a time series analysis, to examine changes across the 80–90 administrative departments. They found that the pattern of crime and violence from 1831 to 1931 did not follow the course of urbanization. Over the long term, property crime decreased, and personal crimes and outbreaks of violence fluctuated, in disregard for the pace of urban growth. They concluded that the milieu of 'urban settings' rather than urbanization as such explained the course of crime. The geographic patterns of crime did not fit the theories advanced for France by sociological historians such as Chevalier. It would be prudent, they advised, to suspend such theories until historians could make more in-depth investigations, and they urged historians to carry out investigations for cities outside of France.[12]

French critics demanded to know why Chevalier offered no data on crime for analysis even though he was aware of detailed crime statistics published by the Ministry of the Interior from 1827. He operated at aggregate level, proposing a link between large patterns, but did not explain how these played out among individuals actually living in the city. Although he claimed that crime was the principal theme of his history of Paris and that statistics provided the necessary framework for understanding, he did not actually devote space to this. Rather, he relied on literature to gather impressions from the working classes. The critics questioned whether the pace of migration brought about the social problems he said it did. If crime was the chief worry of Parisians, it was only because of their fear of migrants, vagabonds and strangers, and this fear preceded the nineteenth century.[13]

Yet, Lane, Monkkonen and Johnson have not had it completely their own way. Studies of urban crime in Canada and England broke with the pattern. John C. Weaver analysed crime and policing in Hamilton, Ontario, from the early nineteenth century to the late twentieth century. He suggested that Lane's trend was more an artefact of changing crime statistics than changing urban locations. To interpret long-term crime trends with confidence required a good knowledge of how and why the statistics were collected. Taking the realities of crime statistics into account complicated the association of rising urbanization with falling crime. In Hamilton, and probably other Canadian cities, there was a significant change in criminal proceedings: the century began with a system of prosecution by private individuals and ended with prosecution by police. This jeopardized the conclusion that crime fell in

the 1800s owing to modernization – the rise of the middle class, increase
of private space and so on. The decline in assaults resulted from changing
criminal justice practices rather than a positive side effect of urbanization.
Weaver worried that in their eagerness to set aside the unsubstantiated
generalization about the growth of cities leading to an increase in crime,
Lane and Monkkonen offered an unsubstantiated generalization of their
own. The 'draftsmen of the grand curves of crime rates' had put their trust
in the power of 'long term trends' to reveal the truth. Yet 'minor historical
events', such as a change in police procedure, comprised a big part of the
interpretation.[14]

Peter King looked at murder rates for counties across England and Wales
in the late eighteenth century and early nineteenth century.[15] Using figures
from parliamentary returns relating to prosecutions for homicides, he
mapped the geography of violence during the pivotal moment of urban and
industrial expansion. Contrary to what Lane, Monkkonen and Johnson had
shown for the United States and Germany, in England and Wales 'there seems
to have been a clear correlation between certain types of urban development
and higher rates of lethal violence'.[16] Small towns located in areas without
rapid industrialization did not have higher murder rates. And, the highest
rates were not found just in big cities, but in urban areas experiencing rapid
growth and receiving large numbers of migrants for the countryside. The
overall pattern supported the theory that violent crime rates were highest in
cities during the transitional stages of industrialization but that the 'mature
years' saw a decline in homicide. A systematic look at key signposts on the
road to urbanization in Britain revealed much higher rates in almost every
region of rapid urban and industrial growth.

Recent interest in cultural history has given Chevalier new life.
Dominique Kalifa's analysis of the cultural landscape of nineteenth-
century Paris portrays an urban population that was deeply affected by
the process of urbanization. Although murders comprised a small portion
of criminal acts, they generated much fear. Newspapers, novels and other
mass circulation texts gave enormous importance to the topic of crime and
had a decisive role in the collective memory of places. The demographic
and economic changes that accelerated in France during the first half of
the nineteenth century shifted the location of crime scenes, specifically, a
process of 'double decentring'. The centre had been the site of overcrowding,
poverty and crime. But criminality moved to the north, changing the spatial
topography of crime; and it moved vertically, to the quarries, catacombs
and sewers under the city. The public at large adjusted their conceptual map
of the city, to take into account changing locations of danger, and changed
their behaviour accordingly. 'Is it necessary', Kalifa writes, with reference
to Chevalier, 'to reiterate the extent to which the capital city, strained by
demographic growth, social changes, and political unrest, made crime one
of its main obsessions?'[17]

The criminal class

In the Victorian era, a common explanation for urban crime was that the city was home to the criminal class of society. Thomas Plint's *Crime in England* (1851) presented this notion as a substantive and unalterable statistical fact.[18] He set out to find the overall trend in criminal activity, and more importantly, what the trend might reveal about the future: whether England was headed for triumph or demise. There had been an increase in the ratio of criminals to population across English counties. During the first half of the century, the average number of criminals per 100,000 population increased threefold, from 54 in 1801 to 156 in 1845. This would appear to indicate a demise, except for his revelation that the increase should not be attributed to the English population as a whole. It was concentrated within a small proportion of people. The evidence indicated that crime within the 'particular social and industrial organisation of society' was 'committed by a comparatively small class, and does not indicate with any accuracy, the general intelligence and morals'.[19]

The rapid growth of the population and aggregation in cities and towns of England, Plint concluded, had been accompanied by a larger growth in the 'criminal or dangerous classes'. These included not only professional thieves, but the vagrant and dissolute. He estimated that about a third of the crimes in any large town could be attributed to the criminal class. He went on to explain how it had come about. It was not a product of the factory system, unsanitary conditions or crowded conditions. It did not result from lack of employment or education or anything to do with social conditions. Rather, the 'large majority is so by descent'.[20] The criminal class stood apart from the English people, in their blood, in their sympathies. Although they were in the community, they were neither *of* the community nor *from* the community. To understand it, it would be necessary to write a 'natural history' of the criminal class, to examine the birthplace, occupation, residence, education and moral influence of that portion of the population responsible for so much crime.

One hundred years later, John J. Tobias revived Plint's explanation. Tobias was suspicious of the methods and motives of the practitioners of the new urban history and adhered to a traditional historicist reading of nineteenth-century literature. The most important way to learn about the past was to find out what people thought at the time based on the documents they left behind, and the most important thing to know about crime in the Victorian era was the part played by the criminal class. It was not, Tobias conceded, a concept that 'appeals to modern thought'. Modern sociologists would no doubt describe the situation in different terms, as a 'lower class' or 'criminal subculture'. To some extent, the difference was 'merely terminology'.[21] Plint was wrong about one thing. The concept could not be examined in statistics, because the organization of criminals was simply not captured in official categories. But he was right – according to Tobias – about the reality of a separate criminal class. There is not a description of crime from about 1815 or so that does not describe crime in terms of the criminal class, and because official statistics are unreliable as a measure of criminal activity, any historian must accept the statements of contemporaries as accurate. 'On the whole', Tobias declared, 'the nineteenth-century concept of a "criminal class" may be regarded as an acceptable explanation of the phenomena of the time.'[22]

If Tobias had a theory in mind when he wrote his history, it seemed to have come more from Dickens than Durkheim. Fagin and the Artful Dodger could live in his pages. Tobias contended that the criminal class was a side effect of the industrial urban environment. The towns of England, especially London, always had a criminal problem different from other areas, and there were groups of people, living in distinct areas, who had evolved a way of life of their own based on unlawful activity. Many young people in cities, without the requisite assistance from families, employers or authorities, and found the means of survival in the techniques, attitudes and habits of criminals. In London, there was a surge in crime in the later eighteenth century and early nineteenth century as a consequence of a society in rapid transition.[23] The criminal class existed, and continued, because it provided support for its members. The 'swell mob' and the 'gang' provided friendship as well as material assistance. Flash houses were headquarters of gangs, sites for training of young thieves, meeting points for exchange of gossip and business. There were boys who specialized in theft; alert and intelligent, they would be recruited by adults for additional training to become experts. If they survived disease and avoided the law, they would grow up to become adult thieves of some standing. The same division took place for girls, the less intelligent being prostitutes, the others thieves who used prostitution to create opportunity.[24]

Using the statistics and methods Tobias rejected, other historians have reached very different conclusions. David Philips analysed offences, and those who committed them, in the Black Country (between Birmingham and Wolverhampton). He tabulated committals to trial based on indictments from 1835 to 1860, including robbery, housebreaking, burglary, forgery, homicides and aggravated and serious assaults. Most crimes cannot be attributed to a professional criminal class. Experienced burglars, pickpockets and thieves committed something like 10 per cent of these offences. Most of the crimes were committed by people who worked ordinary jobs, and on occasion, got into a fight or joined in a robbery. The overall impression of crime in the Black Country in this period is of small amounts pilfered by the poor, thefts and robberies committed with little foresight or planning, and directed at victims as likely to be poor. The picture Tobias gives, of rookeries and flash houses operated by professional criminals, may have been true for London, but London was very different from industrial towns.[25]

Rob Sindall offered a new look at the criminal class using an innovative methodology.[26] Rather than try to estimate the proportion of crime committed by the lower class, he looked into the proportion committed by the middle class. The middle class were preoccupied with threat of the underclass, but what about their colleagues at work? Their next-door neighbours? The shopkeepers they knew? He collected information about all prisoners appearing before quarter sessions and assize courts in London and Birmingham, and he found that 'the middle classes exhibited as many criminal tendencies as the lower classes'.[27] The numbers show, Sindall argued, that crime declined in the nineteenth century, but that decline in middle-class crime was less than that for the lower class. The middle class had the motives, climate and opportunities to turn criminal, and they did in fact demonstrate greater criminality than other classes, except that the increasing tendency of the middle class to commit crimes went unnoticed by Victorian observers. And when crimes of the middle class were discovered, such as fraud and embezzlement, they received lenient treatment from the courts.

Tobias revived the idea of the criminal class as an explanation for urban crime, and historians continued to respond to his proposition in the 1970s, 1980s and 1990s, but it was not much of a debate really. Tobias remained the exception. As Clive Emsley put it in 2005, 'The notion of a criminal class was, indeed remains, a convenient one for insisting that most crime is committed on law-abiding citizens by an alien group. The more historians probe the notion, the more it is revealed to be spurious.'[28] Emsley's language is important here because much historical scholarship on the issue has concentrated on what the idea of the criminal class meant in nineteenth-century contexts. Whether or to what extent there actually was a criminal class does not matter. The point of the story is why people at the time believed in it and the role of this belief in shaping the response to crime.

In nineteenth-century London, as Randall McGowen points out, people learnt about the criminal class from newspapers and periodicals.[29] These literary representations were far from the simple reflections of reality as Tobias suggests. The idea of the criminal class, characterized by its own institutions and customs, had been part of the English imagination since the sixteenth century. None of the Victorians writing about it made points that were original to this period, but repeated claims made over the centuries. What these publications reveal is not the 'reality' of the criminal class, let alone 'proof' of its existence, but the way in which the Victorians convinced themselves of its reality.[30] In the literary imagination, the criminal class used deception as a tactic in commission of crimes, and protected itself by keeping its very existence a secret. In documenting the beliefs, organization and activities of the criminal class, social investigators, novelists and journalists exposed its existence, and at the same time, reassured their readers that it was contained. Knowledge of the criminal class became the key means by which it would be defeated.

Interesting work has also come from histories of cities in Central and South America. The Spanish word *ratero* generally refers to a population of undeserving poor who were thieves mostly because of their aversion to honest work. By looking at the use of this concept by the authorities, and its impact on certain lawbreakers, it is possible to see the invention of a criminal class. Pablo Piccato explains that in Mexico City during the late nineteenth century, concern about urban thieves appeared against wider anxieties about the city's rapid expansion and rising levels of crime. For the majority of the city's inhabitants, *rateros* were simply a fact of everyday life. One had to always be on guard against them because of their special abilities to pick pockets, break into homes, knife their victims and pass as decent citizens. Economic pressures meant the threat would never go away. For the police and policymakers, *rateros* required special measures. Although it is impossible to identify them from judicial records, the police tried to convince the public that they could target *rateros* with campaigns. The police believed that a small group of offenders engaged in theft as a skilled professional trade personified the city's crime problem. Piccato proposes that there was a criminal class in the sense of a population of lawbreakers in regular contact with the authorities. Frequent interrogations by police, and perennial stays in penal institutions, gave *rateros* an identity.[31]

Rateros were also part of the problem in Lima. In about 1860, crime became a major point of public discussion in the city, and the population of unemployed, vagrants and foreign residents took more than their share of the blame. The lower classes presented a threat, Carlos Aguirre writes, not because they were murderers or thieves, but because their presence clashed with the conventions of moderation in lifestyle and respect for the state the decent sector wanted to enjoy.[32] Whenever the police talked about crime in the city, they had in mind an oversupply of *rateros* getting away with thefts. The fact that they continued to be a menace was the fault of the authorities. Although the police and judges did everything they could to see that *rateros* were caught, convicted and sent to prison, the public believed *rateros* enjoyed their status owing to the failure of the authorities. Although the police knew who they were, the authorities never delivered sufficient punishment to put them out of business. And then there were the *faite*, also known as *matón*, who differed from ordinary thieves because they were violent, well-schooled fighters. They lived in the shadows of the city, wherever there was alcohol, prostitution and gambling. Although the authorities saw them as degenerate and vulgar, they were also respected for their bravery and fighting skills. Many worked with the police as informers, and when inside prison, helped in managing prisoners.[33]

The underworld

The 'underworld' has been a popular device for describing urban crime. The idea of a parallel world in the shadows of cityscapes, extensive but invisible to the wider public, retains appeal as a description of urban crime.

Historians have produced numerous studies of the underworld in various cities at different times, although getting a firm grasp on the concept has been difficult. Some doubt remains about whether the underworld exists outside the imagination of historians.[34]

For some historians, particularly those comfortable with criminology, the term is relatively unproblematic. Mark Haller described the underworld of Chicago in the early twentieth century. The 'organized underworld' consisted of professional thieves, business and labour racketeers and contributors to organized crime. Professional thieves included pickpockets, shoplifters, burglars, jewel thieves and confidence men who shared a culture of professional crime. Racketeering took more than one form, but often these criminals took control of unions to steal from members or to arrange 'sweetheart' contracts. Organized crime furnished the most systematic aspect of underworld activity; this included provision of illegal goods and services, such as gambling, prostitution, narcotics and alcohol.[35]

Haller's understanding relied on research carried out in the 1930s by John Landesco, a criminologist at the University of Chicago. In fact, Haller was responsible for the 1968 edition of Landesco's *Organized Crime in Chicago*, originally published by the Chicago Crime Commission. Haller pointed to underworld figures that held important positions as civic leaders and political brokers, and he described the web of interrelationships between underworld figures and other political and economic leaders. The underworld furnished a means of upward mobility for many immigrants who built criminal networks from ties of friendship and loyalty among kin. These relationships fostered a system of favours and rewards among people who shared a similar outlook in the world. Haller insisted on the link between the underworld and cities. He thought of the underworld, and organized crime, as fundamentally connected to city neighbourhoods. Organized crime represented a small-scale and less organized form of business, or a less organized form of small business enterprise.[36]

David R. Johnson urged more historians to follow Haller's lead. Johnson investigated the role of the underworld in the formation of policing. He looked in particular at professional theft, street crime and illicit enterprises including gambling and prostitution. Criminals from these categories comprised a 'highly visible part of an urban underworld whose existence was unquestioned but whose composition and extent were unknown'.[37] Using Philadelphia as a case study, Johnson maintained that urbanization brought opportunities for criminals; thieves benefitted from the increased number of businesses, availability of plunder and density of wealthy targets. Given the criminal imagination, and the inventory of techniques and devices it produced, the ability of the public to shield itself from crime was constantly in doubt. At the same time, gambling and prostitution led to more complex forms of organization. The increase in criminality, combined with organized forms, necessitated a more flexible response to policing than the night watch and constabulary could deliver. Beginning in the 1850s, police organizations began the process of remaking constables into detectives. 'The historical study of crime remains in its infancy ... there is a great need for a general survey of the American underworld.'[38]

The underworld is not limited to historical criminology. Other historians have shown that the underworld was a feature not only of Chicago or even American cities. Richard J. Evans offered a confident account of the underworld in German cities. He refers to an 'underworld of outcasts, people who by trade, occupation, lifestyle or origin had no place in the pre-industrial hierarchy ... but lived, whether by necessity or by choice, in its interstices, beyond its bounds'.[39] He pictured the underworld as several circles that never enclosed another, but intersected at various places. The first and widest circle was formed of vagrants and itinerants, people comprising 3–10 per cent of the population in normal times. Merchants and travelling salesmen did not fit into this group, although some demobilized soldiers, entertainers and pedlars who had no place to be, would have. The second, smaller and more stigmatized circle was formed by the dishonourable: skinners and tanners, shepherds, prostitutes and other people with a means of making a living that was regarded as offensive to the nose or respectability. This category included those frozen out of guilds and city areas: Jews and gypsies. The third, inner circle, were the professional criminals, bandits, robbers, thieves and murderers. These crooks had skills such as housebreaking, deception and disguise, and supporters who purchased their stolen goods. They divided the world into insiders and outsiders, the underworld and the straight world.[40]

Florike Egmond uncovered an underworld operating in the Dutch Republic during the seventeenth and eighteenth centuries. From criminal records (sentences and interrogations) produced by local courts, she gleaned information about individual criminals and their relationships. For Egmond, the underworld can be understood as 'the milieu of professional criminals ... a circuit, a community, a society – in short a world – leading a shady existence'.[41] It is a series of networks or groups in which crime occupied a central place. Members occupy a social position below others in society, although they may have considerable wealth. The records point to an underworld composed of several categories: urban thieves and burglars, southern cliques who operated in their own districts, and bands of gypsies and Jews that operated throughout the Dutch Republic. The Dutch underworld was not the underworld of the capital, but an inter-urban phenomenon extending across principal towns of the Netherlands, including Amsterdam, Rotterdam, The Hague, Delft and Utrecht. These networks extended outside western Netherlands, meaning that there was an 'international urban underworld' linked to Germany.[42]

Deborah Symonds explored hidden activities in nineteenth-century Edinburgh. The city's underworld was populated with men and women who lived by theft, assault, murder and stolen goods. They comprised a 'world' not because of special cultural rules or a curious language of their own. Rather, because of their contribution to the criminal economy of the city which overlapped the legitimate economy for centuries. The thieves and killers who animated this world represent economic actors in a shadow economy, in particular, the trade in corpses. This trade came about because of anachronistic regulations of the state and the church which kept the legal supply too short for demand (autopsy being a key part of surgical training). The underworld was not a separate place, but a world with its own map: locations for prostitutes to find customers, favourite spots for pickpockets to work, shops that purchased watches, clothing and other items with no question asked. 'Underworld, as a term, has fallen out of favour with scholars who associate it with nineteenth century writing about the criminal classes, and especially unscholarly writing about denizens of the underworld, as if they lived in a geographically separate area. I use the term advisedly, then, to refer to public houses, streets, houses and pawnshops that seem to have been frequented by thieves and other criminals, but were also obviously part of the city.'[43]

By the end of the 1990s, however, the scramble in urban history to find a replacement for the urbanization paradigm led to the application of culture as an interpretative framework. The 'cultural turn' altered the view of social groups and also the built environment.[44] It transformed the underworld from a set of social relationships in the urban environment to an idea in the minds of some urban residents about others. The reality of the underworld as a social space became less important than its function as a myth in relation to social tensions and wider politics.

Roshanna P. Sylvester visits Odessa, known during the first decades of the twentieth century as the 'city of thieves'. Moldavanka, a Jewish slum area of the city, was considered home to the criminal underworld. No physical barrier divided this area from the middle class in the central city, but newspaper editors and city authorities imagined a landscape in which the Old Free Port was the fault line in Odessa's cultural landscape. Moldavanka was regarded as a separate and peculiar world, with its own interests, sufferings and prospects. Outside observers took the filthy streets and ramshackle buildings as proof of the moral degeneracy of its residents. Professional beggars, depraved vagabonds, immoral women and savage children filled the lanes and alleys. Moldavanka was also said to house kings and queens, the royalty of the criminal underworld. Pickpockets and fraudsters built luxury flats for themselves, hidden within the squalor. Sylvester argues that Odessa's reputation as a city of thieves was directly tied to Moldavanka's image as home to the criminal underworld. This image came from anti-Semitic Russians and Ukrainians, from city officials and the police who wished to 'contain' the threat of crime, and from criminals who boasted that it was they, not the authorities, that made the rules.[45]

Christian Goeschel examines the so-called *Ringvereine* operating in Berlin during the Weimar period.[46] These were clubs set up in the late nineteenth century by released convicts; the 'rings' claimed to be sporting or wrestling associations. They brought together ex-convicts and members of the underworld, long marginalized in German society, who aspired to bourgeois status and respectability. But in reality, they were engaged in management of the city's night-life, in prostitution and the drug trade. The purpose of the *Ringvereine* went beyond professional criminality; they provided networks for patronage, loyalty and friendship. But, 'the mythical significance of the *Ringvereine*, constructed by the press, political parties and the *Ringvereine* themselves, far outweighed their actual importance'.[47] Goeschel situates the underworld within the romanticized image of organized crime as a self-policing underworld with ancient rules that resonated in Weimar culture, and the mythology of their importance built up by Nazi claims about having effectively suppressed the criminal underworld. The myth surrounding this underworld cannot be accepted at face value but requires critical examination. 'The wider significance of the history of the *Ringvereine* lies in the myth surrounding them.'[48] But dismantling this myth is difficult because of the problems, limitations and biases of the evidence that survives. The belief that interwar Germany was undermined by organized crime was a product of late Weimar activity and Nazi propaganda.

James Alex Garza writes about late-nineteenth-century Mexico City when the 'El Chalequero', the Mexican 'Jack the Ripper', stalked the streets. Francisco Gurrero, El Chalequero, raped and murdered several women, and when the police finally tracked him down, they blamed him for all sorts of crimes, real and imagined. Garza looks in detail at the trials of Gurrero (there were two), and four others involving major criminal cases, found in Mexico City's Archivo General de la Nación, during the government of General Porfiro Díaz. These trials present urban crimes of assault, robbery, rape and murder, and reveal how city officials fashioned a criminal underworld through crime prevention and corruption. Based on real observations and prejudices of the urban poor, this underworld was 'imagined to exist' in the margins of the capital, and 'took a life of its own' in the life of the nation. Fear helped create the imagined underworld; in the 1880s, Mexico City experienced a wave of highly publicized crimes that gave the impression the city was drowning in criminality. For the elite and middle class, this criminal underworld jeopardized Mexico's claim to modern nationhood. The underclass contributed to the construction of Mexican identity, as elites referred to the culture and behaviour of it to demonstrate what their society *was not*. In this way, the government used not only construction projects, modern sports and health programmes, but also criminality, to build the modern state.[49]

Paul Griffiths explains that the idea of a London underworld appears on paper before 1660, in comments on crime by judicial personalities, moralists and social critics.[50] They believed that the city was getting bigger, but not better. And after 1660, there are first-hand accounts of criminal lives which also make reference. Griffiths uses the Bridewell court books to peer into the world of petty criminals in London in the early seventeenth century. Although the Bridewell functioned as a lock-up, it served other functions as well, including a hospital and orphanage. The records do not reveal the complete picture of crime in this period, but as Griffiths explains, there is no better source. They tell the stories of vagrants, beggars, ballad-singers, thieves, tricksters, nightwalkers, porters and a range of characters that animated the night-time streets. Although beadles, magistrates and city officers complained of criminal communities as separate and apart, the records reveal that 'criminals' crossed the spatial, residential and borders of work all the time. Officers took the side of offenders, mixed in criminal circles to the point that some lived double-lives, further blurring the boundaries. The difference between the criminal underworld and conventional society was never more than a 'fluctuating frontier'. The ambiguity of the border makes clear that the 'underworld's margins were political not real'.[51] Although magistrates had their pick of the labels, and controlled the citizen/criminal categories, these were experienced as fuzzy realities.

Timothy J. Gilfoyle has argued that there is much more work to be done: the underworld remains the most under-researched aspect of urban crime. The social environments and networks of criminals, the informal economy and the impact of crime on citizens have been 'relatively unexplored subjects by urban historians'.[52] Gilfoyle examines the underworld of New York in the mid-nineteenth century. 'A new criminal world was born in this period', he writes; 'It was a hidden universe with informal but complex networks of pickpockets, fences, opium addicts, and confidence men who organized their daily lives around their shared illegal behaviors.'[53] He gained entry to the underworld through the writing of George Appo, a professional criminal who left an autobiography. Appo wrote about his experiences in the drug trade, encounters in opium dens, activities of urban gangs, going to jail and serving time in prison. He lived in an invisible world, dependent on camouflage and duplicity, and organized around its own culture. It involved networks of criminals who participated in an underground or informal economy, which from the standpoint of crime history represents 'uncharted territory'.

Urban delinquency

The city has a special relationship to delinquency at least since 1969 when Anthony M. Platt's *The Child Savers* appeared. The book is about the first specialized court for juvenile offenders, the court that originated in Chicago in 1889. Platt, an English sociologist who migrated to the University of California at Berkeley, challenged the Whiggish account of the child-saving movement in the nineteenth century as the product of the 'noble sentiments and tireless energy of middle-class philanthropists'.[54] He brought the sociological approach to deviant behaviour suggested by Howard Becker, who stressed the role of labels in creating deviant identities. 'Labelling theory' concentrated on the ambitions of the rule-makers and their means of rule-making rather than the motives or behaviour of those to whom the rules are applied. The city of Chicago had a major part in the story. Not because of its actual impact on youth, but because of middle-class fears about its impact on youth. The founders of the juvenile court worried that the city embodied everything that was bad about modern life, and their fears led to the establishment of a specialized tribunal for rescuing youth people, especially lower-class immigrants, from city influence. The participation of politically conservative, socially prominent, middle-class women in the child-saving movement reinforced a morality which appeared to be threatened by city life, industrialism and the influx of immigrants.[55]

Platt proposed that the reformers of the early twentieth century created delinquency as an urban problem. 'The child savers went beyond mere humanitarian reforms of existing institutions. They brought attention to – and, in doing so, invented – new categories of youthful misbehaviour.'[56] In this way, he invented delinquency as a topic of historical study with an important contribution to urban history. Delinquency began to attract urban historians after Platt demonstrated the significance of juvenile justice – the establishment of a separate system of laws and institutions for youth within, or beside, criminal justice – as a site for serious historical excavation. He offered a clear 'lesson of history' that resonated with sociologists, criminologists, and lawyers. Historians, however, had some doubts.

Robert Mennel agreed that delinquency was a modern concept; the word seldom appears before 1800. But it 'came of age' in the nineteenth century, not the twentieth century as Platt proposed. As villages became industrial centres, and labour moved from homes to factories, families could no longer absorb indigent and deviant individuals in servant and apprentice roles. As the demands and temptations of urban life threated the disintegration of poor families, loose family members joined crime and poverty in the community. Established citizens in the city created almshouses, asylums and penitentiaries, and children represented a special focus of concern because of the greater potential for reclamation.[57] Platt had demonstrated 'no awareness of refuge philanthropy'. It was precisely because the reform school had proved to be such a notorious failure that the reformers of early twentieth century had turned to juvenile court and probation as alternatives. Platt's mistake was his 'assumption that the child-savers "invented" delinquency whole cloth out of their immediate fears'.[58]

While Mennel questioned the theory, Steven Schlossman challenged the evidence. A key theme of Platt's analysis was that social control had been the overriding ambition of the founders of the juvenile court movement. The reformers set up the court, not to help children in poverty, but to sweep up lower-class immigrants from city streets into institutions where they could be more effectively controlled. 'But rather than testing this argument through analysis of institutional commitments before and after creation of juvenile courts', Schlossman said, 'Platt simply inferred from the reformers' promotional publications what the result must have been.'[59]

Schlossman examined the day-to-day practices of the juvenile system that had emerged at Chicago. He engaged the tools of the new social history, and its emphasis on 'doing history from the bottom up', specifically, using sources that would enable a look at the inner workings of the juvenile court and the reform school. He employed newspapers and juvenile court records from Milwaukee. The Milwaukee reformers were not middle-class women united in a child-saving goal, but men from diverse ethnic, cultural and class backgrounds who disagreed about how to deal with troubled youth. Like Mennel, Schlossman concluded that Platt had misunderstood the purpose of probation: to reunite children with their families rather than confine them in detention homes and reform schools.[60] Platt had, nevertheless, undermined the celebratory view of the juvenile court, and his suspicions about the motives of reformers resonated with academics concerned about the loss of civil rights.

Susan Magarey brought Platt (back) to England. She challenged the view that the problem of delinquency had emerged with the growth of major towns and industrial cities in the mid-nineteenth century. John J. Tobias and other historians had merely parroted the perceptions of the problem of juvenile delinquency uttered by 'property-owning, law enforcing commentators'.[61] There was some justification for property-owners' anxieties in early-nineteenth-century England. Shifts in labour market, crowded housing and disease brought about by industrial capitalism had pushed children from poor and labouring classes into city streets for survival. In law, the position of a child charged with a criminal offence had remained the same from the seventeenth century. Statutes criminalizing behaviours by the young through the enlargement of the criminal code followed from Sir Robert Peel's initiative to make administration of criminal law more efficient. Peel may not have intended to tackle delinquency, but his statutes added to regulation of behaviour of young people and brought it within the scope of criminal justice. Platt's claim that the Chicago reformers 'invented' delinquency may have been an overstatement. But in the case of England between 1820 and 1850, it was surely 'legislated into existence'.[62]

Peter King made an extensive analysis of the problem of delinquency in England between 1780 and 1840. He noted the work of Magarey on the invention of delinquency in the 1820s, 1830s and 1840s, but detected a significant limitation in her analysis. Because no statistics of juvenile offenders had been published before the 1830s, her explanation had been developed without a clear understanding of what was happening in the courts. He collected statistics from court records across England to investigate whether the increase in juvenile prosecutions was in response to an actual increase in criminal behaviour, or changes in attitudes of victims, magistrates and the police to young people's capacity for criminality. He concluded that the city was key. The increase in the portion of indicted offenders who were juveniles was linked to growth of the cities and related changes. Many urban youth were employed in the lowest paid and most precarious jobs, surrounded by open shops displaying the wealth of the prosperous middle class. Scavenging – bordering on theft – did occur. But it took place in the 1780s and 1790s as well. What was new to the nineteenth century was a new vocabulary about the 'alarming increase' of offenders in urban areas. 'The children of the urban poor may well have been driven to adopt new and more extensive appropriation strategies', King concluded. 'What is clear, however, is that victims and criminal justice administrators were beginning to think very differently about how to react to juvenile crime in the big cities of nineteenth-century England.'[63]

The general idea of labelling theory, that is, of interrogating the campaigners rather than the problems they campaigned against, has resonated with historians interested in youth and cities. Peter C. Baldwin did not research the juvenile court, but he did affirm Platt's view of the child-saving movement. From 1880 to 1930, reformers turned their attention to children's access to the city at night. This attention revealed 'cultural conflicts' between middle-class and working-class Americans over night-time leisure activity. Baldwin explained how gas and electric lighting spread throughout the urban landscape, creating, as far as the middle-class urban leaders were concerned, an unnatural environment in which to raise children. He traced the boy's club movement, started by women volunteers in Hartford, Connecticut, who desired to mimic the atmosphere of the respectable home. The clubs were meant to save boys from a life of crime. Reformers also imposed child labour laws, to keep newsboys from the streets at night, and juvenile curfew laws, a practice imported from small towns in Canada, all to keep youth from the streets. None of these were very effective. This framework for controlling youth was largely symbolic; it 'advertised middle class beliefs in the value of scheduling children's lives' and made it a matter of civic policy to assign to each age group 'appropriate activities, spaces and daily routines'.[64]

Other sociological theories have been important as well. Timothy J. Gilfoyle observed that the first histories of urban children and street life had focused on the invention of delinquency and the motivations and behaviours of adult reformers. He aimed to turn this history back to the youth themselves, to an appreciation for the 'subculture' of urban youth. The world of the urban youth was organized around a distinctive, complex and largely unwritten culture. Inspired by the autobiography of George Appo, he examined the activities of child pickpockets in New York City. In some ways, pickpocketing emerged as an underworld alternative to the traditional but disappearing forms of apprenticeship in the emerging urban market economy. Unknown to adults, youths met, socialized and played, and in this way, reproduced their own subculture over time. 'This alternative community of child pick-pockets embodied a new struggle, played out on the streets of America's exploding urban centers', Gilfoyle said, 'between adults with money, consumer goods and power, and unsupervised children with little of each.'[65]

Peter K. Andersson also writes about child pickpockets. But he uses a different sociological theory for his analysis: the symbolic interactionism of Erving Goffman. He examined pickpocket cases from the proceedings of London's Old Bailey and police courts from 1870 to 1900, selected on the basis of their location in crowds, to assess the ways in which the techniques changed in relation to pedestrian behaviour. As Andersson explains, if we think about a pickpocket as someone who operated in crowded public spaces, removed items from pockets without their notice, and disappeared back into the mass of people, then 'pickpocketing is primarily an urban issue and one that presumably proliferates with the growth of public crowding'.[66] Although he remained cautious about the statistics, there appears to have been a rise in pickpocketing in the early nineteenth century followed by a steep decline. This, he suggests, took place in response to changes in the way people behaved in public, and particularly, habits of walking in the urban landscape. The way in which pickpockets operated in Victorian London offers a good example of the sociology of pedestrian behaviour. Goffman had been one of the first sociologists to work out the set of rules which people use to navigate crowded pavements, the 'traffic code'.

Policing the city

There is more to police history than the city, but the city has had a special relationship to policing. In Britain, David Philips explains, the political debate that led to creation of the first police force began in 1792. It was in the great cities, MPs said, where the eighteenth-century system of law and order had broken down. The main argument had been the 'alarming increase' of crime in London. Advocates such as Patrick Colquhoun emphasized the 'unexampled wealth of the Metropolis' as an irresistible temptation to those of 'depraved habits and loose conduct' among the lower classes of people. Riots and disturbances also portended increasing disorder and possible revolution. Sir Robert Peel pushed through his bill for the new Metropolitan Police in 1829 and established the organization (of a centrally coordinated, full-time, paid police force) that would serve as a model for other forces in cities across Britain.[67]

Wilbur R. Miller explained the significance of the new police in his *Cops and Bobbies* (1973), a comparative study of police in London and New York during the mid-nineteenth century. London created the first modern police force in 1829 in the sense that it was a 'preventive police' meant to control crime through prevention rather than merely responding after the fact. Prevention depended on coordination and capacity, pervasiveness, and full-time day-and-night patrols to maintain surveillance at all hours. A final element was visibility; London provided the officers with symbols of authority recognizable by citizens who needed assistance and potential criminals who would be deterred. New York's Municipal Police, established in 1845, represented the preventive ideal, although it differed in various aspects: mission, organization, arrest procedures and response to groups. Between 1830 and 1870, decisions were made that shaped images of urban policing that would endure throughout the nineteenth century.[68]

Roger Swift pointed out that much of discussion of the police concentrated on development of policing in London and the great industrial cities of early Victorian England. He looked at policing in Wolverhampton, York and Exeter between 1835 and 1856. He focused on the circumstances which led to the police, levels of efficiency in enforcement and degree of acceptance they received from the public. Swift found that the level of efficiency attained by these forces remained low in this period, somewhat higher in industrial centres like Wolverhampton than York and Exeter. The experience of York and Exeter demonstrated a great deal of continuity from 'old' to 'new' policing; in fact, aspects of new policing were in these cities rather cosmetic, and traditional reforms of law enforcement (constables, self-help organizations, etc.) remained in play. Further, there were real anxieties on the local level about the coming of the new police. The model policing measures were gradually, and grudgingly, accepted. Finally, the police appeared as part of local government, and changes took place on this level for a variety of reasons.[69]

What the police *actually did* has been subject to some study. Robert Storch said that the elites not only had their reservations about the police, but also ordinary people in cities who regarded them as daily pests. He demonstrated that the urban police began enforcing a new standard of order on the population on the streets around them. The 'new police' represented a significant extension of the moral and political authority of the state. Decades after the establishment of police forces in industrial cities of England, the working class regarded them as unwanted intruders in their neighbourhoods. The police had a wide mandate to detect and prevent crime, but also to maintain constant surveillance over all aspects of working-class life, and to report on political opinions, trade union activities, public houses and recreation. In particular, they arrested people in large numbers for trivial offences, whose definition left wide discretion to the officer: drunkenness, breaches of the peace, gambling, dog-fighting, fist-fighting, playing cricket or football, flying kites or simply gathering. The initiatives of the police cannot be separated from the attitudes, prejudices and reformist impulses of the municipalities, magistrates and local elites who employed them. They were to act as 'domestic missionaries', translating and instilling bourgeois values into working-class districts. No doubt the police, and those who employed them, thought that constant surveillance would diminish after-hours drinking, low theatres, blood sports, public-house gambling and the like. But they succeeded in driving such activities into covert forms. If the upper classes agreed about the mission of the police – to instil bourgeois values into working-class districts – they were unsuccessful.[70]

Eric Monkkonen provides a history of the police in urban America from 1860 to 1920. He could not accept the assumption that the appearance and growth of police was a natural consequence of the growth of cities and urban crime. He also rejected the argument that the police were created by industrialists for the primary purpose of disciplining workers. The formation of modern police forces in various cities followed a common and predictable pattern that had less to do with specific encounters with riots, immigrants and strikes, than a wider history of innovation in urban government, centralization of information and bureaucratization of recruitment procedures. He tracked these influences with a systematic chronology of when police adopted uniforms, a process that began in the late 1850s and concluded by the 1870s. The use of formal arrest powers to maintain control declined considerably during the nineteenth century, but so did police services, such as accommodating overnight lodgers and finding lost children. By the end of the nineteenth century, the police had shifted their focus from class control to crime control, although this would be deemed a failure.[71]

The police spent their time doing social welfare. Greg Marquis has emphasized the social service aspect of urban policing in his study of early-twentieth-century Toronto. The police were not merely a 'coercive agency of social reform'; the working class were not so much their victims as clients. He discussed the Morality Department, which functioned as a domestic complaints bureau and legal aid service. Most of the clients were working-class women unable to afford legal counsel. The Department provided legal advice to battered women, served as a collection agency for support payments for abandoned wives, although these activities followed from a strongly traditional view of the family. Marquis also described the police station shelter and the employment of policewomen as valued interventions in the lives of the poor and vulnerable. It suggests that many members of the working class regarded police stations less as outposts of class authority than neighbourhood crisis intervention centres.[72]

They also spent their time dealing with the impact of new technology in society. The rise of motor traffic had a profound effect on policing during the interwar period. While traffic problems had vexed police in towns from the late nineteenth century, the development of motor cars travelling at much greater speeds brought a problem of new dimensions. By the 1920s, use of the law to regulate motor vehicles had jammed magistrates' courts.[73] As Joanne Klein explained, based on her study of policing in Manchester, Liverpool and Birmingham, traffic duty was given priority over patrol beats, since crashes required immediate attention. Even men not assigned to traffic found more of their time absorbed by it. Because men directing traffic could not leave their posts, regular beat officers were often called on to handle accidents and complaints. The increasing amount of time police spent on traffic, public service duties and paperwork rather than traditional crime prevention duties caused alarm for both police and public. In 1922, the inspectors of constabulary began issuing their annual warning that the proliferation of demands meant that the police were losing ground in the battle for prevention.[74]

What the police *did not do*, Mark H. Haller stressed, was enforce the criminal law. Using the example of Chicago 1890–1925, Haller pointed to the range of activities and the various purposes to which the police were engaged.[75] Police functioned within a system of urban politics which meant that the first officers were not recruited for their legal expertise or social skills but for their political loyalties. The police also developed their own organizational culture, increasingly shaping their own history. They made ties with the underworld, devoting time to drunkenness, gambling and prostitution. They believed that to control crime, it was necessary to regulate vagrants, tramps and other rootless populations. It was not as if the police spent the whole time taking bribes, harassing tramps and consorting with gamblers, Haller stressed. They spent most of their time 'doing nothing at all'.[76] Most of the time walking the beat meant socializing with people or doing things only incidentally related to crime control, such as assisting injured persons, returning lost children to their parents and dragging dead horses from the street.

The relationship between the police and populations within the city, including workers and trade unionists, immigrants and ethnic populations, has been of particular interest. Sidney L. Harring emphasized the class aspect of urban policing. Miller had rightly attributed the tarnished reputation of the police as a legacy of its identification of rough urban politics of the nineteenth century. But, Harring insisted, Miller had neglected to locate the political role of police within its wider class context. Following Marx, Harring discussed the expansion of municipal government as part of the class struggle and labour process of the capitalist city. The city concentrated and sharpened class divisions. The city was a source of cheap labour, a great reservoir of workers, and the police role was one of mediating class conflict. The police served the interests of the bourgeoisie in the class struggle. He examined the role of police in the industrializing cities of the United States between 1865 and 1915. Using examples from Buffalo, Milwaukee and Chicago, he discussed police functions in responding to militant action of trade unions, policing of working-class leisure activity and socialization of immigrant workers. He also discussed crime waves to show class-based aspects of crime prevention.[77]

Greg Marquis and Joanne Klein have examined the class aspect of policing – not police control *of* working class, but police *as* working class. Marquis describes the origins of the Toronto police in the early twentieth century within the matrix of working-class culture. He collected information about staff, including nativity, religion, previous occupation, military experience and residence, for a sample of years between 1910 and 1940. He also looked at police culture through such activities as leisure time. Marquis argues that the Toronto police occupied an ambiguous class position. While those recruited from the working class aspired to bourgeois respectability, their participation in the 'rough culture of the station house' prevented their achievement of middle-class status. The police maintained a suspicion of middle-class professionals they encountered (the social workers, lawyers and reformers), and they valued domestic family life (home ownership and a place in fraternal organizations) as did other workers. Through participation in organizations such as the Police Amateur Athletic Association, they affirmed a working-class appreciation of urban life.[78]

Klein, like Marquis, deals with the first half of the twentieth century. She examines the lives of ordinary police constables in Manchester, Birmingham and Liverpool.[79] Drawing on personnel files, registers and police newspapers, she provides a detailed picture of English policing at its lowest ranks and the impact of relying on men from the lower classes to uphold the law. 'On duty they brought the criminal justice system and working class culture together in unexpected ways, shaping law enforcement through their own notions of what policing meant.'[80] Constables spent much of their time alone, carrying out duties according to their own priorities, and obtaining knowledge about the experience of police on the beat is an essential, but overlooked, part of English policing. 'Many constables came to understand the impact of crime and disorder on ordinary people, as well as the problems facing people living on the fringes of society, in a way the average person could not,' Klein writes. 'But ultimately, the average police constable was trying to do his job without getting into trouble so that he could get paid, hopefully promoted and retire on his pension.'[81]

Marcy S. Sacks looked at the New York Police Department in relation to Black New Yorkers, who were, she argues, 'singled out as targets of police enmity and suspicion'. As the city's Black population began to grow in the late nineteenth century, they became the obsession of police officers and urban reformers. This project began with an anti-vice crusade intended to eliminate the city's vice industry. However, the police spent a great deal of their time to ensure that Black people did not interfere with Whites. This meant that vice flourished in Black districts, primarily because it was allowed to, even encouraged. Harlem became a playground for 'respectable' people. Whites owned most of the saloons, clubs and brothels, and Blacks became the targets of police patrol. The police made stereotypes about Black people into reality, encouraging the idea that they had natural criminal tendencies.[82] Stephen Robertson adds to this portrait with a look at the career of Raymond Claymes, an African-American undercover investigator. Claymes worked for the Committee of Fourteen, a private organization funded by John D. Rockefeller Jr to suppress prostitution. Until 1920, when the Committee found Claymes, they had to rely on White investigators and felt unable to keep track of Harlem. Claymes, a member of the Black middle class, collected evidence on hotels, clubs and other establishments, and subsequently handed this over to the police. Apparently, he was quite good at his job. In 1929, when the commissioner of the police decided to establish a new department of Black undercover detectives, Claymes was asked to train them.[83]

Clifford Rosenberg's *Policing Paris* (2006) examines the role of the Paris police in relation to immigrants during the interwar period.[84] In the decades after the First World War, France supplanted the United States as the world's leading immigrant-receiving nation. The Paris police began enforcing existing laws concerning the residence of foreigners with a new intensity. The police effort to keep track of populations in the city marked a turning point in history between the pre-industrial world, in which people were tied to the land, and the industrial welfare states that kept people out. 'This is the story of the first police force in a major city to enforce systematically the distinctions of citizenship and national origin.'[85] Rosenberg looks into the ways the police used immigration control to manage marginal populations. Police devoted extra attention to immigrant neighbourhoods and made use of the levels of power they had under the immigration laws, ranging from threats to intimidate illegal entrants to expulsion orders. As he points out, the police were preoccupied not with foreigners, immigrants or refugees, but with colonial subjects. He examines the range of programmes created for North African Muslims, most of them French, but not citizens – technically, colonial subjects without the right to vote.

The history of policing, Emsley observes, is to some extent, the history of 'great men' such as Sir Robert Peel, who was crucial to establishment of Metropolitan Police. But assessing the legacy of reformers is complicated by messy social and political history. Peel's role in police history has come under new scrutiny. Susan Lentz and Robert Chaires have written an interesting critique of 'textbook history'. In the American textbooks in criminology courses about policing, the history stresses the importance of the Metropolitan Police Act. Many mention a set of twelve principles emphasizing the preventive power of policing, said to be the guide to development of municipal police forces. These appear under the title 'Peel's Principles', which suggests that Peel was the author of them. Although, Lentz and Chaires observe, no direct source is ever cited. As it turns out, Peel never formulated a set of principles, nor do they represent a collection of quotations he made otherwise. By inventing Peel's Principles, textbook history ties what the police actually did to a theory of what they were meant to do. This reinforces the idea that an innovative step forward in management of cities was accepted by a grateful public and reinforces a particular connection between police, crime and the city.[86]

Conclusion

In their studies of urbanization and crime, Roger Lane, Eric Monkkonen and Eric Johnson took on a significant project: to decide whether sociological theories held up to historical analysis. They found the relationship between urban growth and crime trends to be far less predictable, even for the nineteenth century, than the sociologists said. Lane and the others challenged the conventional wisdom and made an important statement about the value of historical research. But their own model, and even the critique of it by Peter King, sees industrialization as the leitmotif in the music of urbanization and crime. The image of the industrial city has been too prominent. As Timothy Gilfoyle argues, urban crime patterns reflect not only patterns of work, but also leisure, and understanding the organization of leisure activities, legal and illegal, represents an important task for crime historians.

Sociological theories have offered starting points. Not only the grand visions of the nineteenth-century founders, but concepts from twentieth-century sociologists as well. Mark Haller invoked the sociological idea of criminal subculture for his understanding of the underworld. While some historians have found this useful, others have not. Work by Roshanna Sylvester, Christian Goeschel and James Alex Garza insists that the underworld has been less of a real social space than an imaginary cultural space. The labelling theory Anthony Platt used to frame his proposal for the 'invention of delinquency' has had a long influence over historical writing about youth and crime in the city. Again, historical research, initiated by Robert Mennel and Steven Schlossman, has led to rethinking this concept. The experience suggests that historians interested in crime in the city who borrow sociological ideas should proceed with caution. That said, sociology continues to infuse urban history with fresh ideas: Peter Andersson's use of the 'traffic code' for one.

The urban history that has shaped crime history is more accurately described as *American* urban history. This is not completely true, of course. Louis Chevalier produced influential work on Paris, and there have been numerous studies of London and other British cities. But some of the most interesting work in recent years has involved less familiar places, such as Buenos Aires, Lima and Mexico City. This expansion of cities offers increasing possibilities for testing propositions, new ideas for comparative work, and can only be a good thing in terms of improving historical understanding of the city and its criminals.

Notes

1 Louis Chevalier, *Labouring Classes and Dangerous Classes in Paris During the First Half of the Nineteenth Century* (London: Routledge and Kegan Paul, 1973), 2.

2 Chevalier, *Labouring Classes*, 5.

3 Kathleen Neils Conzen, 'Community studies, urban history and American local history', in Michael Kammen, ed., *The Past Before Us: Contemporary History Writing in the United* States (Ithaca, NY: Cornell University Press, 1980), 281.

4   Hugh D. Graham and Ted R. Gurr, *The History of Violence in America: Historical and Comparative Perspectives* (New York: Praeger, 1969).

5   Roger Lane, 'Urbanization and criminal violence in the nineteenth century: Massachusetts as a test case', *Journal of Social History* 2 (1968): 468–83.

6   Roger Lane, *Violent Death in the City: Accident, Suicide and Homicide in Philadelphia 1850-1900* (Cambridge, MA: Harvard University Press, 1979).

7   Eric Monkkonen, 'A disorderly people? Urban order in nineteenth and twentieth-century America', *Journal of American History* 68 (1981): 539–59.

8   Eric Monkkonen, *Murder in New York City* (Berkeley: University of California Press, 2001).

9   Eric A. Johnson, *Urbanization and Crime: Germany 1871-1914* (Cambridge: Cambridge University Press, 1995).

10 Johnson, *Urbanization and Crime*, 158.

11 Julia Kirk Blackwelder and Lyman L. Johnson, 'Changing criminal patterns in Buenos Aires, 1890 to 1914', *Journal of Latin American Studies* 14 (1982): 359–80; Julia Kirk Blackwelder, 'Urbanization, crime, and policing: Buenos Aires, 1880-1914', in Lyman L. Johnson, ed., *The Problem of Order in Changing Societies: Essays on Crime and Policing in Argentina and Uruguay* (Albuquerque: University of New Mexico Press, 1990), 65–87.

12 Abdul Q. Lodhi and Charles Tilly, 'Urbanization, crime and collective violence in 19th-century France', *American Journal of Sociology* 79 (1973): 296–318.

13 Barrie M. Ratcliffe, 'The Chevalier thesis reexamined', *French Historical Studies* 17 (1991): 542–74.

14 John C. Weaver, *Crimes, Constables, and Courts: Order and Transgression in a Canadian City, 1816-1970* (Montreal: McGill-Queen's University Press, 1995), 213–16.

15 Peter King, 'The impact of urbanization on murder rates and on the geography of homicide in England and Wales, 1780-1850', *Historical Journal* 53 (2010): 671–98.

16 King, 'The impact of urbanization', 672.

17 Dominique Kalifa, 'Crime scenes: Criminal topography and social imaginary in nineteenth-century Paris', *French Historical Studies* 27 (2004): 175–94, at 176.

18 Thomas Plint, *Crime in England* (London: Charles Gilpin, 1851).

19 Plint, *Crime in England*, 26.

20 Plint, *Crime in England*, 149.

21 J. J. Tobias, *Crime and Industrial Society in the Nineteenth Century* (London: B. T. Batsford, 1967), 59.

22 Tobias, *Crime and Industrial Society*, 62.

23 Tobias, *Crime and Industrial Society*, 37.

24 Tobias, *Crime and Industrial Society*, 66–7.

25 David Philips, *Crime and Authority in Victorian England: The Black Country 1835-1860* (London: Croom Helm, 1977), 287.

26 Rob Sindall, 'Middle-class crime in nineteenth-century England', *Criminal Justice History: An International Annual* 4 (1983): 23–40.

27 Sindall, 'Middle-class crime', 23.

28 Clive Emsley, *Crime and Society in England 1750-1900*, 3rd edn (Harlow: Longman, 2005), 178.

29 Randall McGowen, 'Getting to know the criminal class in nineteenth-century England', *Nineteenth Century Contexts: An Interdisciplinary Journal* 14 (1990): 33–54.

30 McGowen, 'Getting to know', 35.

31 Pablo Piccato, *City of Suspects: Crime in Mexico City, 1900-1931* (Durham, NC: Duke University Press, 2001) and Pablo Piccato, '*Cuidado con los rateros*: The making of criminals in modern Mexico City', in Ricardo D. Salvatore, Carlos Aguirre and Gilbert M. Joseph, eds, *Crime and Punishment in Latin America: Law and Society Since Late Colonial Times* (Durham, NC: Duke University Press, 2001), 233–72.

32 Carlos Aguirre, *The Criminals of Lima and their Worlds: The Prison Experience, 1850-1935* (Durham, NC: Duke University Press), 80.

33 Aguirre, *The Criminals of Lima*, 120–3.

34 Andy Croall, 'Who's afraid of the Victorian underworld?', *The Historian* 84 (2004): 30–5; Heather Shore, 'Criminality, deviance and the underworld since 1750', in Anne-Marie Kilday and David Nash, eds, *Histories of Crime: Britain 1600-2000* (London: Palgrave Macmillan, 2010), 120–40.

35 Mark H. Haller, 'Urban crime and criminal justice: The Chicago case', *Journal of American History* 57 (1970): 619–35; Mark H. Haller, 'Organized crime in urban society: Chicago in the twentieth century', *Journal of Social History* 5 (1971): 143–63.

36 Matthew Yeager, 'Fifty years of research on illegal enterprises: An interview with Mark Haller', *Trends in Organized Crime* 15 (2012): 1–12.

37 David R. Johnson, *Policing the Urban Underworld: The Impact of Crime on the Development of American Policie 1800-1887* (Philadelphia: Temple University Press, 1979), 4.

38 Johnson, *Policing the Urban Underworld*, 9.

39 Richard J. Evans, *The German Underworld: Deviants and Outcasts in German History* (London: Routledge, 1988), 1.

40 Evans, *The German Underworld*, 1–2.

41 Florike Egmond, 'Multiple underworlds in the Dutch Republic of the seventeenth and eighteenth centuries', in Cyrille Fijnaut and Letizia Paoli, eds, *Organised Crime in Europe: Concepts, Patterns, and Control Policies in the European Union and Beyond* (Dordrecht: Springer, 2006), 77, 77–107.

42 Florike Egmond, *Underworlds: Organised Crime in the Netherlands 1650-1800* (Cambridge: Cambridge University Press, 1993).

43 Deborah Symonds, *Notorious Murders, Black Lanterns, and Moveable Goods: The Transformation of Edinburgh's Underworld in the Early Nineteenth Century* (Akron, OH: University of Akron Press, 2006), 146.

44   Timothy J. Gilfoyle, 'White cities, linguistic turns, and Disneylands: The new paradigms of urban history', *Reviews in American History* 26 (1998): 175–204.

45   Roshanna P. Sylvester, 'City of thieves: Moldavanka, criminality, and respectability in prerevolutionary Odessa', *Journal of Urban History* 27 (2001): 131–57.

46   Christian Goeschel, 'The criminal underworld in Weimar and Nazi Berlin', *History Workshop Journal* 75 (2013): 1–13.

47   Goeschel, 'The criminal underworld', 6.

48   Goeschel, 'The criminal underworld', 18.

49   James Alex Garza, *The Imagined Underworld: Sex, Crime, and Vice in Poririan Mexico City* (Lincoln: University of Nebraska Press, 2007).

50   Paul Griffiths, *Lost Londons: Change, Crime and Control in the Capital City, 1550-1660* (Cambridge: Cambridge University Press, 2008).

51   Griffiths, *Lost Londons*, 178.

52   Timothy J. Gilfoyle, 'New perspectives on crime and punishment in the American City', *Journal of Urban History* 29 (2003): 519–24.

53   Timothy J. Gilfoyle, *A Pickpocket's Tale: The Underworld of Nineteenth Century New York* (New York: W. W. Norton, 2006), xiii.

54   Anthony M. Platt, *The Child Savers: The Invention of Delinquency* (Chicago: University of Chicago Press, 1969), 10.

55   Platt, *The Child Savers*, 177.

56   Platt, *The Child Savers*, 3.

57   Robert M. Mennel, *Thorns and Thistles: Juvenile Delinquents in the United States, 1825-1940* (Hannover, NH: University Press of New England, 1973).

58   Robert M. Mennel, 'Juvenile delinquency in perspective', *History of Education Quarterly* 13 (1973): 275–81.

59   Steven Schlossman, 'End of innocence: Science and the transformation of progressive juvenile justice, 1899-1917', *History of Education* 7 (1978): 209.

60   Steven Schlossman, *Love and the American Delinquent* (Chicago: University of Chicago Press, 1977).

61   Susan Margarey, 'The invention of juvenile delinquency in early nineteenth-century England', *Labour History* 34 (1978): 12 (11–27).

62   Margarey, 'The invention of juvenile delinquency', 24–5.

63   Peter King, 'The rise of juvenile delinquency in England 1780-1840: Changing patterns of perception and prosecution', *Past and Present* 160 (1998): 165 (116–66).

64   Peter C. Baldwin, '"Nocturnal habits and dark wisdom": The American response to children in the streets at night, 1880-1930', *Journal of Social History* 25 (2002): 605–6.

65   Timothy J. Gilfoyle, 'Street rats and gutter snipes: Child pickpockets and street culture in New York City, 1850-1900', *Journal of Social History* 37 (2004): 868 (853–82).

66 Peter K. Andersson, '"Bustling, crowding, and pushing": Pickpockets and the nineteenth-century street crowd', *Urban History* 41 (2014): 293 (291–310).

67 David Philips, '"A new engine of power and authority": The institutionalization of law-enforcement in England 1780-1830', in V. A. C Gatrell, Bruce Lenman and Geoffrey Parker, eds, *Crime and the Law: The Social History of Crime in Western Europe since 1500* (London: Europa, 1980), 155–89.

68 Wilbur R. Miller, *Cops and Bobbies: Police Authority in New York and London, 1830-1870* (Chicago: University of Chicago Press, 1973).

69 Roger Swift, 'Urban policing in early Victorian England, 1835-86: A reappraisal', *History* 73 (1988): 211–37.

70 Robert D. Storch, 'The plague of blue locusts: Police reform and popular resistance in Northern England, 1840-1857', *International Review of Social History* 20 (1975): 61–90; Robert D. Storch, 'The policeman as domestic missionary: Urban discipline and popular culture in Northern England, 1850-1880', *Journal of Social History* 9 (1976): 481–509.

71 Eric H. Monkkonen, *Police in Urban America 1860-1920* (Cambridge: Cambridge University Press, 1981).

72 Greg Marquis, 'The police as a social service in early twentieth-century Toronto', *Social History* 25 (1992): 335–58.

73 Clive Emsley, '"Mother, what *did* policemen do when there weren't any motors?" The law, the police and the regulation of motor traffic in England, 1900-1939', *Historical Journal* 36 (1993): 357–81.

74 Joanne Klein, 'Traffic, telephones and police boxes: The deterioration of beat policing in Birmingham, Liverpool and Manchester between the world wars', in Gerald Blaney, ed., *Policing Interwar Europe: Continuity, Change and Crisis, 1918-40* (London: Palgrave Macmillan, 2007), 215–36.

75 Mark H. Haller, 'Historical roots of police behavior: Chicago, 1890-1925', *Law and Society Review* 10 (1976): 303–23.

76 Haller, 'Historical roots', 321.

77 Sidney L. Harring, *Policing a Class Society: The Experience of American Cities, 1865-1915* (New Brunswick, NJ: Rutgers University Press, 1983).

78 Greg Marquis, 'Workingmen in uniform: The early twentieth century Toronto police', *Historie Sociale—Social History* 20 (1987): 259–77.

79 Joanne Klein, *Invisible Men: The Secret Lives of Police Constables in Liverpool, Manchester and Birmingham, 1900-1939* (Liverpool: Liverpool University Press, 2010).

80 Klein, *Invisible Men*, 3.

81 Klein, *Invisible Men*, 10.

82 Marcy S. Sacks, '"To show who was in charge": Police repression of New York City's black population at the turn of the twentieth century', *Journal of Urban History* 31 (2005): 799–819.

83 Stephen Robertson, 'Harlem undercover: Vice investigators, race and prostitution, 1910-1930', *Journal of Urban History* 35 (2009): 486.

84 Clifford Rosenberg, *Policing Paris: The Origins of Modern Immigration Control between the Wars* (Ithaca, NY: Cornell University Press, 2006).

85 Rosenberg, *Policing Paris*, xv.

86 Susan A. Lentz and Robert H. Chaires, 'The invention of Peel's principles: A study of policing "textbook" history', *Journal of Criminal Justice* 35 (2007): 69–79.

Further reading

Adler, Jeffrey. *First in Violence, Deepest in Dirt: Homicide in Chicago, 1875-1920*. Cambridge, MA: Harvard University Press, 2006.

Beattie, J. M. *Policing and Punishment in London 1660-1720: Urban Crime and the Limits of Terror*. Oxford: Oxford University Press, 2001.

Davies, Andrew. 'The Scottish Chicago? from "hooligans" to "gangsters" in interwar Glasgow'. *Cultural and Social History* 4 (2007): 511–27.

Gilfoyle, Timothy J. 'New perspectives on crime and punishment in the American City'. *Journal of Urban History* 29 (2003): 519–24.

Johnson, Eric and Eric Monkkonen, eds. *The Civilization of Crime: Violence in Town and Country Since the Middle Ages*. Urbana, IL: Northern Illinois University Press, 1996.

King, Peter. 'The impact of urbanization on murder rates and on the geography of homicide in England and Wales, 1780-1850'. *Historical Journal* 53 (2010): 671–98.

Larson, Erik. *The Devil in the White City: Murder, Magic and Madness at the Fair that Changed America*. New York: Doubleday, 2008.

Shore, Heather. *Artful Dodgers: Youth and Crime in Early Nineteenth Century London*. Woodbridge, UK: Boydell Press, 1999.

Stovall, Tyler. 'Murder in Montmarte: Race, sex, and crime in Jazz Age Paris', in Françoise Lionnet and Shu-mai Shih, eds, *Minor Transnationalism*. Durham, NC: Duke University Press, 2005, 135–52.

CHAPTER SIX

Foucault's project

It would be difficult to exaggerate the influence of Michel Foucault on the writing of crime history. He brought an incredible imagination to the study of crime in the past that introduced a fresh theoretical framework, sparked new methodological strategies and opened up new topics for study. He engineered the post-structuralist turn in crime history, a turn that revolutionized the way in which the history of crime would be written. Before Foucault, crime history belonged to social history, pursued along the lines of quantitative techniques, Marxist analysis or urban sociology. After Foucault, crime became part of the 'new cultural history', pursued along the lines of linguistics and literary theory.

Foucault resisted the idea that he followed a generalizable method. His later books do not acknowledge his earlier work, perhaps to avoid giving the impression that knowledge can accumulate. Rather, he improvised theories and methods to fit current projects. He referred to his early studies in medicine and psychiatry as 'archaeologies'; his subsequent work on the prison as 'genealogies'; and his later work on sexuality as 'problematizations'. At the same time, the approaches do not dislodge one another. They can be described as complementary alternatives to the conventional study of history.[1] The overall project furnished theories and concepts for historians working in various fields, and an extensive commentary about what he really meant. Foucault's work attracted criticism, even as his conceptual vocabulary became ubiquitous.

This chapter examines the impact of Foucault's project on crime history. We begin in the 1970s, the moment when crime historians encountered Foucault. Part 1 recalls the big splash made by his work on the emergence of the modern prison. We then return to the 1960s to uncover the intellectual origins of his approach. Part 2 considers Foucault's version of post-structuralism and how it led to writing the history of criminology. The final parts try to explain the effect of his work on crime history and the possibility that his influence has faded only in recent years. Part 3 considers his role in the new cultural history and the diversity of topics that resulted. Part 4 imagines a post-Foucault history with a discussion of the recent history of the crime museum.

The birth of the prison

Crime historians learnt about Foucault with the publication of *Discipline and Punish* (1979).[2] Or I should say English-speaking crime historians, because 'the Foucault phenomenon' was already underway in France. In the 1950s and 1960s, he held a series of university posts, authored several books, including a bestseller, and achieved the status of a public intellectual. He was awarded a chair at the Collége de France in 1970. Foucault styled himself as professor of the 'history of systems of thought' which put him in the territory of intellectual or cultural history. But he offered a kind of theoretical or speculative history that did not fit within the boundaries of orthodox history writing. He was more philosopher than historian.[3]

Ostensibly, *Discipline and Punish* is an account of the origins of the modern prison.[4] The book opens with a description of punishment under the monarchic, aristocratic regime that operated in France from the fifteenth to the eighteenth century. Foucault details the execution of Robert-François Damiens, who tried to kill King Louis XV in 1757, and the procedures of physical torture used to extract a confession. Foucault narrated the 'gloomy festival' of public punishment and the message intended for its audience, followed by the reforms of the Enlightenment and early experiments with incarceration. In the final part, he examined the legacy of the reformers as reflected in the systems of punishment they sought to introduce. To show the significance of prison discipline, he moved away from the legal realm to other institutions in society: the military, the factory and the school. He presented Jeremy Bentham's proposal for the panopticon, or 'the all-seeing eye', an architectural plan for a circular building enabling continuous and effortless surveillance. Punishment has shifted, not merely from the body to the mind, but to a new system that brought body and mind within a more pervasive regime of social control.

Whether Foucault ever intended to contribute to prison history remains clouded. There were philosopher-historians before Foucault, but they had gone about the trade in a different way. Their strategy had been to read historical works to establish the chronology of events, and then to reflect on these events and propose a larger meaning across the whole of them. Foucault did not confine himself to secondary sources, but looked into archives and documents. This resembled the craft of conventional historians, and although Foucault used these documents as no historian would, it made him appear as if he was following traditional methods.[5] Except that he did not adhere to the conventions of historical scholarship and made amateurish mistakes. Did Foucault want us to believe that a philosopher of the past had immunity from the demands of historical research? Had he invented a 'new' way to write history that transcended 'old' ideas about chronology, agency and causality? Did he even intend to be taken as a historian, or was the prison merely a metaphor for his vision of life in modern society? *Discipline and Punish* left historians bewitched, bothered and bewildered.

'In his empirical statements, Foucault was often wrong', Eric Monkkonen said of *Discipline and Punish*; 'Any careful reader of Foucault realizes that Foucault's thesis has no relationship to empirical work, perhaps not even to reality.'[6] But Foucault had, as Monkkonen observed, already shielded himself from this form of scrutiny. Foucault produced a synthesis, a grand vision that neither stood nor fell on its empirical presentation or actual analysis of the criminal justice system at work. The criteria of evidence, proof and explanation accepted by most historians were part of the problem in Foucault's view, the expected result of the legerdemain of power that operates in the modern world. To note Foucault's mistakes of fact is to miss the point of his work. A revolution in the present, not an argument about the past, is what he was really trying to get across.[7] As Peter Burke put it, 'Many sound second-rate historians can correct Foucault's errors, but are unable to produce a single new idea.'[8]

In large part, *Discipline and Punish* was read as a history of punishment because it appeared about the same time as two other histories of confinement. In *The Discovery of the Asylum* (1971), David Rothman said that the spread of prisons in the United States took place in the early nineteenth century as a part of a wider movement for planting total institutions, including poorhouses and insane asylums. Inspired by a vision of order in democratic society, reformers in the 1820s and 1830s saw confinement as a curative to crime and deviance. Michael Ignatieff's *A Just Measure of Pain* (1978) examined the model penitentiaries and the practice of solitary confinement in the early nineteenth century. He anchored the rise of prisons in England to changing economic conditions and class divisions brought about by the Industrial Revolution. Ignatieff, Rothman and Foucault – according to Ignatieff – provided a 'revisionist' account of the prison, which dislodged it from the cheerful story of humanitarian aspirations, and re-shelved it alongside schemes for effecting greater control over deviants in society.[9]

The revisionists quarrelled among themselves about a point or two, but agreed that the 'birth of the prison' took place between 1760 and 1840, the period of the Enlightenment. They doubted what the founders of these institutions claimed they were doing and portrayed the institutions they created as having a darker purpose. According to the 'social control school' of history, the reform programmes delivered in prisons did not embody ideals of absolution or redemption so much as strategies of power and domination. Prisons were merely one method of formal social control, among others that were less obvious, such as asylums, factories, schools and hospitals.[10] Further, formal social control was less important to understand than *informal* social control. Aspirations for reform, the language of care, even campaigns of opposition concealed the curtailment of personal freedom. Discipline was diffused throughout society, operating continuously, invisibly and efficiently, through forms of surveillance Bentham himself could not have imagined. The march of social control operated like a 'Whig history in reverse', a step-by-step descent into a dark cellar of restrictions on the human spirit.[11]

The 'functionalist' aspect of *Discipline and Punish* came closest to a conventional historical argument, and so the revisionists planted their flag on it as territory belonging to their empire. Foucault had not bothered to critique the Whig histories, but did seem to address the question of the function or role of the prison in society. He suggested that prisons functioned as a tactic of, or in the interests of, class domination. Prisoners represented a dangerous class that could be sliced off from the respectable class, and within the boundaries of the prison and under the supervision of the warders, allowed to work.[12] However, if this was the intention, it invited questions that required further elaboration. How did 'social discipline' acquire its social or class character? If the prison figured into social struggles, who or what calculated its effects? Foucault saw power everywhere; even institutions meant to limit power, such as the legal procedures and constitutional rights, merely offered a cover for its exercise. Human agency disappeared under the weight of invisible forces.[13]

Pieter Spierenburg denied there was a revolutionary break in punishment, that is, whether the problem Foucault solved about the 'birth of the prison' was ever a problem to begin with. Foucault was so preoccupied with finding discontinuities, radical breaks or ruptures, that he lost sight of the *longue durée* in which change occurs so gradually as to be invisible. The workhouses in Holland and Germany, and bridewells and houses of correction in England, represented a prison in the modern sense because they incorporated inmate labour and implemented reform of criminals. No revolutionary break occurred during the Enlightenment because governments had already put institutions for confinement in place. Foucault offered an ad hoc explanation of a change that occurred between 1760 and 1840. But the real source of change leading to the shift from the spectacle of the scaffold to the modern prison took place over the long term, beginning in 1600 or so and continuing into the nineteenth century.[14] Spierenburg viewed the houses of correction as the first step in the history of confinement. He emphasized conceptions of the pauper, a change that took place in Protestant as well as Catholic areas of Europe. He also emphasized the role of the state within the wider and longer process of secularization.[15]

Robert Nye complained that Foucault made his allegations stick only by ignoring the wider institutional setting within France at the time.[16] To present a coherent narrative, Foucault overlooked the diversity of points of view. Across institutional settings, there were conflicts among founders and disputes among policymakers. It was contrived to put the criminal policymaking process of France between 1780 and 1850 midway on an imaginary continuum between simple-medieval and complex-modern policymaking processes. Centralization and codification of secular law was an important element of medieval state-building, and ecclesiastical sanctions continued for some time after, 'making the task of combining the various corporate discourses into a synthetic national one virtually impossible'.[17] Foucault's concept of legal-penal process as a bourgeois strategy of social discipline extending throughout every dimension of modernizing society applies to relatively brief periods of time in European history. To apply Foucault's concept of the relationship between penal law and human sciences to France after 1850, it would be necessary to break down the various interests engaged in formulation of criminal policy in a more detailed manner than he does for the earlier period. Decision-making about crime in the Third Republic was complex, and there were discourses within the political class and the rhetoric of philanthropic societies in addition to those Foucault targeted.

In discussing the transition from one form of discipline to another, Richard Evans observed that Foucault lapsed into the passive voice.[18] Foucault claimed that discipline had been embodied in the sovereign and became diffused throughout the whole of society, from family to prison. Yet, he neither attempted to find out how or why this transition took place, nor to identify those responsible, nor to determine who benefitted from it, nor to trace its relation to social, economic and political realities. Foucault overestimated the disorderliness of early modern executions because he treated the entire period as a unity and failed to understand why they broke down in specific places for particular reasons. He knew little of the practices in early modern society, and seriously underestimated the importance not only of ritual and ceremony, but also of religion and magic in giving meaning to people's lives. At every stage, Foucault discounted informal notions of justice and retribution read onto the formal penal system, and failed to think through the multiple meanings of punishment in structures of popular culture, consciousness and experience.[19]

Heinz Steinert rejected Foucault's claim about the historical development of the prison because *Discipline and Punish* failed to connect the dots between asylums in the seventeenth century and rise of prisons in the nineteenth century. The ambiguity in Foucault's point of view represents an essential weakness as a historical explanation; Foucault declined to explain the connection between general forms of domination in society and specific forms of institutional control. If he intended to portray discipline as a social movement, as reflected in institutions of confinement, he would have needed to show how these institutions actually introduced elements of discipline before it was more widely reproduced in society. If he intended to say that discipline was limited to institutions of confinement, and was not connected to any wider understanding of the state, then his argument loses its significance. He would need to make a stronger argument for the effectiveness of the 'carceral system' in disciplining inmates. The idea that domination is not limited to institutions of confinement is a useful insight, but power is less mystical than Foucault makes out.[20]

Alternatively, Michael Meranze saw room for application of Foucault to prisons in the United States. Using Philadelphia as the central site, he traced the replacement of a penal system based on public capital and corporal punishment to one centred on penitence and solitary confinement.[21] The late eighteenth and early nineteenth centuries saw the proliferation of disciplinary techniques throughout the city. Whether the target was prostitution, criminality, poverty or idleness, reformers believed that problems could be tackled through reformation of character, and this reformation was best achieved in environments where it could be managed and controlled. 'These laboratories of virtue assembled spaces separate from daily life, arranged according to carefully specified rules and overseen by hierarchical organizations. They sought to inculcate the habits of labor, personal restraint, and submission to the law.'[22] Social discipline does not aim to capture some transhistorical need for 'social control' or present individual 'self-discipline' as a form of malevolence. Instead it is a historically specific way of governing groups and individuals. Meranze presents social discipline as the 'equivalent of wage labour' and the 'effective underpinning of liberal democracy'.[23] Just as wage labour bound workers to coercions of the market, so discipline tied individuals to the threat of authorities to expand their power.

In 2006, more than two decades after *Discipline and Punish* had first appeared, Pieter Spierenburg decided that his original critique had been too harsh. He had rejected Foucault's version of the birth of the prison in favour of Elias's view, but having reflected further, decided there was more to like in Foucault's account than he had seen at first. Over the years, layers of interpretation and reinterpretation had accumulated on Foucault's book, which made it difficult to find the author's real intention. The appropriation of Foucault by Rothman and Ignatieff as a revisionist had confused his true identity. But from a close reading, it was possible to glimpse the 'real Foucault'. While Foucault appeared to be saying that changing sensibilities played little part in the rise of the modern prison, he actually made space for a change in attitudes towards suffering as part of a multi-causal explanation. Foucault differed from Elias in his approach and methods, but like Elias, preferred a long-term exploration, a high level of generalization and a concern with power.[24]

Where does this leave the birth of the prison? Certainly Foucault's study made the prison a worthy subject for historical study. And, decades after writing about prisons in Europe and North America, historians carried their copy of Foucault's work overseas. *Discipline and Punish* has become, Mary Gibson argues, 'the master text consulted by most prison historians'. She points to Foucault's influence in historical studies of prisons to show how he 'created a paradigm shift in historical explanation' and provided 'the touchstone of prison history worldwide'.[25] Traces of Foucault's narrative appear in histories of prisons in Asia, Africa and the Americas, from China and Japan to the United States and Peru. Although prisons outside of Europe appeared in the late nineteenth century, or even the twentieth century, they suggest Foucault was right about the role of incarceration in modern society. Foucault's language has had an even bigger influence. *Discipline and Punish* followed on from his earlier philosophical work in which he brought an arsenal of concepts to academic writing. It is in his conceptual vocabulary that Foucault's perspective 'pervades, sometimes imperceptibly, the entire contemporary history of crime and punishment'.[26]

Taylor C. Sherman is not so sure. Also thinking about the Foucault effect, she assesses his influence on the study of prisons in Asia, Africa, South America and the Caribbean.[27] True, he inspired a generation of historians. But in adhering to the model of *Discipline and Punish*, this generation became 'locked in an historiographical cul-de-sac'.[28] In moving the analysis overseas, Foucault's generation found that when exported to colonial settings, the modern prison did not follow the course it did in Europe. They pointed to the 'undisciplined colonial prison', a place where violence was common, labour reflected a preoccupation with profit rather than discipline, and surveillance was impeded by the very warders meant to oversee these functions. There emerged an unhelpful debate over the extent to which the colonial prison could be understood as a modern prison and the introduction of arguments that colonial prisons managed only a pre-modern or partially modern development. 'It is clear that the field is in need of a new conceptual framework', Sherman concludes. 'Foucault's *Discipline and Punish* provided fresh inspiration twenty years ago, but it has long been clear that his model does not "fit" in colonial Asia, Africa or Latin America.'[29]

History of criminology

The popularity of *Discipline and Punish* drew crime historians to Foucault's earlier works. As English translations of his books appeared, and historians began to situate what Foucault said about prisons within his overall philosophy, it became clear that his 'history of the present' did not match any familiar category of historiography. He denounced 'scientific history'. Empirical evidence cannot be made to support any claim of recovering the past for what it really was. He was unconcerned with obtaining knowledge of the past for its own sake, but for revealing traces of the past in the present. Although he used narrative, his method subverted the usual presentation of history. He rearranged the evidence, denied its conclusions and appropriated its resources for his own purposes. His method was 'counter history' and 'social critique'.[30]

Foucault's project originated in structuralism, a theory of language instigated by Ferdinand de Saussure, a Swiss linguist. In a collection of writings published after his death, Saussure suggested the possibility of finding a common internal structure across languages. He proposed to abandon the search for any pattern linking spoken sounds with objects or experiences in the external world. Only when the sounds or words were detached from their referents and modelled as a formal system could progress be made. Saussure concentrated on the smallest units of speech able to convey meaning and found pairs of opposites that changed what was being said. The key was the relationship between the sounds, not the sounds themselves. There was no necessary connection between any particular name, or signifier, and the thing it referred to, the signified. This was the paradox of language: it was composed of elements that were signifiers but elements that in themselves signified nothing. Or, to put it another way, language was not a vehicle for communicating meaning, but rather, meaning was an artefact of language.

In France, in the 1960s, structural linguistics began to spill over the banks. The search began for the hidden symmetries not only in language, but behind the array of cultures and ideas that shaped the twentieth century. Structuralists brought Saussure to places he had not intended to go: Claude Lévi-Strauss, anthropology; Louis Althusser, Marxist theory; and Jacques Lacan, psychoanalysis. Initially, Foucault was happy to be known as a structuralist. The word 'structure' appeared throughout the original edition of *The Birth of the Clinic* (1963). The book examined the origins of clinical medicine in France from 1769 to 1825, drawing close links between the accumulation of medical knowledge and institutional practices. In this discussion, he introduced the concept of 'gaze'. But as the structuralist movement became more popular in France, he became less content to be categorized in this way. The student demonstrations of May 1968 in Paris rejected structuralism as the old guard of an archaic university system ('Structures don't take to the streets' became a student slogan), and intellectuals began to run from the label. Foucault, who was relatively young and already engaged in politics, escaped denunciation, and he did not look back.

He also began to distance himself from the post-structuralists. Jacques Derrida, the leading post-structuralist in literary studies, theorized that people move within structures, or more precisely, linguistic structures, which they do not determine, but instead, determine them. He promoted a method he called 'deconstruction'. This was built on the idea that texts had no reference to external reality, rather, the meaning was found within the text itself. Further, texts are not only independent of the context in which they were produced, but independent of the author who produced them. In other words, the intention of the author, and the context in which the text was written, offered no clues to grasping the significance of the text. Foucault broke with Derrida by insisting on the importance of history. Unlike Derrida, Foucault said, he was not interested in language as such. Rather, he was interested in the 'accumulated existence of discourses' and the 'analysis of discourse in its *archival* form'.[31] In this way, Foucault pioneered post-structuralist history. He did not study language in relation to itself, but in relation to the past, and if social relations were structured like language, it was possible to see binary opposition in relationships: medicine/illness, rationality/insanity, criminology/criminality. Foucault used the term 'discourse analysis' to mean the study of language in relation to power.

The Order of Things (1970), previewed at his induction to the Collége de France, delivered his proposal for viewing intellectual history as a contest of rival discourses.[32] The book traced the origins of discourses of economics, linguistics and biology from the fifteenth century to the nineteenth century. In the final chapter, Foucault dealt with the nineteenth-century origins of the human sciences: history, sociology, psychoanalysis and ethnology. In *The Archaeology of Knowledge* (1976), Foucault elaborated his method of discourse analysis.[33] He developed the idea of 'discursive formations' in which common rules, specific gaze and a consensus about the object of study brought together actors from different backgrounds. A scientific discourse is less important for what the scientists have to say, or as a statement about their focus of study, than for the knowledge it creates. He was interested in the process by which one discourse became more important than another. The knowledge supplied by the human sciences is not based on demonstrating a superior understanding of the world, but on what it has managed to exclude over the years. A discourse, he said, created knowledge by crowding out others. This is why so much of Foucault's writing concerns discourses employed to contain deviant behaviour, and why he chose to write about madness, illness and criminality.

In addition to *Discipline and Punish*, Foucault presented his theory of discourse in another book about crime history that appeared just before it. *I, Pierre Rivière* (1975) has received far less attention because it reveals the problem with Foucault's conceptualization of discourse for crime history. While collecting archival material in the early 1970s, Foucault came across the case of a peasant condemned for murdering his mother, sister and brother. It was an unusual case, not because of mistaken identity or any mystery about motives, but rather the opposite. Rivière left a forty-page account of his life, his family relations and the reasons for his crimes. The case was heard in 1836, at a time of uncertainty in French procedure over the place of psychiatric concepts in the law. The psychiatrist who testified at the proceedings used Rivière's statement to prove his insanity. Foucault and collaborators produced a book that contained the unedited account of this text alongside the statements of the officials who decided the case. Foucault wanted to avoid offering an interpretation, because to do so would fall into one of the discourses (medical, legal, psychological, criminological) under examination. Rather, he wanted the voices of the murderer and his inquisitors to reveal the formation of power/knowledge.[34]

The problem, Patricia O'Brien pointed out, is that the killer has an exemption. The other narratives, legal, psychiatric, etc., are juxtaposed against each other, competing in power-knowledge. But, not so with the killer. Foucault allows the killer's account to speak for itself, as if it was the standard by which the others could be assayed for their power-knowledge content.[35] The 'excluded' assume a privileged place in Foucault's scheme, a place that has no justification in Foucault's view of the past. Recovering the voices of those who have been crowded out has appeal when discussing the diseased or mentally ill. But this does not work in quite the same way in crime history. It is possible to find a case like Damiens, the pathetic individual crushed by the full might of sacred and secular authorities because he dared to threaten the king. But Rivière is no Damiens. He murdered poor peasants and had the arrogance to write about his experiences, his feelings, his life. The 'excluded' would not be Pierre, but the voices of those he silenced: his dead mother, brother and sister.

At the end of the day, Gareth Steadman Jones insists, Foucault did not really set the agenda for a new kind of history as he claimed to have done.[36] Foucault popularized a linguistic approach, and the term 'discursive approach' came to be taken as another name for Foucault's writings. But 'discursive analysis' does not provide a suitable platform for building historical understanding, not even for Foucault. Historians in the English-speaking world accepted Foucault's promise of a new agenda without realizing the extent to which it relied on Marxist theory. Foucault's conception of a novel method of inquiry amounted to an inferior or counterfeit version of the 'old' social history. Foucault offered a variant of Marxist conclusions: a conception of law as no more than a veiled form of violence and reluctance to accept any normative conceptions of moral right. He offered a reworking of the state as a mere superstructure that left no basis for distinguishing between states that abided by legal norms from those that did not. This resulted, not in a viable alternative to social history, but a 'crude functionalist notion of social control' that managed to deliver only the 'reductionist practices of the gauchest sociology and social history of the 1970s'.[37]

In *Discipline and Punish*, Foucault mentioned writing a 'history of the present', that is, an alternative to ordinary history. Robert Castel, who knew Foucault when they both worked at Vicennes, explained how difficult, or impossible, this would be to achieve. By what right may one give a different reading to historical material, including what is written by historians, if one knows no more (and arguably less) than a conventional historian? In choosing to ignore, or transcend, historical scholarship, Foucault assigned himself two Herculean tasks. The second makes clear why the first is so difficult. First, his approach must contribute something to what has already been achieved by conventional historical approach. He needs to say something more than what social history has said. Second, what a history of the present contributes to our understanding must not come at the price of our knowledge of the past. In other words, this alternative account can be refuted if it contradicts historical knowledge, and only historians are the judges of that. 'The right to choose one's materials and to refocus them in light of a current issue, to place them in different categories – sociological categories, for example – is not permission to rewrite history.'[38]

Nevertheless, 'discourse' and 'discursive' became ubiquitous in crime history. Assembling a collection of texts, whether prison reports, police records, newspaper articles or court cases, and treating these as a discourse about crime, became a popular way to proceed. From a social history point of view, much of this material would be regarded as the official or top-down view, and as such, in need of amendment by rarer sources offering a floor-up view. But the point of a Foucault-inspired story is that there is no objective criminality at issue (or that whether there was or was not is less important than the effect of claiming that there was), but in seeing the way in which this discourse related to wider social or cultural anxieties. In an interview, Foucault suggested that criminology should be taken as a discourse about crime. In this statement, he offered justification for why it would be worthwhile to write the history of criminology. He initiated a branch of crime history devoted to the 'birth of criminology', which led to further debates and discussion.

Prior to Foucault, criminology had no history. It was unimportant to social, cultural or intellectual history, and if anything, had been a chapter (footnote?) in the history of science. In the 1950s, the editor of the *Journal of Criminal Law, Criminology and Police Science* commissioned a series of articles on the lives of 'great figures of the past ... who anticipated modern criminological research'. The essays later appeared in a collection edited by Hermann Mannheim with the title *Pioneers in Criminology* (1960).[39] Robert Nye continued with the history of science approach, albeit with greater appreciation for how what the criminologists of the late nineteenth century connected within a wider intellectual history. Nye reported on an early debate between the Italian founders, who favoured a biological explanation for crime, and French counterparts, who advocated social milieu. He argued that the biological view had been displaced, by the French in the 1880s, several decades before it was 'disproved' by statistical studies at the time of the First World War.[40]

David Garland's *Punishment and Welfare* (1985) discussed the rise of criminology within a history of prisons.[41] The book introduced Garland's general strategy of adopting Foucault's style while arguing against specific points. Foucault had described how discourses related to institutions, theory to practice and knowledge to power. Garland said he wanted to do this in a concrete way, through analysis of empirical evidence, specifically, through scrutiny of government reports relating to prison and social policy in the late nineteenth and early twentieth centuries. Just as Foucault had argued that the clinic formed the basis for medicine, there was a link between criminology and a specific institution. Garland referred to 'discursive and technical resources' and their 'organisational basis and social support', including criminology alongside welfare-oriented schemes. He argued that modern penality in England emerged in the brief period from 1895 to 1914, later than Foucault had suggested for France. And, it did not embody a specific logic of a disciplinary society, but was constructed around eclectic and contradictory forms, including punishment and welfare. But Foucault was right about the necessary relationship between criminology and the prison. The prison acted as an 'institutional surface of emergence' for criminology, an 'experimental laboratory' in which the new knowledge, 'the science of criminology', could develop. 'While modern penality cannot be understood without reference to criminological discourse, the reverse is also true in a profound and fundamental sense.'[42]

Piers Beirne examined the intellectual history of criminology from the mid-eighteenth century to the early twentieth century. Or, more specifically, 'positivist criminology' by which he meant 'a discourse about crime' based on the assumption of a harmony between natural and social sciences, and that held theory to be independent of its objects or people to be studied.[43] Beirne saw an intellectual pathway from Italian legal reformer Cesare Beccaria's pamphlet on crimes and punishments in 1764 to English statistician Charles Goring's statistical report on the English convict in 1913 (an unusual move in terms of theoretical criminology). While Foucault's idea of discourse supplied the unifying theme for the essays in the book, he objected to Foucault's specific theory of criminology. Foucault said that criminology emerged in France in the 1820s as a calculated response to the need for an official discourse to justify new strategies of punishment. Such a comment assumed a connection between the first criminologists, such as Quetelet, and conscious objectives of French penal policy. While criminology emerged from state practice, it was not an expression of state or even class interests. Rather, positivist criminology emerged from the intersection of two previously unrelated domains of state activity: institutions/penality and the statistical movement.[44]

Richard Wetzell started from Foucault's suggestion that criminological knowledge had a large part in the development of criminal justice. Although, Wetzell explained, he wanted to avoid the 'functionalist approach of Foucault and others in the social control school'.[45] He charted the history of criminology in Germany from the reception of Lombroso's theories and criminal psychology in Imperial Germany, through criminal-sociological and criminal-biological research in the Weimar era, to criminology within the Nazi regime. He showed that many prominent criminologists were eager to connect their work with the agenda of Nazi biological politics. However, 'Nazi criminology' was complex. Not all science and medicine in the National Socialism era was completely Nazi. Criminologists pursued ideas about criminality as an inherited tendency and increasing methodological sophistication, leading to the conclusion that crime resulted from a complex interaction of heredity and environment. Even within Nazi Germany, the history of criminology cannot be reduced to a mechanism of social control. There were tensions in the relationship between criminological knowledge and penal policy that Foucault's theory had overlooked.

Peter Becker and Richard Wetzell rely directly on Foucault for *Criminals and Their Scientists* (2006), an edited collection devoted to the history of criminology. Their book contains essays on criminological writing across Europe, but also Argentina, Australia and Japan as well the United States. The essays deal with the conceptual foundations of criminology found in forgotten controversies among German psychiatrists, medical debates in France and psychoanalysis in Austria. While the various chapters engage different methodological strategies, Foucault's concept of 'discursive formation' supplied a useful way for organizing the book as a whole. Unlike other modern disciplines, criminology coalesced from various sites: medicine, prisons and police, as well as legal. They saw a close association between discourse and institutional practice.[46] Becker's own chapter in the book, 'Criminological Discussions at the end of the Nineteenth Century About the Underworld', elaborated on Foucault's archaeology of knowledge as a method of writing about history. He compared the views of professional criminals found in Hans Gross's forensic science and Richard von Krafft-Ebing's psychiatric classifications.[47]

Daniel Vyleta agreed with Foucault in the general characterization of criminology as 'a tale of knowledge turned into power directed against society's unwanted'.[48] But, he suggests that a willingness to accept Foucault's overall framework has meant that historians have overlooked or discounted debates within criminology. Vyleta insisted that criminology was not a science centring on the deviance of the criminal. Through a careful examination of the texts of Hans Gross, and debates in Austria and Germany in which he took part, he revealed a more complex conception of criminology. Historians had assigned Gross a place in the history of forensic science, but his work actually had much more importance to theoretical foundations of criminological analysis. His publications, the *Handbuch für Untersuchungsrichter* (Handbook for Investigative Judges) and *Criminalpsychologie* (Criminal Psychology), have been read as practical manuals for forensic techniques. But these involved a sophisticated system for reading emotion and intention from clues. Contrary to Wetzell, Vyleta insisted that Gross should be categorized as contributing to a long tradition in criminology arguing against an anthropological or psychological difference between criminals and non-criminals.

Variations on culture

Discipline and Punish not only established prison as a worthy topic in the history of crime, but affirmed the importance of culture. By the 1970s, most crime history was written within the broad framework of social history. By the 1980s, 'new cultural history' would challenge this hegemony and Foucault was a major reason why.

Foucault's project has some resemblance to that of the *Annales* school. The *Annales* historians avoided political events as the foundation of historical study in favour of the deep structures that lie beneath. They wrote about 'mentalities', cultural forms which regularize mental activity, including aesthetic images, linguistic codes, religious rituals and social customs. Foucault, too, looked for common codes of knowledge through which the world is perceived. His concept of discourses is something like what Febvre called 'mental equipment', both of which seek to map the mental structures through which people organize their activities and classify their perceptions of the world.[49] However, Foucault dismissed the *Annalistes*' ambition of finding the 'total history' or laws of cohesion that define a historical period. According to total history, economic structures, mental outlooks, social institutions and political conduct are governed by the same causality. Foucault rejected the technique of constructing the past around a single centre, whether a world view or source of change. He offered 'general history', an attempt to find forms of social categorization or systems of thought, without falling back on any theory of causation (such as the economy, geography, psychology and biology).[50]

Foucault broke the monopoly, Patricia O'Brien explains, that social history held over writing the history of crime by dynamiting the very foundation on which it is built: that society itself is the reality to be studied. Foucault said he wanted to 'create a history of the different modes by which, in our culture, human beings are made subjects'. He studied culture through technologies of power. He denied that power was held in the hands of the state; he offered no theory of how government operated. Instead he wrote of 'micro-powers' through dispositions, manoeuvres, techniques and tactics activated through cultural space.[51] Understanding the history of crime and punishment from the perspective of cultural narrative had startling implications. In looking back at documents, it removed any distinction between factual and fictional accounts. Official reports, social surveys, journalistic investigations and the like lost any significance as descriptions of what was going on in society, but had equal weight with detective novels and tattooed bodies as 'crime stories'. More than one historian objected to this kind of textual analysis. For professional historians, it was not a blueprint for a wonderful postmodern future but a collective suicide note.[52] In any event, the effect of this was to greatly expand the array of possible topics for crime history. Given the significance of microphysics of power, anything and everything had significance. Cultural artefacts, from police photographs to artwork by murderers to clothing of prisoners, all revealed the hidden dynamic of power.

Judith Walkowitz targeted two series of news stories in late-nineteenth-century London: journalist W. T. Stead's exposé of the 'White slave trade' and the 'Jack the Ripper' murders. Stead claimed that child prostitution was rampant in London and 'proved' this by buying a girl for £5 with the connivance of the girl's own drunken mother. 'By focusing on narrative', Walkowitz explained, she wanted to 'explore how cultural meanings around sexual danger were produced and disseminated in Victorian society, and what were their cultural and political effects'.[53] She discussed how the theatrical characters of the innocent and wronged heroine appealed to working-class women and galvanized women reformers, and how the 'facts' of London life contained in the social surveys of Mayhew and Booth convinced Parliament to enact legislation. And she discussed how the ripper stories operated as a form of control over women, a counterweight to a rising tide of female emancipation. She reinforced the 'history of the present' by ending with a discussion of the 'Yorkshire Ripper' murders of the 1980s.[54]

Marie-Christine Leps followed Foucault's lead in her analysis of late-nineteenth-century discourses of crime. Like Walkowitz, she digested the press coverage of the ripper murders of 1888 alongside other sources, this time, criminological texts and detective novels. The rise of mass journalism, the emergence of scientific criminology and expanding crime fiction represented 'institutional places' from which the 'discursive practices' of criminality spread from institutions, such as the prison, to the wider society. The power visible in prisons, courts and schools gained currency from crime stories circulated in the press, the criminality as the object of scientific study, and the criminal at the centre of fictional detective narratives. The effect is to reinforce the lack of any meaningful distinction between true and fictional accounts. Regardless of the writer's intention, or the evidence they might have had for their claims, they collectively reveal the way culture reproduced the relationship between knowledge and power. Leps offered an elaboration and not a critique of Foucault's philosophical strategy.[55]

Claire Anderson has written about the criminal body as seen from the management of prisoners in South East Asia during the colonial era. From the late eighteenth to the mid-twentieth centuries, the British transported tens of thousands of Indian convicts to penal settlements in South East Asia, Mauritius and the Andaman islands. She explores colonial efforts to make the bodies of prisoners 'legible' through the use of signs to connect individuals to written records. That the authorities tried a number of methods, including photographs, measurements, fingermarks and tattoos, suggests the extent to which they failed. She looks at the ways colonial authorities appropriated the Indian body to construct new social categories. They used clothing, uniforms, hair cutting and forms of shackles to demarcate status within prisoner hierarchies. She also looks at jails as a metaphor for broader social practices in the construction of colonial knowledge. Convict populations in the colonies became a convenient sample for research into questions, the answers to which contributed to administration.[56] Her study of convicts' clothing shows how prisoners proceeded through a hierarchy of tasks and locations in these settlements, and the most immediate marker of their status was dress. By the mid-nineteenth century, a complex system of clothing had been developed, informed by the experience of the Australian colonies. Clothing was not simply utilitarian, but symbolic on many levels. It established the power in social relations at levels of colonial society; it was a means by which individuals chose their self-image and understood their identity. It was a means by which individuals and populations had their identities fashioned for them.[57]

Todd Herzog has examined the meaning of crime in interwar Germany.[58] Weimar Germany presents an interesting case study because although there is evidence to suggest that levels of crime were not particularly high, government officials, social critics, novelists and other opinion-makers were convinced that it was. Herzog focused on a curious series published in 1924–5, *Aubenseiter der Gesellschaft: Die Verbrechen der Gegenwart* (Outsiders of Society – The Crimes of Today). Edited by a well-known literary figure and political activist, Rudolf Leonhard, the series included investigative case studies into recent sensational criminal cases by Ernst Weiss, Iwall Goll and Alfred Döbbin. Herzog found a 'criminalistic fantasy' characterized by its willingness to situate criminals in the ordinary world of everyday life, and implicitly, a critique of Foucault's projection of increasing delineation, discipline and surveillance. He had expected, following Foucault, to find a story now familiar to cultural historians. He thought he would have seen the 'dangerous individual' of the late nineteenth century, and then would see the criminalization of this individual in the early twentieth century, culminating in the criminalization of Jews in the Third Reich. The Weimar period would display a separation of the criminal from the non-criminal. The 'psychiatrization of criminal danger' and the formation of the 'scientifico-legal complex' would lead to objectification of the criminal not only as distinct from the non-criminal, but identified and disciplined through examinations. Instead, Herzog found a discourse not of increasing separation, but a fusion of 'other' and 'non-other' in the ordinary and normal individual. Popular, scientific and literary discourse blurred distinctions between criminality and civility.[59]

Cultural analysis à la Foucault rehabilitated the career of Cesare Lombroso. Looking back for the scientific foundations of criminology had relegated the Italian founder of criminal anthropology to a footnote: he represented a false start to producing knowledge about crime. However, Lombroso achieved a prominent place in the 'new cultural history'. As Mary Gibson has explained, the scientific texts of Lombroso and his colleagues did not represent examples merely of flawed scientific work, but rather of cultural claims about crime. By inserting short stories in between statistical evidence, Lombroso attempted to convince by means of cultural evidence. Internal inconsistences and factual errors in the texts are less important than understanding their ability to persuade. She presented examples of cultural production in criminology drawn from popularized texts. She discussed an article Lombroso wrote for an Italian magazine, a chapter by Guglielmo Ferrero in a book on famous trials, and a lecture given by Salvatore Ottolenghi to a class of police cadets. The texts illustrate the use of narrative for Italian criminal anthropologists to prove the value of their 'scientific theory'.[60]

Using the texts produced by Lombroso, David Horn explored the 'idea that bodies can testify (or be made to testify) to legal and scientific truths'. He focused on nineteenth-century Italy because it was the site of 'the emergence of a family of discourses and techniques intended to qualify and quantify the bodies of dangerous persons'.[61] The accounts of social historians had positioned the Italian criminologists behind the French criminologists, who demonstrated the contradictions, inconsistencies and errors in the Italian presentations. Horn insisted that Lombroso was less important for their theories, than for an emerging culture of science built on measurements, photographs and drawings, graphs and tables. Horn's book reprinted a fabulous array of illustrations from Lombroso, including peculiarities of the ear, ceramics decorated by criminals, symbolic tattoos and judicial astrology, although with an assortment of devices, the Landolt campimeter, Anfossi craniograph, Mosso plethysmograph and volumetric glove. Foucault supplied the opening quote about interrogation of the body.

Foucault's way is not, of course, the only way to think about culture. Norbert Elias's civilizing process presents another version of a deep structure in history. The slow modification of social conventions, table manners, sexual etiquette, rules of language and so on, represent the transformation of sensibilities. As a marker of long-term change in sensibilities, Elias spoke of the 'threshold of shame'. The threshold of shame reveals the tolerated social behaviour in a given historical moment.[62] David Nash and Anne-Marie Kilday, in their work on crime and punishment in Britain from the seventeenth to the nineteenth centuries, discuss the importance of shame. They cover attitudes towards child murderers, the case of a disgraced parson, and the reactions to wife abuse over an extended period. Foucault implied that shame would have disappeared with the arrival of modern prison surveillance punishment over brutal corporal punishment, yet shame continued into the nineteenth century. Although they conclude that Elias, too, got it wrong. In describing the gradual evolution of manners, he referred to the transition from 'shame culture' to 'guilt culture'. 'In making us modern, Elias would have been anxious for us to leave the phenomenon of shame behind.'[63] Shame seems to be an anachronistic, primitive, pre-modern social attitude.

The practitioners of microhistory wanted to escape the overemphasis on institutional and legal history. The leading figure has been Carlo Ginzburg, a founding editor of the *microstorie* series. He wrote about the lives of people living in sixteenth-century Rome and Bologna, and he treated them as if they were citizens of another country. Through the intense scrutiny of a few legal documents, especially records of interrogations, he recovered interactions between elite culture and popular culture. The microhistorians wanted to avoid the preoccupation with quantification and abstract sociological concepts. Above all, they did not believe in using the past to satisfy present concerns. The microhistorians delighted in recovering details of forgotten individuals: what the residents of a mountain village dreamed about, a single incident that took place among the servants in a grand house. Not people who would have a claim to determining the course of history, but those lost to history because their lives are judged as insignificant: criminals and heretics, unwed mothers and peasants. Italian microhistorians reduced the scale of historical research in order to test many of the abstractions in social thought, and to find an alternative means for evaluation of historical evidence, the 'evidential paradigm'.[64]

The evidential paradigm proposes that history can be best recalled through single, seemingly insignificant clues, rather than through the application of laws derived from repeatable and quantifiable observations. It resembles the search for clues, Ginzburg said, along the lines of Freud's psychiatric diagnosis, or forensic detection, as portrayed by Conan Doyle's Sherlock Holmes. Freud revealed the unconscious by attending to inadvertent gestures and fragments of speech; Sherlock Holmes reconstructed criminal events from trivial aspects of locations and persons. The evidential paradigm could be seen, perhaps most clearly, in the artistic connoisseurship of Giovanni Morelli. To detect forgeries, Morelli taught, it was necessary to concentrate on minor details, especially those least significant within the painter's school: the depiction of fingernails, the positioning of feet, the shape of the ears. Using the ear as a signature of the masters, he corrected mistaken attributions in galleries across Europe.[65]

Edward Muir combined the techniques of Italian microhistory with a wider approach to cultural history. He produced, along with Guido Ruggiero, more than one volume dealing with crime. *Microhistory and the Lost Peoples of Europe* (1991) contains essays set in the sixteenth century about a Jew hiring a mason to destroy the Christian images in another Jew's house, episodes of pillaging property after the death of a bishop or pope, the lives of unwed mothers caught between hospitals and the Inquisition, and how the myth of the armies of dead warriors led to sightings of an apparition. *History from Crime* (1994) presents essays that originally appeared in *Quaderni Storici*. It contains essays on cohabitation, witchcraft, magic, corruption, counterfeiting and infanticide.[66] The events take place in different settings, a seventeenth-century village in north-eastern Italy and early-twentieth-century Vienna. These essays use a particular criminal event as a point of departure for investigating society and culture from the perspective the records can provide.

The microhistorians share Foucault's interest in the deviant and abnormal, the targets of inquisition, criminals and insane persons, and in institutions created in response to them, prisons, hospitals and asylums. Their analyses reveal how dominant habits of thought dismiss alternatives as illicit, heretical and irrational. They appreciate the value of narrative. Both have excelled in telling engaging stories. They also share an attitude towards progress. Microhistorians expressed doubts, as did Foucault, about modern culture. They do not accept that modern cultures have allowed for greater freedom of movement than medieval cultures. But microhistorians deny any kinship with Foucault. Ginzburg referred to Foucault's project (in *The Order of Things*) as 'not so interesting' and 'even weak'. To begin with, Ginzburg said, Foucault's theories defy verification. According to Foucault's scheme, the standards of truth come from a modern academic discipline that reconquers the past, to make it conform to the uses of the present. For Ginzburg, this is an evasion. It is not easy to examine the long dead, but this does not authorize misrepresentation and distortion. The past must be explored through concrete evidence, not intellectual techniques which are artificial constructs. Foucault consciously inserts himself between the past and the present; he diverts attention from the subjects of history to his own activities as a scholar.[67]

Crime history post-Foucault

Twenty years after it appeared, everyone was still talking about *Discipline and Punish*. On his deathbed, even Leon Radzinowicz was said to have been reading Foucault.[68] After *Discipline and Punish*, Foucault began writing what he proposed would be a six-volume history of sexuality. He continued to give lectures at the Collége de France, and one of them on 'governmentality', became extremely influential as well. It seemed to reinstate the power of Foucault to initiate whole areas of study across the social sciences and humanities. But within crime history in the past decade or so, his influence has declined. One of the ways this has become clear is in the emerging history of the crime museum.

The crime museum would seem to be ready-made for Foucault's analysis. A collection of objects for display, significant for their criminological value, categorized according to the criminal sciences. Indeed, some accounts of prison museums do invoke Foucault's concepts. Allie Terry references Foucault in his study of the Bargello, the infamous prison house in Florence. Originally, it served as the residence of the chief magistrate who in the fourteenth century received permission to use torture in the process of justice. During this time, frescoes with religious themes covered walls and ceilings to portray the choice between heaven and hell. The building remained a prison as the years went by, although the authorities covered the frescoes with whitewash and destroyed the instruments of torture. Then in 1858 the building became the National Museum. The new scheme restored the original interiors and imported new artwork into the galleries of the former prison. The criminal bodies within the Bargello were replaced by the elite of society, who came to see a portrait of Dante among other treasures. But Terry insists that despite the change of audience and functions of the site, violence remained part of the encounter. Indeed, the exterior of the building remained as it was. It contains effigies to shame those who transgressed against the authority of the government, such as the figure of a man hung upside down by one foot. In this way, the building brought crime under Foucault's 'collective gaze'.[69]

Michael Welch and Melissa Macuare find a space for Foucault in their mapping of the Argentine Penitentiary Museum in Buenos Aires. As the museum suggests, prisons represented a site where state power is exercised, and the ways in which it was linked with the new science of surveillance, control and discipline is on display. They rely on Foucault, supplemented by Geertz's method of 'thick description', to describe the items in the museum collection, revealing the penal apparatus of modern Argentina. The museum, which opened in 1980, is located in a prison built in 1860. As they see it, the Argentine Penitentiary Museum intends to give visitors an 'official' version of the state's penal history. The museum operates as a 'technical-cultural institution' with the expressed purpose of revealing penitentiary life. Yet although it reveals the construction of a narrative about the birth of the modern Argentine prison, Welch and Macuare insist that it contains more than a single story of reliance on disciplinary and surveillance technologies geared at transforming convicts into workers. It also embodies socio-religious themes, including a narrative of purification.[70]

However, Susanne Regener makes no reference to Foucault in her study of the most famous crime museum of all, the museum built by Cesare Lombroso housed at the Institute for Medical Jurisprudence at Turin. The collection contains display cases and cupboards, boxes, glass containers, wax models and human bones. There are photographs depicting criminals, psychiatric patients and prostitutes; objects made by inmates of prisons and asylums; brains and complete heads suspended in liquid; tools used for crime and photographs of criminals with their tools; plaster masks of fugitives, plaster moulds of ears and hands, preserved slices of tattooed skin, and many skeletons and skulls. Such a bizarre assortment of artefacts, justified by their significance to criminal anthropology, is virtually Foucault's playground. Yet, Regener does not mention his name.[71] Nor does Silvano Montaldo in his account of the Lombroso Museum. The museum, closed at the time of Regener's analysis, reopened in 2009, on the hundredth anniversary of Lombroso's death. Montaldo explains how Lombroso's collection survived over the years and how it became the public museum. The exhibitions aim to present the 'science' of criminal anthropology in the context of the wider social and cultural history of the period.[72]

Carolyn Strange and Michael Kempa have written about Alcatraz and Robben Island, former sites of punishment and incarceration that have become tourist sites. Drawing on policy documents, onsite observations and interviews of staff, they discuss the phenomenon of 'dark tourism'.[73] Laura Huey has written about the Vienna Kriminalmuseum and its strange celebration of the 'sublime in crime'. She describes the displays – poisoning, stabbing, shooting, bludgeoning and strangling – in graphic detail. She examines the rise of such sites as places of leisure and the ostensible purpose of the museum: to offer an alternative account of the history of Vienna and of the development of jurisprudence, police work and forensic investigation. Like Strange and Kempa, and Wilson, Huey's article links to dark tourism. But, aside from a brief mention, she ignores Foucault.[74] Amy Chazkel has put together a special section of *Radical History Review* on police museums in Latin America: the legal Medicine in Cuba and police museums in Argentina and Mexico. The museums represent shrines to policing, gruesome displays of criminal activity and anachronistic cabinets of forensic curiosities. The museums pursue a vision of order, not merely a chronological narrative. Yet again, Foucault is nowhere to be seen.[75]

How can it be that Foucault makes no appearance? Could it be that he has lost his power to shock, amuse, evoke? He has not disappeared from the stage altogether. The fact that these authors do not cite him does not mean that he has had no influence. There is evidence of the Foucault phrasebook in use. Regener mentions the 'scientific discourse and the practice of collecting', the 'power for imparting knowledge' and 'mechanisms for segregation and exclusion'.[76] Wilson has a section entitled 'representing the other' and 'frozen narratives'.[77] Foucault's ideas have become so ubiquitous, so embedded in cultural analysis, that they need not be cited.

At the same time, the authors of recent histories of crime museums declare that Foucault simply does not fit. Jean Comaroff and Joel Comaroff discuss 'criminal obsessions, after Foucault' with reference to the South African police museum in Pretoria. The collection began in the 1960s as a jumble of relics from criminal cases: murder weapons, photographs of mutilated bodies, the effects of a notorious female poisoner. The museum, housed in a building from the 1930s where the national police headquarters had been located, displayed artefacts from cases that ended in convictions. It catalogued the triumph of law and order over the enemies of the state: apprehension of spectacular criminals and protection of the 'national security' against the threat of terrorism. But this was the same building where the infamous national security service had made interrogations; the museum exhibits were below the interrogation facility. By the 1990s, in post-Apartheid South Africa, such a building had become abhorrent. Some efforts were made to add fresh exhibits to the museum, adding the possibility of different readings of history. But it was not enough. The museum, under the jurisdiction of an ANC-administered Ministry of Safety and Security, became the space of contest and argument as never before, and closed because of its own contradictions. The Comaroffs observe that far from a desire to make power invisible and subtle, the police museum condensed power in order to make it visible, tangible, accountable. 'What we have here, in other words, is an *inversion* of the history laid out by Foucault in *Discipline and Punish*, according to which, famously, the theatricality of premodern power gives way to ever more implicit, internalized, capillary kinds of discipline.'[78]

Alejandra Bronfman sets aside Foucault as well. Foucault had used the example of the taxonomy of animals (allegedly taken from a Chinese encyclopaedia) to argue for what he called the grid of 'identities, similitudes and analogies'. Foucault rooted his argument in a spatial metaphor. The grid arranges the categories and therefore, by their proximity, represents a site where meaning is derived from the intersection of language and space. Bronfman emphasizes that the diverse items at the Museum of Legal

Medicine at the University of Havana fit awkwardly together. There is no unifying logic. Some, such as tattooed mulatto skin, are the efforts of criminological science to grasp criminality. Others, such as a flying donkey built from bread crumbs by a prisoner, suggest a chamber-of-horrors approach intended to reveal tangible products of the criminal mind. Bronfman acknowledges the relevance of Foucault's grid of categories and conceptual map, but such collections mix the grotesque, banal and sinister, with no hidden logic of power. The collections represent cultural spaces where coherence falls apart.[79] The material culture of criminality is not displayed with a clear narrative, whether triumph of police or success of criminological science, but the opposite: the failure to contain, the inability to categorize and catalogue.

Jacqueline Z. Wilson has nothing to say about Foucault, except that he was wrong. In *Prison: Cultural Memory and Dark Tourism* (2008), she refers to her study of decommissioned prisons in Australia converted into tourist sites. Australians have a special relationship with prisons – 'the country having been founded as a jail' – especially where prison history involves convicts. She recovers the lost narratives, those of the inmates 'othered' by society at the time but also by public history since then. The narratives challenge the 'established' view, as dominated by the voices of custodial staff, policymakers and media based on interviews with tourists, curators, managers and former prison staff, and anthropological reading of the site, including physical sources of architecture and graffiti. Foucault, Wilson explains, is the primary culprit for spreading the myth that Bentham's panopticon was central to Britain's penal philosophy. The Home Office never put Bentham's design into practice in Britain, nor anywhere in the empire, and especially not in Australia. His theory of the 'surveillance society' has some resonance with diffusion of closed-circuit television in modern society, but the 'theory's translation to English, and its consequent implied applicability to the British correctional paradigm, tends to be historically misleading'.[80]

Conclusion

Foucault broke into crime history with an imaginative history of the prison. His style of presentation, the examples he used and his scepticism about the purpose of punishment attracted wide interest. He established the prison as an intellectually serious topic for historical study, and even if this was all he did, it would have been a significant contribution. But Foucault's project was much larger than writing prison history.

Foucault brought post-structuralism to crime history. He reinvigorated conversations among historians about historical evidence, the role of theory in understanding the past, and the use of history in the present. He shifted the frame of reference away from cities, economic changes and topics in social science, towards literary theory and cultural studies. The idea that the architectural drawings for a prison that was never built revealed the mental structures of western civilization continues to intrigue and inspire. But what was radical has now become mainstream. The words 'discourse' and 'discursive' appear so often in histories of crime, they hardly need a reference to Foucault. It is easy to collect a few literary sources from the past and pronounce them a 'discourse' to justify their selection and significance. Too easy, it seems, because numerous articles pressed from this mould are published year after year.

Nevertheless, the linguistic aspect remains important. The cultural aspect, too. It is hard to imagine the array of topics now seen as crime history without Foucault's influence. But the most lasting legacy of Foucault has been the importance attached to theory. He organized history not around sources of evidence, the sequence of events or wider aspects of society, but around concepts that contributed in some way to a larger intellectual whole. Foucault made historical research secondary to the theoretical explanation in the writing of crime history, and he established a standard of measurement. As measured against Foucault, leading historians deal with the ideas and second-raters worry about the details.

Notes

1 Thomas Flynn, 'Foucault's mapping of history', in Gary Gutting, ed., *The Cambridge Companion to Foucault* (Cambridge: Cambridge University Press, 2005), 29, 29–48.

2 Norbert Finzsch, '"Comparing apples and oranges?" The history of early prisons in Germany and the United States', in Norbert Finzsch and Robert Jutte, eds, *Institutions of Confinement: Hospitals, Asylums and Prisons in Western Europe and North America 1500-1950* (Cambridge: Cambridge University Press, 1996), 213–33.

3 Patrick H. Hutton, 'The Foucault phenomenon and contemporary French historiography', *Historical Reflections/Reflexions Historiques* 17 (1991): 77–102.

4 Michel Foucault, *Discipline and Punish: The Birth of the Prison* (Vintage: New York, 1979); originally, *Suveillier et Punir: Naissance de la prison* (Paris, 1975).

5 Gérard Noiriel, 'Foucault and history: The lessons of a disillusion', *Journal of Modern History* 66 (1994): 548–9.

6 Eric H. Monkkonen, 'The dangers of synthesis', *American Historical Review* 91 (1986): 1153.

7 Monkkonen, 'The dangers of synthesis', 1154.

8 Peter Burke, *Critical Essays on Michel Foucault* (Cambridge: Scholars Press, 1992), 8.

9 Michael Ignatieff, 'State, civil society and total institutions: A critique of recent social histories of punishment', in Stanley Cohen and Andrew Scull,

eds, *Social Control and the State: Historical and Comparative Essays* (Oxford: Robertson, 1983); Robert P. Weiss, 'Humanitarianism, labour exploitation, or social control? A critical survey of theory and research on the origin and development of prisons', *Social History* 12 (1987): 331–50.

10　David Rothman, 'Social control: The use and abuses of the concept in the history of incarceration', *Rice University Studies* 67 (1981): 9–20.

11　David Garland, 'Foucault's *Discipline and Punish*: An exposition and critique', *American Bar Foundation Research Journal* 11 (1986): 847.

12　Ricardo Salvatore, 'Criminology, prison reform, and the Buenos Aires working class', *Journal of Interdisciplinary History* 23 (1992): 279–99.

13　Michael Donnelly, 'Foucault's geneaology of the human sciences', *Economy and Society* 11 (1982): 363–80 (378).

14　Pieter Spierenburg, *The Spectacle of Suffering: Executions and the Evolution of Repression* (Cambridge: Cambridge University Press, 1984); Pieter Spierenburg, 'Punishment, power and history', *Social Science History* 28 (2004): 607–36.

15　Pieter Spierenburg, 'From Amsterdam to Auburn: An explanation for the rise of the prison in seventeenth-century Holland and nineteenth-century America', *Journal of Social History* 20 (1980): 441.

16　Robert A. Nye, 'Crime in modern societies: Some research strategies for historians', *Journal of Social History* 11 (1978): 491–507.

17　Nye, 'Crime in modern societies', 5.

18　Richard J. Evans, *Rituals of Retribution: Capital Punishment in Germany 1600-1987* (Oxford: Oxford University Press, 1996).

19　Evans, *Rituals of Retribution*, 880–1.

20　Martin Dinges, 'Michel Foucault's impact on German historiography of criminal justice, social discipline, and medicalization', in Norbert Finzsch and Robert Jutte, eds, *Institutions of Confinement: Hospitals, Asylums and Prisons in Western Europe and North America, 1500-1950* (Cambridge: Cambridge University Press, 1996), 162, 155–74.

21　Michael Meranze, *Laboratories of Virtue: Punishment, Revolution and Authority in Philadelphia, 1760-1835* (Chapel Hill: University of North Carolina Press, 1996).

22　Meranze, *Laboratories of Virtue*, 4.

23　Meranze, *Laboratories of Virtue*, 14.

24　Pieter Spierenburg, 'Punishment, power, and history', *Social Science History* 28 (2004): 607–36.

25　Mary Gibson, 'Global perspectives on the birth of the prison', *American Historical Review* 116 (2011): 1040–63.

26　Gibson, 'Global perspectives', 1041.

27　Taylor C. Sherman, 'Tensions of colonial punishment: Perspectives on recent developments in the study of coercive networks in Asia, Africa and the Caribbean', *History Compass* 7 (2009): 659–77.

28 Sherman, 'Tensions in colonial punishment', 665.

29 Sherman, 'Tensions in colonial punishment', 668–9.

30 Thomas Flynn, 'Foucault's mapping of history', in Gary Gutting, ed., *The Cambridge Companion to Foucault* (Cambridge: Cambridge University Press, 2005), 29–48, 33–7.

31 Clare O'Farrell, 'Michel Foucault: The unconsciousness of history and culture', in Nancy Partner and Sarah Foot, eds, *The Sage Handbook of Historical Theory* (London: Sage, 2013), 165, 162–82.

32 Michel Foucault, *The Order of Things: An Archaeology of the Human Sciences* (London: Tavistock, 1970); originally, *Les Mots et les choses* (Paris, 1966).

33 Michel Foucault, *The Archaeology of Knowledge* (London: Tavistock, 1972); originally, *L'Archéologie du savoir* (Paris, 1969).

34 Michel Foucault, *I, Pierre Rivière, Having Slaughtered My Mother, My Sister, and My Brother ...* (New York: Random House, 1975).

35 Patricia O'Brien, 'Crime and punishment as a historical problem', *Journal of Social History* 11 (1978): 508–20 (514–15).

36 Gareth Steadman Jones, 'The determinist fix: Some obstacles to the further development of the linguistic approach to history in the 1990s', *History Workshop Journal* 42 (1996): 19–35.

37 Steadman Jones, 'The determinist fix', 25.

38 Robert Castel, '"Problematization" as a mode of reading history', in Jan Goldstein, ed., *Foucault and the Writing of History* (Oxford: Blackwell, 1994), 237, 237–52.

39 Herman Mannheim, *Pioneers in Criminology* (London: Stevens and Sons, 1960).

40 Robert Nye, 'Heredity or Milieu: The foundations of modern European criminological theory', *Isis* 67 (1976): 334–55.

41 David Garland, *Punishment and Welfare: A History of Penal Strategies* (Aldershot: Gower, 1985).

42 Garland, *Punishment and Welfare*, 261.

43 Piers Beirne, *Inventing Criminology: Essays on the Rise of 'Homo Criminalis'* (Albany: State University of New York Press, 1993), 3.

44 Beirne, *Inventing Criminology*, 68.

45 Richard F. Wetzell, *Inventing the Criminal: A History of German Criminology, 1880-1945* (Chapel Hill: University of North Carolina Press, 2000), 2.

46 Peter Becker and Richard F. Wetzell, eds, *Criminals and Their Scientists: The History of Criminology in International Perspective* (Cambridge: Cambridge University Press, 2006), 4.

47 Peter Becker, 'The criminologists' gaze at the underworld: Toward an archaeology of criminological writing', in Becker and Wetzell, *Criminals and Their Scientists*, 106.

48 Daniel Mark Vyleta, 'Was early twentieth-century criminology a science of the "Other"? A re-evaluation of Austro-German criminological debates', *Cultural and Social History* 3 (2006): 406–23.

49   Patrick H. Hutton, 'A history of mentalities: The new map of cultural history',
     History and Theory 20 (1981): 252.

50   Patricia O'Brien, 'Michel Foucault's history of culture', in Lynn Hunt, ed.,
     The New Cultural History (Berkeley: University of California Press, 1989), 27,
     25–46.

51   O'Brien, 'Michel Foucault's history', 35.

52   Richard Evans, *In Defence of History* (London: Granta, 1997).

53   Judith Walkowitz, *City of Dreadful Delight: Narratives of Sexual Danger in
     Late-Victorian London* (Chicago: University of Chicago Press, 1992), 83.

54   Walkowitz, *City of Dreadful Delight*.

55   Marie-Christine Leps, *Apprehending the Criminal: The Productive of Deviance
     in Nineteenth Century Discourse* (Durham, NC: Duke University Press, 1992).

56   Claire Anderson, *Legible Bodies: Race, Criminality and Colonisation in South
     Asia* (Oxford: Berg, 2004).

57   Claire Anderson, 'Fashioning identities: Convict dress in colonial south and
     southeast Asia', *History Workshop Journal* 52 (2001): 153–74.

58   Todd Herzog, *Crime Stories: Criminalistic Fantasy and the Culture of Crisis in
     Weimar Germany* (New York: Berghan Books, 2009).

59   Herzog, *Crime Stories*, 5–8, 37.

60   Mary Gibson, 'Science and narrative in Italian criminology, 1880-1920',
     in Amy Srebnick and René Lévy, eds, *Crime and Culture: An Historical
     Perspective* (Ashgate: Aldershot, 2005), 37–47.

61   David G. Horn, *The Criminal Body: Lombroso and the Anatomy of Deviance*
     (London: Routledge, 2003), 1.

62   Hutton, 'A history of mentalities', 248.

63   David Nash and Anne-Marie Kilday, *Cultures of Shame: Exploring Crime and
     Morality in Britain 1600-1900* (London: Palgrave, 2010), 15.

64   Muir and Ruggiero, *Microhistory and the Lost*, viii.

65   Anna Davin, 'Morelli, Freud, and Sherlock Holmes: Clues and the scientific
     method', *History Workshop Journal* 9 (1980): 5–36.

66   Edward Muir and Guido Ruggiero, eds, *History from Crime* (Baltimore, MD:
     Johns Hopkins University Press, 1994).

67   Muir and Ruggiero, *Microhistory and the Lost*, xiii.

68   Daniel Maier-Katkin, 'On Sir Leon Radzinowicz Michel Foucault: Authority,
     morality and the history of criminal law at the juncture of the modern and
     postmodern', *Punishment and Society* 5 (2003): 155–77.

69   Allie Terry, 'Criminals and tourists: Prison history and museum Politics at the
     Bargello in Florence', *Art History* 33 (2010): 836–55.

70   Michael Welch and Melissa Macuare, 'Penal tourism in Argentina: Bridging
     Foucauldian and neo-Durkheimian perspectives', *Theoretical Criminology* 15
     (2011): 401–25.

71   Susan Regener, 'Criminological Museums and the visualization of Evil', *Crime,
     History and Societies* 7 (2003): 2–13.

72 Silvano Montaldo, 'The Lombroso Museum from its Origins to the present day', in Paul Knepper and P. J. Ystehede, eds, *The Cesare Lombroso Handbook* (London: Routledge, 2013), 98–112.

73 Carolyn Strange and Michael Kempa, 'Shades of dark tourism: Alcatraz and Robben Island', *Annals of Tourism Research* 30 (2003): 386–405.

74 Laura Huey, 'Crime behind the glass: Exploring the sublime in crime and the Vienna Kriminalmuseum', *Theoretical Criminology* 15 (2011): 381–99.

75 Amy Chazkel, 'Police Museums in Latin America', *Radical History Review* 113 (2012): 127–33.

76 Regener, 'Criminological Museums', 2.

77 Wilson, 'Australian prison tourism', 566.

78 Jean Comaroff and John Comaroff, 'Criminal obsessions, after Foucault: Postcoloniality, policing, and the metaphysics of disorder', *Critical Inquiry* 30 (2004): 800–24 (804).

79 Alejandra Bronfman, 'The fantastic flying Donkey and the Tattoo', *Radical History Review* 113 (2012): 134–42.

80 Jacqueline Z. Wilson, *Prison: Cultural Memory and Dark Tourism* (New York: Peter Lang, 2008), 37.

Further reading

Brown, Mark. *Penal Power and Colonial Rule*. London: Routledge, 2014.

Dodsworth, F. M. 'The idea of police in eighteenth-century England: Discipline, reformation, superintendence, c. 1780-1800'. *Journal of the History of Ideas* 69 (2008): 583–604.

Evans, Robin. *The Fabrication of Virtue: English Prison Architecture 1750-1840*. Cambridge: Cambridge University Press, 1982.

Garland, David. *Punishment and Welfare: A History of Penal Strategies*. Aldershot: Gower, 1985.

Garland, David. 'What is a "history of the present?" On Foucault's genealogies and their critical preconditions'. *Punishment and Society* 16 (2014): 365–84.

McMullan, John L. 'The arresting eye: Discourse, surveillance and disciplinary administration in early English police thinking'. *Social & Legal Studies* 7 (1998): 97–128.

Meranze, Michael. 'Michel Foucault, the death penalty and the crisis of historical understanding'. *Historical Reflections* 29 (2003): 191–209.

Simon, Jonathon. *Governing Through Crime: How the War on Crime Transformed American Democracy and Created a Culture of Fear*. New York: Oxford University Press, 2007.

Walkowitz, Judith R. *City of Dreadful Delight: Narratives of Sexual Danger in Late-Victorian London*. Chicago: University of Chicago Press, 1992.

Ward, Tony. 'An honourable regime of truth? Foucault, psychiatry and English criminal justice', in Helen Johnston, ed., *Punishment and Control in Historical Perspective*. London: Palgrave Macmillan, 2008, 56–74.

CHAPTER SEVEN

Women, gender and crime

Quite a lot has been written about the history of women and crime, and all of it within the past few decades. The 'new social history' put crime on the map. But, the leading historical figures – the British Marxists, Foucault, the *Annalistes* – neglected to mark the position for women. Instead, the task was done by others. Historical writing about women, gender and crime developed rapidly as crime historians read the emerging women's history, and feminist historians took an interest in crime, police and prisons.

Women's history took off in the wake of the feminist movement of the 1960s. At first, there was an effort to include women in discussions which had previously involved only men. As the field of women's history expanded, conversations began about whether to focus on women or gender, about the importance of gender compared to class and ethnicity, and whether gender included masculinity. The post-structural movement led to further expansion with renewed discussions about appropriate methodologies and theoretical frameworks. Each new area brought work on women and crime. The results have not only built up women's history by adding topics that had gone unnoticed, but have changed the way the history of crime in general has been written. Writing the history of women and crime introduced new subjects of study, revised interpretative frameworks and provoked questions about research methods.

In this chapter, we will examine how women became a topic of crime history, and how writing the history of women and crime changed with each development in women's history in general. Part 1 reviews statistical studies of female criminality and specifically the debate initiated by Malcolm Feeley and Deborah Little about the 'vanishing female'. Part 2 looks into the influence of feminism and the search for role models among the first women in criminal justice professions. This includes work by Estelle Freedman, Philippa Levine and Louise Jackson. Part 3 discusses the significance of gender as a topic of history with reference to work by Patricia O'Brien,

Nicole Rafter and Lucia Zedner. Part 4 introduces masculinity as a topic of analysis with reference to Martin Wiener's work and the reactions to it. Part 5 considers several examples of the new cultural history of women, specifically, studies of female murderers.

Measuring female criminality

In the 1970s, historians published studies of female criminality using court records. Curiously, the initial frame of reference was not feminism, but criminology. These historians compared women to men, and they consulted British and American criminologists to interpret what they found. But this changed as feminists joined the discussion.

Barbara Hanawalt examined women criminals in the late medieval period. Using circuit court records for several counties, coroners' rolls, and records of two manorial courts, she investigated the amount of, motivation for, and types of, criminality for women and men. Such a study, she explained, afforded valuable information on one aspect of women's lives in medieval society, and was 'helpful in giving historical perspective to modern criminal statistics'.[1] Women did not limit themselves to crimes such as larceny and counterfeiting which required more cunning than physical strength. Half of the felonies women committed involved violence to persons and property. Receiving was the only crime which seemed a female offence, partly because of a familial duty to receive family members, although their motivation for other crimes covered the same range as men. Women differed somewhat in what they stole; men and women tended to steal livestock, although women displayed more of an inclination to take household goods, clothing and foodstuffs.[2]

John Beattie studied indictments in Surrey from 1663 to 1802.[3] He found that women participated in the same range of crimes as men – property offences being the most common for men and women – but the numbers involved were 'markedly different'. Men outnumbered women in all categories, especially in property offences and personal violence. 'A strikingly lower level of criminality of women is clearly apparent.'[4] For women more than men, it was theft and related offences that most often brought them into trouble with the law. The explanation for the overall pattern of women's criminality, he proposed, had less to do with biological and emotional factors than social realities, relationships between women and men, and in general, the place of women in society.[5] Beattie affirmed these conclusions in his book, *Crime and the Courts in England 1660-1800*, published in 1986, and by this time, a debate about the interpretation of female crime statistics began to brew.[6]

Gayle Rowe looked at women and crime in late-eighteenth-century Pennsylvania. He gathered statistics concerning criminal allegations against women from 1763 to 1790 using legal records for a dozen counties. The time frame allowed for examining the impact of the revolution. Rowe found that a smaller portion of the cases coming before the courts were against women compared to what Beattie reported for England, and this was particularly true for property crimes. He found a case of one woman who had appeared before the courts several times and gained the reputation for being 'a Notorious Thief'. Most of the other women who came to court did not have such a lengthy criminal career and committed crimes, such as assault, that seemed much more impromptu and temporary. Rowe acknowledged that crime statistics do reflect women's behaviour; he had more confidence that changes in the statistics revealed priorities, assumptions and capacities of court personnel. Rowe found that judicial authorities chose not to prosecute cases such as fornication, adultery and bastardy, choosing instead to view these as family matters. After the war, authorities choose to pursue women's property crimes less diligently and to concentrate on punishing men for offences associated with the revolution.[7]

Natalie Hull brought a similar approach to Massachusetts.[8] The ledgers of the superior court from 1673 to 1774 revealed that women were charged with a variety of serious crimes, including assaults, burglary and homicides. The pattern was different from what Beattie described, but the explanation is consistent with his conclusions about women and crime. Compared to men, who were most often charged with crimes against property, women came to court for crimes against persons. However, women committed fewer crimes than men. Despite being assigned to an inferior social status, they obeyed the law. Women did not resort to subterfuge or violence to express contempt. The fact that homicide was the most frequent charge made against women who came to court for a felony reflected the limited social sphere in which women lived their lives. It is the exception that proves the rule. Broader economic opportunities did not exist, so women rarely got the chance to commit property crimes. Women were largely confined to the home, so the only crimes they could commit generally concerned domestic relationships. Most of the victims of women murderers were their own children.[9]

Then, Malcolm Feeley and Deborah Little set the kettle to boil with the publication of their work on 'the vanishing female'. Using records from the Old Bailey between 1687 and 1912, they looked at serious felonies ranging from larceny to murder.[10] They observed a trend in the figures that suggested an overall decline in the criminality of women. In the eighteenth century, a high proportion of women appeared in the court, followed by a falling off over the next 150 years to the twentieth-century level. The 'central mystery ...', they propose, 'is the marked decrease in women's criminal involvement that appears to have taken place over the course of the eighteenth and early nineteenth centuries'.[11] The case of the 'vanishing female' challenges the conclusion that criminal activity *has always been* a male phenomenon. Feeley and Little thought about the reasons for this decline. After ruling out changes in court jurisdiction, demographic shifts, the impact of women's offences, and women as accomplices of men, they concluded that it was best explained by a combination of changes in the economy, sexual relations within the family, roles of men and women in society and cultural values. Wide-scale social changes from the 1700s to the 1900s led 'toward a greater range of social controls that restricted women to domestic life' and that 'provided some protections for women against economic uncertainties of life in London'.[12]

Robert Shoemaker found the empirical situation Feeley and Little uncovered believable. He agreed that 'the proportion of defendants accused of serious crime who were female declined dramatically over the course of this period'.[13] In the first half of the eighteenth century, women accounted for 35 per cent of felony indictments at the Old Bailey. The proportion fell steadily during the nineteenth century, so that by 1850, 15 per cent of those accused were women. But he advised caution. The vanishing female amounted to 'a hypothesis' that requires more tests before it can be accepted. The decline likely had less to do with changes in women's behaviour and more to do with changing methods of prosecution than Feeley and Little believed. The statistics 'demonstrate unquestionably' that attitudes towards female criminality changed significantly over this period. 'What is impossible to say', Shoemaker emphasizes, 'is whether patterns of male and female crime actually changed, or whether changing conceptions of proper public behaviour for men and women simply led to a redefinition of crime, which increasingly meant property crime, as a quintessentially male activity.'[14]

Feeley has continued to believe that what he saw in London was real: females vanished over time. In the seventeenth century and eighteenth century, women accounted for 30–50 per cent of criminal cases, and in the late nineteenth century and twentieth century, this dropped to 5–15 per cent. To fortify his argument, he has marshalled evidence from other cities. Trends in crime for Amsterdam, Ghent and Toronto also registered a decline in women's involvement. The vanishing female pattern appears to hold true for minor and serious offences but not for violent offences. It also appears that women's crime was higher in cities than in small, rural communities. But, Feeley argues, by concentrating on local conditions, historians have missed cross-national patterns. He returned to social, economic and cultural changes for his explanation. A relaxing of 'patriarchal controls' accounts for the decrease relative to women's greater involvement in crime in the seventeenth century.[15]

But, drawing on various data sets from English and Welsh counties from 1750 to 1850, Peter King raised new suspicions. As he pointed out, given that the Old Bailey dealt almost exclusively with felony cases, the vanishing female argument distils down to a claim about indictable crimes only. He did not see the same pattern outside London. The proportion of female offenders among indictments in Essex from 1740 to 1847 did not reveal a decrease. There are some fluctuations, reflecting the number of men tried during times of war and peace, but there was no discernible long-term decline. Further, statistical information from Berkshire, Somerset,

Cornwall and Gloucestershire revealed a common pattern: very little long-term change from 1750 to 1850 in the proportion of indictable offenders who were female.[16] King has also pointed to jurisdictional changes at the Old Bailey. Feeley and Little were aware of this, but discounted it in their explanation. King maintains that the unreliability of indictments as a measure of crime prevents any straightforward model of long-term change in levels of female involvement in recorded crime. There was an exceptional period around 1700, when the proportion of those indicted for theft at the Old Bailey reflected a high involvement of women. And, only by taking this moment as the starting point of a trend does the proportion of women seem to decline. From 1750 to 1850, and almost certainly from 1650 to 1750, the proportion of female offenders found among those indicted varied only slightly. 'On closer inspection therefore', King concludes, 'the vanishing female offender vanishes.'[17]

Feeley acknowledged King's 'rigorous examination' of the data. King had good reasons for his reservations about the 'broad pattern' and 'local explanations' for the London trend. Still, Feeley believes there to have been a decline of female criminals after 1800. He referred King to the data from England, the Netherlands, France and Sweden showing that the trend since 1800 holds across Europe. (Feeley might also have mentioned Russia where figures are available from the early nineteenth century.)[18] Feeley has affirmed his explanation. The vanishing female resulted from a broad social transformation from public to private patriarchy that occurred in domains of both work and family. But, the important point, Feely insisted, remains: historical studies of women and crime refute the assumption that crime has always been a male phenomenon. Women were present in courts as criminal defendants in larger numbers in the pre-industrial era. No longer is this the case in the modern era.[19]

Feeley emphasized the significance of the vanishing female argument for criminology. Theories of female crime had been based on the assumption that crime was overwhelmingly a male activity. The realization that women's lower involvement in crime was in historic terms a recent phenomenon would mean a shift in theories away from conceptions of the female mind or female body and towards theories of political, economic and social factors. Alternatively, the founders of women's history saw themselves engaged in a political effort to challenge the authority of the academic profession of history and to change the way history was written. An important aim of feminist history was to pursue women in the past *on their own terms*, wherever this might lead.[20] Feminist historians wanted to avoid re-creating a masculine world with women added in. They challenged historians' assumptions about the past, such as periodization, as well as methods and interpretation evidence. The kettle was about to boil over.

Garthine Walker and Jenny Kermode doubted whether quantification is the right way to study women and crime in history. The image of the law-abiding woman in history was an artefact of the way the history of crime had been researched. The methodological and conceptual frameworks have been calibrated for men although these settings remain unacknowledged. 'Prevalent methodologies of historians of crime', Walker and Kermode said, 'have restricted rather than facilitated our understanding of female criminality in the past.'[21] In aggregating data and analysing patterns, historians have categorized criminal activity in a way that discounts women. Walker analysed records of quarter and assize courts for Cheshire in England. Counting those prosecuted by recognizance, as an alternative to formal indictment, revealed greater numbers of women as complainants and defendants. It was also necessary to go beyond counting of offences for men and women, to consider narrative sources. These revealed the importance of the social context in which women committed crimes. The social networks in which women participated, such as the household, characterized the choice of items to steal.

Few of the defendants in Cheshire county courts were women, but looking closely at these records, Walker found an identifiable pattern among women charged with theft. Women participated in burglaries and housebreakings, and they tended to work with other women rather than men. The women did not necessarily steal goods of lesser value than men, but there was a difference in what women took. While clothes and household linens were the most common targets for men and women, women had a far greater propensity to steal these items. Female targets included cooking utensils, cloth, wool and yarns because they knew the value of such things in the day-to-day activities of households. Preference for household items did not reflect a lack of courage or initiative, but restricted opportunity, as they were excluded from paid, skilled work of guilds. Women controlled the distribution of stolen clothes, linens and household goods; stealing, receiving, disposing, searching and trading information was 'women's work'. Recognizing the participation of women in various social networks of exchange, and unravelling the gendered organization of them, is key to the pattern of women's participation in crime.[22]

Walker's point has been developed further. Peter King has observed that historical analyses based on 'counting and comparing indictments' are 'extremely limiting'.[23] They reveal nothing about the characteristics of the offender, the relationship between the victim and the offender, or the context in which the victimization occurred. He combined information from the Old Bailey Session Papers with the Newgate Calendars, the lists of London prisoners awaiting trial at the Old Bailey. They provide more information, including information about the backgrounds, family circumstances, etc. King offered a 'much more deeply contextualized account' of female offenders in late-eighteenth-century London to explain why women were more vulnerable to prosecution for theft at certain points in their lives. In the late eighteenth century, the vulnerability of women in London to prosecution for property crime was closely related to their changing work experiences and the life cycle. To grasp women's criminality, it is important to see it within the context of migration, marriage, childrearing and work opportunities for women.[24]

Jennine Hurl-Eamon studied petty violence committed by women in London from 1680 to 1720. By 'petty violence', she means 'acts of aggression – physical or verbal – that were viewed by their contemporaries as relatively minor, but nonetheless unacceptable'.[25] To find this, she looked at court records for the Westminster Quarter Sessions, specifically, all recognizances in which the word *assault* was used. The recognizances are found in small slips of parchment, numbered and bound with the court rolls of the quarter sessions. While seldom used by historians, this method of prosecution was popular in eighteenth-century London. She found that women did resort to physical aggression in many situations, and in this way, women contributed to the banality of violence in early modern London. Fewer women, compared to men, engaged in violent acts against the state. When they did, it was in response to neighbourhood tensions and smaller community concerns rather than for broader political reasons. Women came to court for inciting crowds to riot.

The search for role models

The first kinds of history to emerge out of the women's movement have been characterized as 'compensatory history' or 'contribution history'. Essentially, these histories kept the same questions from traditional history and tried to fit women's past into the blanks on the form left by the exclusive focus on men.[26] Political, diplomatic and military history made no space for women, and women's history went about recovering the women who had been left out. These were women who were worth remembering because they had made a contribution to the major events otherwise credited to men. The history of female criminals found its place in this context.

'In the new field of women's history', Mary S. Hartman exclaimed in 1974, 'the study of crime offers some intriguing possibilities.'[27] She explored 'domestic crime' among middle-class women, the counterpart she suggested to 'white collar crime'. Information about middle-class perpetrators was not to be found in crime statistics, so she turned to legal journals, literary reviews, diaries and other narrative sources for French and English women from 1830 to 1880. She theorized that female criminality for this population was linked to moments of crisis or stress in women's lives during the nineteenth century. Hartman developed her study into a book about murder by 'respectable women' in France and England during the nineteenth century.[28] She found thirteen women notorious in the Victorian era for committing murder. They included wives and daughters of industrialists, professional men and shopkeepers. They killed husbands, lovers, siblings and children; they used suffocation, blows, guns, knives and poison. These women were not heroines, yet by their actions achieved a place in women's history.

Murderesses were scarce, and without knowing something of the total number of women who came to trial, it is impossible to say exactly how atypical they were. But they were not atypical in the sense that the problems and tensions their trials brought to light were common to a large number of households. They were, as Hartman puts it, 'ordinary women who found extreme solutions to ordinary problems'.[29] Using newspaper accounts of trial proceedings, she examined the motives of the women in their social context and commented on a pattern of alleged crimes. She concluded that the circumstances which led respectable women to contemplate murder did shift during the period. This was a process of modernization in which women carved out greater autonomy, taking advantage of increased incomes to improve their lives, in a context shaped by a code of manners which 'defined the proper young woman as a frail but appealing, intellectually inferior but morally superior being'.[30]

Feminism encouraged historians to look for the origins of women's oppression and to document various forms of resistance to it. Criminal women challenged the stereotypes of passive, frail, subservient women dependent on men. The point of these histories was to show that women were not the silent victims of patriarchy, but spirited, rebellious and stubborn characters. It showed notorious women who refused to accept the place prepared for them in a male-defined society. The women transported to Australia have been particularly useful from this perspective. Kerry Wimshurst wrote about girls in reformatory schools in the late nineteenth century, during a time when the female reformatory system in Australia was repressive and punitive. Women suffered excessive drudgery and repression not only because they were 'bad' but because they were female. They were meant to receive 'domestic training' to teach them how to be virtuous wives and mothers, although essentially this meant mountains of laundry work. The girls earned a reputation for being the most rebellious and incorrigible element within the female reformatory population. The case files revealed riotous behaviour, absconding and property damage. Through these disturbing and unsettling activities, they waged a persistent campaign of resistance to 'state moral coercion' that was more consistent and imaginative than anything the boys came up with.[31]

Kay Daniels recalled the rebelliousness of women in the female factories of Tasmania (Van Diemen's Land).[32] Although convict women have been portrayed as disobedient, rather than rebellious, they did engage in riot and other displays of mass disobedience. In one such incident in 1833, women at the female factory at Hobart greeted a visit of the governor's wife by baring their bottoms en masse. There were reports of a 'flash mob' of women who had money, rings and other jewellery, and served as the ringleaders of women's society within the prison. Daniels describes an internal subculture within the female factories in which the women recreated and mocked elements of the dominant male culture of society outside. Intrinsic to this subculture was an internal economy of 'trafficking' which undermined the official authority and entrenched power of its leaders. 'Far from being the passive victims of the system ... women reshaped the prison environment to their own needs and interests.'[33]

Heather Shore and Diedre Palk portray women before the courts as clever defendants that gave the authorities a considerable challenge. Shore looks at two women in London who, beginning in the 1720s, 'played the justice system' for years. Mary Harvey and Isabella Eaton, both keepers of taverns, were well known to the authorities. They appeared in court for various offences including theft, perjury, abusing a constable and keeping a disorderly house. Despite numerous trials, and considerable efforts by several powerful justices to snare them, they avoided conviction. Shore concludes that in the 'unusual case', women took 'advantage of the flexibility and discretion inherent in the early eighteenth-century system'.[34] Palk has looked at female forgers. The introduction of paper currency took place in the early nineteenth century when war with France had prompted the Bank of England to prefer payment in paper notes rather than gold. The appearance of low-value paper notes created a temptation for criminal enterprise that some found hard to resist. Men and women were prosecuted for offences and sent to prison, ultimately bound for the colonies. But while waiting in Newgate, sometimes for months, for passage to Australia, they wrote letters for relief and other favours. Most of these letter writers were women, and many were successful in portraying themselves as 'fit objects for mercy'. Women in particular knew the rules of the charitable system and the sort of rhetoric that would appeal to male prosecutors.[35]

John Carter Wood examined the case of Beatrice Pace who was tried in 1928 for the murder of her husband, Harry. Beatrice and Harry lived in a cottage near Fetter Hill in Gloucestershire. When he died after an illness, his family made accusations, leading to an inquest. Scotland Yard reported the cause of death to be arsenic poisoning and charged Beatrice with wilful murder. During the trial, the public learnt of Harry's abuse and came to sympathize with Beatrice. She was acquitted and went on to write her memoirs, having gained a reputation as 'the most remarkable woman in England'. Through a thorough search of records, including witness statements, police reports and Beatrice's letters from prison, as well as local and national press coverage, Carter Wood shows how the public came to view her as a martyr, although details of her private life suggest a woman considerably different from this image.[36]

The feminist ideas that inspired historians to find rebels and rioters among women criminals also generated interest in women who wanted to save them. Feminist historians looked back to the leaders of the women's movement, to suffragists who campaigned for equality, to reformers who improved lives of women and to founders of institutions established to meet women's needs. This was a search for models for use in the present, for women of the past who could show the way forward. Or as Estelle B. Freedman put it, studying the women's movement of the late nineteenth and early twentieth centuries could generate knowledge of 'female institution building'. Examining feminist leaders, including Jane Adams in Chicago, Katherine Bement Davis in New York, and Julia Lathrop in Washington DC, she advocated a 'strategy of creating a strong, public, female sphere'.[37]

In *Their Sisters' Keepers* (1981), Freedman considered the founding of reformatories for women in the United States in the late nineteenth century. In Indiana, New York and Massachusetts, women established prison regimes guided by feminine ideals and staffed by women. The movement to aid female prisoners had roots in the decades before the Civil War, in the separation between domestic and public work. Women reformers held a view of women's separate nature, which limited their own power and stifled the inmates they sought to aid. As Freedman explained, women's prison reform had a complicated relationship to feminism. She explores the eccentricities of reformers like Eliza Farnham: feminist, atheist, phrenologist and matron at New York's Sing Sing penitentiary. These women had important insights. They identified sexual inequalities and spoke against them. But rarely did they become activists for women's rights. Rather, they wanted to improve the institutions that confined women and became keepers of their own institutions.[38]

Annemieke van Drenth and Francisca de Haan studied the lives of two nineteenth-century feminist icons: Elizabeth Fry and Josephine Butler. The lives of Fry and Butler are significant because they embody the ideal of care in Western culture, which is connoted as feminine. During the nineteenth century, women began to feel responsible for their own sex and developed a sense of gender identity. This, in turn, led to female organizations and the beginning of the women's movement. Elizabeth Fry improved conditions of imprisoned women in England, and Josephine Butler campaigned for repeal of the Contagious Diseases Act in the Netherlands. Van Drenth and de Haan pursue the themes of power, religion and gender in promotion of 'caring power', a term inspired by Foucault's 'pastoral power'. They see caring power as a new humanitarian sensibility that merged with Protestant religious fervour; it spread across England, the continent and the United States, culminating in the modern welfare state.[39]

Freedman's work established women's participation in criminal justice as a part of the early feminist movement. This led to critical biographies of the early pioneers: who should, and who should not, merit the title of 'feminist', as well as the organization of, and motivations for, women's organizations. Ann Logan examined the overlap of the feminist movement and criminal justice in Britain. She looked into the late nineteenth century, at the time Josephine Butler became well known for her campaign against wife abuse. But, Logan devotes most of her energy to the decades of the twentieth century after women achieved the right to vote. For Logan, 'feminist' refers to those who perceived gendered inequality in social relationships and access to power, and took some action to improve the status or condition of women. Feminists took greater interest in criminal justice than has been appreciated. Using records of organizations that made up the women's movement and penal reform groups, such as the Howard League and Magistrates Association, Logan identified a 'feminist criminal justice network'. Not a pleasing phrase perhaps, but an important idea. There was an overlap of women's groups and other organizations that campaigned for criminal justice, in which feminist women, mostly from the middle and upper classes, urged reforms of juvenile justice, criminal courts, penal reform and treatment of victims.[40]

Logan argues that in more than one way, the introduction of women magistrates in England was a logical outcome of the struggle for women's suffrage and citizenship rights. She shows how this was not inevitable or automatic, but a deliberate effort on the part of women determined to make good the promise of equal citizenship. The office of justice of the peace originated in the twelfth century but was rarely occupied by women until the twentieth century. To introduce women to the post, beginning in 1910 or so, women's organizations marshalled arguments available to them, including strategies that had been used in the struggle for women's suffrage. Within a few decades, women magistrates made up nearly a quarter of all justices of the peace. In a generation, the place of women on the bench had become a common sight.[41] She shows the difference this made in the overall role. The introduction of women was a factor that led to the Magistrates Association. Although the office of JP was that of a 'lay magistrate', women transformed the role through their willingness to receive education and training. The women's drive for professionalization encouraged men and helped ensure the survival of the lay element in criminal justice through the twentieth century.[42]

Lucy Bland and Philippa Levine studied the introduction of women into police patrols in England, also in the twentieth century. Bland examined the aspirations and practices of women police during the First World War. Led by the National Vigilance Association, the wartime campaign brought women into policing organizations to assist in patrol of military camps. She concluded that in their attempts to protect women and girls, 'protection' became surveillance. Worse still, the authorities used women in their policing role to protect men from women rather than women from men. To shield soldiers from venereal disease, the authorities targeted the leisure behaviours of women around military camps. Or, in other words, the men's need for protection derived from an assumption of women's inherent vulnerability. The fear of 'polluting females' meant women police spent more of their time watching other women than men. Policing of women meant women police as well as women being policed.[43]

Levine points out how the new women of the patrols had ambitions of creating a permanent female officer corps.[44] The very first women in policing began at the Metropolitan Police in 1889. The 'police matrons' were attached to police stations for the purpose of looking after women taken into custody. There was reluctance to institutionalize this role. But the war years provided the organizational impetus. Levine points to diversity within the women's movement. While Bland emphasizes the arguments of feminists along moral lines (social purity), rather than political, Levine shows a wider argument for women police, including appeals to medical knowledge. 'The varied motives that brought women into police work thus go well beyond any simple equation with feminist movement.'[45] Wartime policing of sexuality infringed in distinctive ways on those women suffering from venereal disease. Levine emphasizes the dilemma. Ambitions of women in policing were realizable only in the framework that stressed special female attributes, yet institutionalization of women in policing was only possible by drawing them away from women and towards men. The women police of the war years could only claim their place within policing by asserting a female role which accepted constraints of family and femininity. Their activities, coupled with methods and assumptions necessary to maintain credibility, left many of their procedures open to criticism.

Louise Jackson moved the history of women in policing away from institutional histories and the achievements of notable policewomen to examine more carefully what women in policing actually meant. She looked at policing in the United Kingdom, finely tuned to the relationship between justice and welfare, policing and child welfare. Throughout the twentieth century, women police had a central role in detection and prevention of child abuse, child neglect and the 'policing of families'. The relationship between care and control was ambivalent; even though they were meant to be engaged in crime prevention, women police were required to share tasks with social workers. Jackson's research concentrated on the period between 1915 and 1975 when women police succeeded in negotiating their own occupational identity in relation to masculine police cultures and professional groups. Women police pursued a distinctly feminine professional identity in relation to probation officers and social workers. She used a range of documentary sources retrieved through archival research, including autobiographical statements. She also conducted interviews with women who joined police between 1938 and 1973. This has provided for an understanding of the aims, identities and work experiences of women and the complexities of their position beyond the 'pioneering' and 'heroic'.[46]

Jackson's work involved women in undercover work. In addition to uniformed roles for women in policing organizations, women worked in plain clothes. The Criminal Investigations Department (CID) of the London Metropolitan Police deployed women in decoy, observations and undercover work. Plain-clothed women policed the city vice resorts, brothels, and illegal gambling and drinking clubs. Jackson examines the public fascination with the idea of women detectives working for the CID, and the stereotyped images of women who could pass because they were feminine and did not look like a woman police officer.[47] Women also made careers for themselves as private detectives. Women detectives became popular in crime fiction from the 1970s, but little historical research had been done on the lives of actual women operatives. Jackson recalls the career of Annette Kerner, who opened in 1946 her Mayfair Detective Agency at 231 Baker Street. While Kerner and others did not see themselves as feminist pioneers, they did succeed in a male-dominated profession, successfully negotiating professionalism, femininity and urban space.[48]

Stephanie Limoncelli focuses on the role of women's organizations in the white slavery campaign through comparison of four national contexts: Britain, the Netherlands, France and Italy.[49] Although conceived by feminists to protect women from sexual exploitation, the movement fell short of its goal. Instead of promoting international humanitarianism, it gave way to nationalist preoccupations with undesirable immigrants and the mobility of women. State officials sought to preserve authority to regulate (and retain) prostitution in metropolitan and colonial areas in support of military and migrant labour. The officials were able to do so in part because the women's groups driving the anti-vice campaign were divided in their approach to prostitution: some advocated regulation, others prohibition. Limoncelli pursues a 'broad level of analysis from a global vantage point' which allows us to see the workings of international government and non-governmental organizations and often contradictory outcomes of humanitarian efforts in international governance. 'The anti-trafficking movement ended up reinforcing rather than challenging state power as state officials selectively used reforms as mechanism to realise their own interests in maintaining and controlling women's mobility and sexual labor.'[50]

Gender history

Gender was always part of women's history, but by the 1980s it became a theoretical framework to rival feminism. Gender went beyond biology and the essentialism it implied. It drew on linguistic concepts of difference and sociological ideas about social roles assigned to women and men. Gender examined female and male as social categories and the perceptions of femininity.[51] It emphasized the impossibility of a single identity for women. Gender extended women's history by examining the way women were perceived, difference in identities for women and men, and formation of institutions based of these differences.

Patricia O'Brien explains how shoplifting became 'a woman's crime'.[52] In nineteenth-century France, a society marked by new consumer behaviour in the marketplace, *kleptomania* became a popular diagnosis. She looks at case studies and discussions by forensic specialists. Shoplifting, or more specifically, theft from department stores, was on the rise and there was concern about an 'epidemic' of stealing after 1880. The crime was committed almost exclusively by women; the only other crime with a similar profile was prostitution. These acts were explained by what were regarded as women's illnesses; kleptomania was seen as a women's sickness like hysteria. Elaine

Abelson investigated the situation in England. She examined social attitudes towards middle-class women engaged in retail theft during the late Victorian era. The late nineteenth century brought a new form of retail, the department store, and with it, a new category of criminal, the middle-class woman, and a new justification, kleptomania. In the 1890s, the terms 'shoplifter' and 'kleptomaniac' were used interchangeably. Kleptomania was something women had, an eccentric, yet natural element of the feminine chemistry. It became an explanation of women's criminality in popular culture, as women took on the role of shopping in urban areas. During the twentieth century, the image of the woman shoplifter, as defined in biological terms, was replaced by that of the psychiatric theory of unconscious motivation.[53]

Tammy Whitlock examined the issue of shoplifting against the backdrop of the English retail environment in the late nineteenth century. For Whitlock, the link between femininity and retail theft did not emerge with the department store, but with anxieties about the role of women in consumer culture. The small family shops of the eighteenth century gave way to new forms: multiple employee bazaars and emporiums, followed by department stores. Records of trials and newspaper stories reveal how women who entered this new realm of conspicuous consumption generated a host of anxieties. While Victorian society accepted men in the vigorous pursuit of capitalism, it was uncomfortable with women in urban shopping culture. Shoplifting trials and fictional accounts illustrate how the role of women, particularly middle-class women as unrestrained consumers, clashed with the home-centred image. Although it might be romantic to cast women shoplifters in the role of reluctant participants rebelling against capitalism, Whitlock explains that they accepted it. Women who shoplifted often stole from the very stores where they purchased goods for their families, unlike professional thieves who rarely stole from the same store more than once.[54]

Barry Godfrey has uncovered gender-ordered patterns of employee theft in the industrial era. He reviewed records for petty sessions of the West Riding of Yorkshire and those of the Worsted Committee and their Inspectorate (a private policing agency established for textile manufacturers) for the nineteenth century. Few of those prosecuted for workplace appropriation were women – less than 15 per cent. Those women who had a criminal propensity had less opportunity to take workplace goods given supervision of female workers within the factory. Male workers, employed in occupations which enabled them to move about the factory, had more opportunity. When they did steal, women were less likely to be prosecuted. Overseers preferred to deal with women informally; as workers, they could be more easily replaced. Women themselves appear to have preferred this as well. Given their role in the factory, they could have challenged work rules and destabilized the informal rules based on gender and class. But most cooperated with the process.[55]

The significance of gender as a historical perspective is not only that it enabled an understanding of the criminality of women, but that it led to a revision of the historical accounts which had been written as if women did not exist. Feminist historians pointed out that the British Marxist Historians had neglected to think about women. E. P. Thompson had written about culture of working-class men as if it was the culture of the working class in general. (Marxist feminism would appear, however, and it would be of particular significance to the emergence of women's history in Britain.) Foucault, too, left out women in his influential history of prisons. Michelle Perrot, Patricia O'Brien and Nicole Rafter noticed that the 'revisionist' account of the prison forgot about women.

Gender, O'Brien pointed out, had been the basis for differences in institutional responses in France throughout the nineteenth century. 'For most of the century', she observed, 'men in groups were regarded as dangerous; women were not ... the rehabilitation of women did not primarily emphasize vocational training; instead the importance of religion and an autonomous moral sense were recognized and indispensable.'[56] She surveyed the development of prisons in France from 1810 to 1885, and by sifting through the wealth of archived materials, produced a history of the prison concerned with the individuals that shaped the new system. She concentrated on the experience of the imprisoned, separate from the ideals of those who administered prisons, and arranged her history from the 'inside out' in the same way crowds had been studied from the 'bottom up'. She included a discussion of gender: differences in women and men prisoners, the causes of criminality for women and men and the formation of institutions for women and men.[57]

Nicole Rafter emphasized that the emergence of prison history in the 1970s neglected to consider women. This led to an incomplete, if not mistaken, understanding of the purpose of prison in society. When David Rothman referred to the doctrines of separation, obedience and labour as the 'holy trinity' around which authorities organized prison regimes in the early-nineteenth-century United States, he had not taken into account that these institutions housed women as well as men. Women experienced little separation, no supervision and few opportunities for labour. These institutions had been designed by men to confine men, and the few women confined in them had very different experiences because no provision had been made for them. Had Rothman thought that his trio of doctrines applied mostly to men, he might have concluded that the earliest prisons were organized around idealized aspects of masculinity.[58]

Lucia Zedner contributed a study of crime and prisons in England in the Victoria era, which focused on 'the role of gender in determining attitudes and responses to criminality'.[59] The history of crime, she emphasized, had been written from the understanding that crime was simply something men did. Women represented a fifth of those convicted for crime in the late nineteenth century (a significantly higher portion than the late twentieth century), and they generated a great deal of attention from the authorities. She examined the convict prisons of Millbank and Pentonville, and also local prisons, which contained most of those confined in Britain. Along with reports, official papers and writings of reformers, she sifted through day-to-day records to see prison life as experienced by inmates and workers. The treatment women received, Zedner emphasizes, was not because the founders of prisons failed to think about what their confinement would mean. The issue of women's criminality provoked significant discussion in the Victorian era, and policymakers debated the appropriateness of emerging penal policies to women. At the end of the century, policymakers became disillusioned about the efficacy of confinement. They worried about the persistence of habitual criminals who remained impervious to reform. Women figured prominently in the debates as they presented the most serious problem, and in these debates, attention was focused on two groups of recidivists, habitual inebriates and the feeble-minded. Zedner pointed out that middle-class women had a significant influence on shaping the regimes of femininity from which those in prison had escaped.

The awareness of gender led to questions about discrimination against women or gendered justice. Were women treated with greater leniency due to paternalism, chivalry and the like? Or, did they receive more harsh or humiliating punishments for betraying the ideals of feminine virtue? Rafter characterized the treatment women received as 'partial justice'. Prison governors reacted to women with leniency; generally, they excused women from rules to which men were subjected. This did not result in better conditions so much as different conditions: freedom from harsh labour but fewer opportunities for exercise and fresh air. Even when administrators pursued impartiality, women suffered more because they were kept in improvised spaces of buildings designed for men. When several women were confined together, they had less contact with staff, and experienced greater isolation. Women had to endure childbirth, and manage care for infants, in masculine environments. Given the relatively small numbers within state prison systems, partial justice remained the leitmotif of women's confinement well after the nineteenth century.[60]

At the same time, Carolyn Conley's study of Irish courts from 1865 to 1892 suggests that women as a class did not receive gendered justice. Judicial authorities treated women as individuals, as subjects with rights under the law. They granted that women had the right to fight back in brawls and domestic arguments and accepted that women had a physical disadvantage and needed protection. In treating sexual assaults, an area likely to be influenced by preconceptions of gender, Irish courts tended to regard them as crimes, regardless of the social status of the victim. The reasons for 'this surprisingly progressive outlook' among judges in the country, especially when compared to their counterparts in England, are not obvious. Conley surmises that Irish exceptionalism may have had to do with the shared experience of responding to famine and greater awareness of the demands of individual survival.[61]

Judith Knelman's study of women murderers, most of whom were 'underclass', found that many avoided the ultimate penalty. She collected information for fifty murder trials covered by newspapers from the 1840s. Overall, about twice as many men were tried for murder as women, though a much smaller portion of the women were actually executed. In one five-year period between 1847 and 1852, thirteen women were executed for murder, and nine were sentenced to hang but were reprieved.[62] There were limits to leniency, she points out, and these had to do with gender expectations. 'Child murder, especially by women, was tolerated; other, more threatening types of murder were not.'[63] Expectations about criminal behaviour were different for women and for men, in part because they were based on the fears and insecurities of the dominant social group – men. What most threatened the dominant group – subversive aggression by subordinates – was the most reviled. For this reason, women convicted of domestic poisonings and suffocations received a lenient response, and women convicted for murders outside these circumstances did not.

Femininities and masculinities

Whether to concentrate on women or gender remains an important conversation in feminist history. Gender in its social science form pluralized the category of women to include differences of class, race/ethnicity and sexuality. It is easy to see that these differences matter; women's history should be about more than what White European middle-class women were doing. But if there are so many differences, what constitutes the common ground for feminist historians to organize a coherent approach?[64]

Feminist histories of crime observed that as important as the distinction between men and women was, class divisions mattered. Barbara Brenzel framed her account of the first reformatory for girls in the United States around class. The Lancaster Industrial School, opened in Massachusetts in 1856, was built on the cottage plan. Most of the girls were sent not for criminal offences, but moral offences, such as vagrancy, idleness, and lewd behaviour that threatened the moral order. The state did not scoop up these girls and deposit them, rather, the girls were turned over to the authorities by their families who worried they were on the path to promiscuity. The model worked in the sense that it kept the girls from prostitution and that it was not harsh or repressive. Nevertheless, Brenzel said, the reformers operated from a limited vision. The school concerned itself with forming the 'daughters of the poor' rather than ameliorating social ills contributing to impoverishment.[65]

Shani D'Cruze assembled a collection of essays concerning gender, class and 'everyday violence' in Britain. Everyday violence, she explains, 'eventuates out of people's ordinary, routine and mundane interaction'; it refers to 'violence in familiar places: the home and the neighbourhood, the pub or the workplace; the street or the backyard'.[66] The contributions cover wife beating, child murder, youth gangs, domestic murder, rape and violence against women. The essays are linked by a focus on the intersection of class and gender, the mechanism through which women experienced differences in power. Violence occurred within the middle class, and offenders received punishment, but only when their actions proved impossible to ignore or redefine. While historians of the 1970s had viewed violence among working class as resistance to institutions of 'social control' created by the middle class, the contributions showed how working-class people took steps to regulate themselves. Through 'everyday violence', working-class men exercised control over women.

Nicole Rafter analysed gender, class and race in her study of the national movement to construct separate prisons for women from 1800 to 1935. Using case studies of women's imprisonment in New York, Ohio and Tennessee, she assessed the treatment that women who were confined in men's prisons received and the variations for White women and Black women. While White women supplied most of the inmates for reformatories, Black women filled the custodial prisons in the South and elsewhere. Rafter rejected the claim that the founding of reformatories for women was an essentially humanitarian initiative by women campaigners to help their fallen sisters. It was a middle-class movement, related to other progressive campaigns aimed at establishing control over working-class women, who through their behaviour, challenged conventional standards for true womanhood.[67] Building on Rafter's work, Anne Butler examined how gender and race shaped prison life for women. In the 'Wild West', Black women prisoners were few and far between. They never presented large numbers and conditions varied from state to state. African-Americans had, like others, looked to the frontier with the hope of a more promising future. But they found that they could not escape attitudes and treatment. Racial values characteristic of the South remained a powerful force. Racism, persistent even after the end of slavery, shaped the quality of life for Black women. 'Black women found that, in the West, a forge of racism reshaped the chains of slavery into bars of a penitentiary.'[68]

Kali N. Gross analysed Black women who committed crimes in Philadelphia from 1880 to 1910. She built a social profile of Black female criminals from prison and penitentiary records. Intake records from these institutions contain information about crime, sentence, marital status and education. She combined this with information from available trial transcripts, as well as material from the city's newspapers.[69] In some cases, their crimes revealed greed, ruthless gain, self-hatred and a willingness to resort to violence. But in many more cases, the women were railroaded by the criminal justice system. Although it is difficult to generalize, their crimes often illustrate circumstances and themes as well as motivations different from other social categories of offenders, that of White women, White men and Black men. Crimes of Black women reflected poverty and racial exclusion; they also provided additional income and a means of grasping autonomy. The legal response to women was not only about gender. From the state's point of view, Black female crime justified a set of urban reforms that affirmed White middle-class authority and fitness to govern.

Perceiving women's history as gender history expanded the understanding of women in society, but also allowed for perceiving men's history as gender history. Masculinity mattered as well as femininity.[70] Masculinities seem a tailor-made explanation for some forms of criminality, such as duelling. Historians have looked at the duel, a ritualized form of violence between men that took place across Europe and the Americas. In France, duels happened between soldiers in military settings, and in Germany, academics at universities got involved. Swords, and later, pistols were the weapons of choice, but knives also proved popular in Amsterdam and Rome. By the beginning of the nineteenth century, duelling had disappeared from England, while on the continent, and in the United States, duelling remained. In Italy and France, knife fighting persisted until the First World War.[71]

Robert Shoemaker examined the decline of the duel in London. He tracked down evidence of 206 duels between 1660 and 1800, a portion of an unknown number that took place.[72] The association of duels was regarded as behaviour fitting aristocrats, and men engaged in them to confirm their elite status. The encounters were meant to demonstrate courage rather than skill or prowess with weapons. Although courage was the point of the exercise, duellists preferred to avoid an audience, and instead chose a time and place that was private. Over time, weapons changed from swords to firearms, increasing the risk of serious injury and death. Until the 1720s, it was fashionable to wear swords in London, and duellists could engage immediately. But compared to swords, duels with pistols were likely to take place after some delay (to fetch pistols). Despite the increasing lethality, duellists remained true to form. 'What is impressive is how robust the rules for maintaining fair play and reducing bloodshed actually were.'[73] Over time, the frequency of duels declined. Gentry culture increasingly condemned violent behaviour, and by the late eighteenth century, gentlemen were meant to subdue their angry impulses and display empathy for feelings of others.

Gang warfare is another form of masculine violence. Andrew Davies has written about 'scuttling', that is, fighting by opposing bands of youth using various weapons, in nineteenth-century Manchester.[74] Scuttling appears in newspapers from the 1870s and reached highest incidence in 1889. The participants appear to have been from Manchester and the borough of Salford. And, the participants appear to be mostly men. In a sample of 250 gang crimes of violence reported in the press, nearly 94 per cent were men. (Davies points out that the smaller number of women who took part were more rebellious than the men and transgressed codes of conduct in Victorian ideals of femininity.)[75] The fights do not appear to be motivated by short-term economic gain or ethnic tensions. Rather, 'scuttlers both dramatised and endorsed the customary association between "hardness" and masculine status which permeated life in working-class districts'.[76] Rival gangs of men competed according to masculine notions of honour and reputation in an era when 'hardness' or toughness was considered a quintessential masculine virtue.

Martin Wiener studied the response to criminal violence in nineteenth-century England. During the reign of Queen Victoria, the behaviour of men came under increasing scrutiny, and this 're-imagining of gender played a crucial if as yet unappreciated role in criminal justice history'.[77] He constructed a data set from thousands of court cases, including every case of spousal murder that went to trial, and other domestic homicide and rape cases. Violence committed by men, particularly against women, he proposes, came to be viewed with ever greater disapproval and was treated with greater severity. The Victorian idea of manliness was not merely a hypocritical instrument of male domination, but a reconstruction of relationships of power and existing social relations. While men's prerogatives over women expanded in some directions, they contracted in others. Even as violence directed towards women in domestic settings was tolerated, in public spheres it was investigated, censured and punished by more engaged agents of criminal justice. Newer expectations for men moved from gentlemen to *all men*, and from public violence between men to private violence directed at women. As a consequence, the male proportion of those prosecuted at the Old Bailey rose from about 75 per cent in the 1830s to 90 per cent by 1900. Wiener said his emphasis on male violence was in response to feminist theories, which stressed the impact of nineteenth-century conceptions of domesticity, patriarchy and separate spheres, and neglecting changes in social attitudes towards men.

John Tosh declared his support for the idea. Criminal violence declined in the Victorian era, and a changing culture of manliness seems a good explanation. 'This process is still poorly understood', he says, 'but it must certainly be attributed to something more profound than improved policing.'[78] But others are less sure. Shani D'Cruze and Louise A. Jackson do not accept Wiener's evidence that 'chivalric and restrained masculinity became hegemonic within middle class and "respectable" working class circles'.[79] Homicide was an extreme form of violence, far less common than common assault tried by magistrates. So homicide cases were atypical. Further, Wiener misread the evidence from rape cases. In citing an increase in rape cases coming for trial, he overlooked the removal of the death penalty in 1841 which had made juries less likely to convict. Also, he failed to mention that a majority of rape and sexual assault cases were acquitted or dealt with as common assault.[80]

Clive Emsley agrees with Wiener about how, in the early nineteenth century, violence came to be articulated in England as a social problem related to the ideal of the English gentleman. While men were expected to be aggressive in sports, or when defending family and country, this combativeness was supposedly reined in by notions of fairness and openness. The English people themselves, as well as observers from abroad, perceived the capacity for restraint as a particularly English characteristic. But it was not only about national identity: 'Englishness was gendered.' Women were not expected to be physical, except in the sense of bearing children and nurturing them. The belief in restraint likely had an effect on actual behaviour. But Emsley does not think it is possible to see the impact of restraint in the crime statistics available. Finding proof of the impact of belief in restraint on nineteenth-century crime trends, like the broader idea of English as a non-violent people, is beyond the reach of the evidence that can be gathered by historians.[81]

The virtual woman

In the 1990s, the post-structural movement took women's history in yet another direction, with its emphasis on discourse analysis, textual criticism and postmodern scepticism of the difference between fact and fiction. The point of these histories is not to explain women's behaviour, but the way in which women's behaviour was understood by men, and what that says about culture as a medium of power.

Many of these studies have borrowed analytical strategies from Foucault following the example of Judith Walkowitz's *City of Dreadful Delight* (1992). Walkowitz discussed the 'the ripper' story together with the press campaign against the 'white slave trade' in the 1880s. Although these narratives originated from different politics, both accessed 'similar cultural themes and rhetorical strategies'.[82] They afforded women, and men, the opportunity to discuss 'sexual danger', to voice their own anxieties about passion, lust and violence. Walkowitz explained that her 'cultural history' examined certain myths about prostitution that came into view while looking back from the late twentieth century, and she drew parallels from the 'ripper' of the 1880s to concepts of male dangerousness and female vulnerability surrounding the 'Yorkshire Ripper' case of the 1980s. The events, whether in the nineteenth century or the twentieth century, reveal the 'operation of power in the Foucauldian sense, as a dispersed and decentred force that is hard to grasp and possess fully'.[83]

Ruth Harris examined the discourse surrounding the women accused of crimes of passion in late-nineteenth-century France. Hundreds of cases by women and men came before the assize courts between 1880 and 1910 claiming to be *criminelles passionnelles*. The cases involved rival discourses: the official masculine world of psychiatric assessment and judicial analysis versus the feminine arena of dramatic self-presentation and retrospective rationalization. The courtroom language revealed varying interpretations of women's nature, sexuality and psychology. Criminological knowledge entered at trial revealed gender as a key factor in determining the form, style and nature of criminality. Here, Cesare Lombroso's conception of the female criminal was important. The woman who committed a crime of passion placed herself before the court, asking the judicial authorities to acknowledge her honourable intentions and excuse the harm resulted. The fact that the juries responded with leniency had to do, Harris proposed, with their comparing these women to exemplars of crime of the era furnished by criminologists. The female criminals overcome by emotion contrasted with evil women who acted with stealth, cunning and heartlessness.[84]

Women who committed murders have been especially popular for the new cultural history of women's criminality. Ann-Louise Shapiro looked at interpretations of 'female criminality' in fin-de-siecle Paris. Because women contributed only a small and declining portion of crimes prosecuted, their offences did not seem to threaten public order. However, lawyers, doctors, journalists, politicians and other professional men commented extensively on the problem of the female criminal. Female criminality amounted to a code that condensed wider concerns about sexual difference and legitimized the gender conventions of domestic and public life. In the 1890s, a new type of criminal woman appeared that corresponded with the feminist agitator. Both came to be seen as dangerous forms of aggressive femininity that threatened male authority and signposted national decline.[85] Lucy Bland recalled the story of Marie Marguerite, who shot dead her Egyptian, multimillionaire husband, Kamel Bey Fahmy. During the trial, which took place at the Old Bailey in 1923, Marie admitted to the killing. At first she declared it was an accident; later, she said it was an act of self-defence and finally claimed that she had been 'driven to desperation' by the 'brutality and beastliness' of her husband. Marguerite was a woman with a past: she had given birth to a daughter outside of marriage, divorced her first husband and had affairs with married men. But the negative image of Kamel Bey, Bland says, proved more powerful. He was portrayed as a foreigner who had wanted to 'own' Marie and use her to satisfy his bizarre sexual demands. It was a sensational trial, with her life subject to speculation by media and gossip. But she got away with it because his race made it seem justifiable.[86]

Elizabeth Miller discusses crime narratives concerned with the 'new woman criminal'. Three new crime genres emerged at the end of the nineteenth century: the detective series, the crime film and the terrorist novel. These narratives had little to do with real, historical criminals who committed ordinary crimes, often within domestic settings. The new woman criminals committed their shocking acts in the public arena to signpost the dangers of transgressing social conventions, but also to suggest its illicit pleasures. Miller describes the overlap of imperialism, consumerism and feminism in the fictionalized account of hair-dresser Madame Rachel, convicted of fraud in 1868. Rachel's story was rewritten to appear in *The Sorceress of the Strand* (1902) detective series. She appears as a beautiful but evil genius, whose knowledge of cosmetics and commerce enables her to foil the detectives. Foucault taught historians to see literary depictions of criminality in the Victorian era as an extension of surveillance, power diffused throughout popular culture, and illustrating the criminal 'other'.

Miller shows how this conception of the criminal subject contributed to overlooking the new woman criminal.[87]

Recent studies by Lizzie Seal and Laura Downing fit squarely in this genre. Seal's book, which appears in the Palgrave Cultural Criminology Series, offers a 'feminist reading' of gender representations of women murderers using Foucault's version of discourse analysis. She presents a typology of women murderers, such as the masculine woman, the muse/mastermind and damaged personality, from a selection of murders across a range of times and places. She then analyses a dozen cases of women accused of murder in mid-twentieth-century Britain. The period of the 1950s and 1960s was a pivotal period in the construction of gender. Through the analysis of 'gender construction in a particular time and place', Seal explores 'how these representations of women accused of murder articulated cultural anxieties about the nature of post-war British society'.[88]

Downing examines nineteenth-century discourses, medical, literary and popular, about the female murderer in France. She examines the way the discourses of criminology furnished by Lombroso and Lacassagne shaped gendered ideas of deviant behaviour. The 'creative female murderer was constructed as the most deviant and monstrous of social subjects by her contemporaries'.[89] Downing discussed the case of Marie Lafarge, a Frenchwoman sentenced to life imprisonment for poisoning her husband in 1841. The trial and imprisonment of Lafarge attracted significant attention in France during the 1840s and supplied the material for the emerging science of criminology. Lombroso used her case study as an example of the inborn female criminal. The spectre of the violent murderous female jeopardized gender expectations in an era when women's civic freedom was under scrutiny. The association of women with poison was an old association, although Lombroso made it the exemplary 'women's crime', the embodiment of the new type of 'criminal woman'.[90]

Conclusion

The historiography of women and crime has expanded rapidly in the past few decades, driven by trends in the history of women. The results have not only built up women's history by adding topics that had gone unnoticed, but have changed the way the history of crime in general has been written. Writing the history of women and crime introduced new subjects of study, revised interpretative frameworks and suggested new research methodologies.

Feminist perspectives have brought a great deal to crime history. The 'vanishing female' controversy had raised important questions about women's participation in crime. And a larger question, suggested by feminist history, is Garthine Walker's point about whether crime statistics are the best means of understanding female criminality. To understand women's criminality, historians cannot rely on the same sources of evidence or the same analytic techniques as used for men's criminality. It is an important issue because it implies a fundamental reorientation. But, feminist historians have presented women who as criminals challenged social roles, and women as reformers who reshaped prisons and police organizations. This, too, is important although it has entailed issues of lesser importance. There is, for example, the ongoing conversation about which of the early reformers should be awarded the title of 'feminist'. Retrofitting a label that emerged in the late twentieth century to anyone who lived in the nineteenth century is always going to be a problem because of the unavoidable anachronism.

The arrival of 'gender history' added another dimension to the history of women and crime. Examining the role of women in relation to wider society and culture, along the lines of Patricia O'Brien's thieves, Nicole Rafter's prisoners and Judith Knelman's murderers, has been beneficial. The examination of masculinities and crime, as Martin Wiener insists, certainly draws attention away from the task of recovering the women 'hidden from history'. Masculinities does explain duelling and other forms of crime. And, the 'masculinities and crime approach' arguably leaves more room for women than the post-structuralist approach. The new cultural history of women, as informed by Foucault, relegates women to an image in the minds of men. It suggests a male-centred history in which women cease to exist.

Notes

1   Barbara Hanawalt, 'The female felon in fourteen-century England', *Viator* 5 (1974): 253.

2   Hanawalt, 'The female felon', 267.

3   John Beattie, 'The criminality of women in eighteenth-century England', *Journal of Social History* 8 (1975): 80–116.

4   Beattie, 'The criminality of women', 80.

5   Beattie, 'The criminality of women', 116.

6   John Beattie, *Crime and the Courts of England 1660-1800* (Oxford: Oxford University Press, 1986), 238.

7   G. S. Rowe, 'Women's crime and criminal justice administration in Pennsylvania, 1763-1790', *Pennsylvania Magazine of History and Biography* 109 (1985): 335–68.

8   N. E. H. Hull, *Female Felons: Women and Serious Crime in Colonial Massachusetts* (Urbana: University of Illinois Press, 1987).

9   Hull, *Female Felons*, 46.

10 Malcolm M. Feeley and Deborah Little, 'The vanishing female: The decline of women in the criminal process, 1687-1912', *Law & Society Review* 25 (1991): 719–58.

11 Feeley and Little, 'The vanishing female', 720.

12 Feeley and Little, 'The vanishing female', 749.

13 Robert Shoemaker, *Gender in English Society 1650-1850* (Harlow, England: Longman, 1998), 302.

14 Shoemaker, *Gender in English Society*, 304. Robert B. Shoemaker, 'Print and the female voice: representations of women's crime in London, 1690-1735', *Gender & History* 22 (2010): 75–91.

15 Malcolm Feeley, 'The decline of women in the criminal process: A comparative history', *Criminal Justice History: An International Annual* 15 (1994): 25–274.

16 Peter King, *Crime and Law in England, 1750-1840: Remaking Justice from the Margins* (Cambridge: Cambridge University Press, 2006).

17 King, *Crime and Law*, 220.

18 Stephen P. Frank, 'Narratives with numbers: Women, crime and judicial statistics in imperial Russia, 1834-1913', *The Russian Review* 55 (1996): 541–66.

19 Malcolm M. Feeley and Hadar Aviram, 'Social historical studies of women, crime and courts', *Annual Review of Law and Social Science* 6 (2010): 151–71; Malcolm Feeley and Hadar Aviram, *The Vanishing Offender: The Decline of Women in the Criminal Process, 1650-1900* (Columbus: Ohio State University Press, in press).

20 Gerda Lerner, 'Placing women in history: Definitions and challenges', *Feminist Studies* 3 (1975): 6.

21 Garthine Walker and Jenny Kermode, 'Introduction', in Jenny Kermode and Garthine Walker, eds, *Women, Crime and the Courts in Early Modern England* (London: UCL Press, 1994), 4.

22 Garthine Walker, 'Women, theft and the world of stolen goods', in Jenny Kermode and Garthine Walker, eds, *Women, Crime and the Courts in Early Modern England* (London: UCL Press, 1994), 81–105.

23 Peter King, 'Female offenders, work and life-cycle change in late eighteenth-century London', *Continuity and Change* 11 (1996): 62.

24 King, 'Female offenders', 85.

25 Jennine Hurl-Eamon, *Gender and Petty Violence in London, 1680-1720* (Columbus: Ohio State University Press, 2005), 2.

26 Gerda Lerner, 'Placing women in history: Definitions and challenges', *Feminist Studies* 3 (1975): 5–14; Natalie Zemon Davis, '"Women's history" in transition: The European case', *Feminist Studies* 3 (1976): 83–103.

27 Mary S. Hartman, 'Crime and the respectable woman: Toward a pattern of middle-class criminality in nineteenth-century France and England', *Feminist Studies* 21 (1974): 38.

28 Mary S. Hartman, *Victorian Murderesses: A True History of Thirteen Respectable French and Englishwomen Accused of Unspeakable Crimes* (London: Robson Books, 1977).

29 Hartman, *Victorian Murderesses*, 3.

30 Hartman, *Victorian Murderesses*, 2.

31 Kerry Wimshurst, 'Control and resistance: Reformatory school girls in late nineteenth-century Australia', *Journal of Social History* 18 (1984): 273–387.

32 Kay Daniels, 'The flash mob: Rebellion, rough culture and sexuality in the female factories of Van Diemen's Land', *Australian Feminist Studies* 8 (1993): 133–50.

33 Daniels, 'The flash mob', 148.

34 Heather Shore, '"The reckoning": Disorderly women, informing constables and the Westminster justices, 1727-33', *Social History* 34 (2009): 409–27.

35 Deidre Palk, '"Fit objects for mercy": Gender, the Bank of England and currency criminals, 1804-1833', *Women's Writing* 11 (2004): 237–58; Deidre Palk, *Crime, Gender and Judicial Discretion 1780-1830* (Woodbridge, Suffolk: Boydell Press, 2006).

36 John Carter Wood, *The Most Remarkable Woman in England: Poison, Celebrity and the Trials of Beatrice Pace* (Manchester: Manchester University Press, 2012).

37 Estelle B. Freedman, 'Separatism as strategy: Female institution building and American feminism, 1870-1930', *Feminist Studies* 5 (1979): 513.

38 Estelle B. Freedman, *Their Sisters Keepers: Women's Prison Reform in America, 1830-1930* (Ann Arbor: University of Michigan Press, 1981).

39 Annemieke van Drenth and Francisca de Haan, *The Rise of Caring Power: Elizabeth Fry and Josephine Butler in Britain and the Netherlands* (Amsterdam: Amsterdam University Press, 1999).

40 Anne Logan, *Feminism and Criminal Justice: A Historical Perspective* (London: Palgrave Macmillan, 2008).

41 Anne Logan, 'In search of equal citizenship: The campaign for women magistrates in England and Wales, 1910-1939', *Women's History Review* 16 (2007): 501–18.

42 Ann Logan, 'Professionalism and the impact of England's first women justices, 1920-1950', *The Historical Journal* 49 (2006): 833–50.

43 Lucy Bland, 'In the name of protection: The policing of women in the First World War', in Julia Brophy and Carol Smart, eds, *Women in Law: Explorations in Law, Family and Sexuality* (London: Routledge and Kegan Paul, 1985), 23–49.

44 Philippa Levine, '"Walking the streets in a way no decent woman should": Women police in World War I', *Journal of Modern History* 66 (1994): 34–78.

45 Levine, 'Walking the streets', 49.

46 Louise A. Jackson, *Women Police: Gender, Welfare and Surveillance in the Twentieth Century* (Manchester: Manchester University Press, 2006).

47 Louise A. Jackson, '"Lady cops" and "decoy Doras": Gender, surveillance and the construction of urban knowledge 1919-59', *London Journal* 27 (2002): 63–83.

48 Louise A. Jackson, 'The unusual case of "Mrs Sherlock": Memoir, identity, and the "real" woman private detective in twentieth-century Britain', *Gender and History* 15 (2003): 108–34.

49 Stephanie Limoncelli, *The Politics of Trafficking: The First International Movement to Combat the Sexual Exploitation of Women* (Stanford: Stanford University Press, 2010).

50 Limoncelli, *The Politics of Trafficking*, 2–3.

51 Joan W. Scott, 'Gender: A useful category of analysis', *American Historical Review* 91 (1986): 1053–75; Gisela Bock, 'Women's history and gender history: Aspects of an international debate', *Gender and History* 1 (1989): 7–30.

52 Patricia O'Brien, 'The kleptomania diagnosis: Bourgeois women and theft in nineteenth century France', *Journal of Social History* 17 (1983): 65–77.

53 Elaine S. Abelson, *When Ladies Go A-Thieving: Middle Class Shoplifters in the Victorian Department Store* (Oxford: Oxford University Press, 1989).

54 Tammy C. Whitlock, *Crime, Gender and Consumer Culture in Nineteenth-Century England* (Ashgate: Aldershot, 2005).

55 Barry Godfrey and David Cox, *Policing the Factory: Theft, Private Policing and the Law in Modern England* (London: Bloomsbury, 2013); Barry Godfrey, 'Workplace appropriation and the gendering of factory "law": West Yorkshire, 1840-80', in Margaret L. Arnot and Cornelie Usborne, eds, *Gender and Crime in Modern Europe* (London: UCL Press, 1999), 137–50.

56 Patricia O'Brien, 'Crime and punishment as a historical problem', *Journal of Social History* 11 (1978): 517.

57 Patricia O'Brien, *The Promise of Punishment: Prisons in Nineteenth-Century France* (Princeton: Princeton University Press, 1982).

58 Nicole H. Rafter, 'Gender, prisons, and prison history', *Social Science History* 9 (1985): 234.

59 Lucia Zedner, *Women, Crime and Custody in Victorian England* (Oxford: Clarendon, 1991), 1.

60 Nicole Rafter, *Partial Justice: Women in State Prisons 1800-1935* (Boston, MA: Northeastern University Press, 1985), xxx.

61 Carolyn A. Conley, 'No pedestals: Women and violence in late nineteenth-century Ireland', *Journal of Social History* 28 (1995): 801–18.

62 Judith Knelman, *Twisting in the Wind: The Murderess and the English Press* (Toronto: University of Toronto Press, 1998), 15.

63 Knelman, *Twisting in the Wind*, 8.

64 Joan W. Scott, 'Women's history', in Peter Burke, ed., *New Perspectives on Historical Writing*, 2nd edn (Cambridge: Polity Press, 2001), 43–70.

65 Barbara Brenzel, 'Lancaster industrial school for girls: A social portrait of a nineteenth-century reform school for girls', *Feminist Studies* 3 (1975): 40–53.

66 Shani D'Cruze, ed., *Everyday Violence in Britain, 1850-1950: Gender and Class* (Harlow: Pearson Education, 2000), 1, 11.

67 Nicole H. Rafter, *Partial Justice: Women, Prisons and Social Control*, 2nd edn (New Brunswick, NJ: Transaction, 1990), xiii.

68 Anne M. Butler, 'Still in chains: Black women in western prisons, 1865-1910', *Western Historical Quarterly* 20 (1989): 18–35 (35).

69 Kali N. Gross, *Colored Amazons: Crime, Violence, and Black Women in the City of Brotherly Love 1880-1910* (Durham, NC: Duke University Press, 2006).

70   John Tosh, 'What should historians do with masculinity? Reflections on Nineteenth-century Britain', *History Workshop Journal* 38 (1994): 179–202.

71   Pieter Spierenburg, ed., *Men and Violence: Gender, Honor, and Rituals in Modern Europe and America* (Columbus: Ohio State University Press, 1998).

72   Robert Shoemaker, 'The taming of the duel: Masculinity, honour and ritual violence in London, 1660-1800', *The Historical Journal* 45 (2002): 525–45.

73   Shoemaker, 'The taming of the duel', 533.

74   Andrew Davies, 'Youth gangs, masculinity and violence in late Victorian Manchester and Salford', *Journal of Social History* 32 (1998): 349–69.

75   Andrew Davies, 'The viragoes are no less cruel than the lads: Young women, gangs and violence in late Victorian Manchester', *British Journal of Criminology* 39 (1999): 72–89.

76   Davies, 'Youth gangs', 363.

77   Martin J. Wiener, *Men of Blood: Violence, Manliness, and Criminal Justice in Victorian England* (Cambridge: Cambridge University Press, 2004), 3.

78   John Tosh, 'Masculinities in an industrializing society: Britain, 1800-1914', *Journal of British Studies* 44 (2005): 330–42.

79   Shani D'Cruze and Louise A. Jackson, *Women, Crime and Justice in England Since 1660* (London: Palgrave Macmillan, 2009), 23.

80   D'Cruze and Jackson, *Women, Crime and Justice*, 22–5.

81   Clive Emsley, *Hard Men: The English and Violence since 1750* (London: Hambledon, 2005), 10, 179.

82   Judith R. Walkowitz, *City of Dreadful Delight: Narratives of Sexual Danger in Late-Victorian London* (Chicago: University of Chicago Press, 1992), 5.

83   Walkowitz, *City of Dreadful Delight*, 8.

84   Ruth Harris, 'Melodrama, hysteria and feminine crimes of passion in the fin-de-siecle', *History Workshop Journal* 25 (1988): 31–63.

85   Ann-Louise Shapiro, *Breaking the Codes: Female Criminality in Fin-de-Siècle Paris* (Stanford, CA: Stanford University Press, 1996).

86   Lucy Bland, 'The trial of madame Faymy: Orientalism, violence, sexual perversity, and the fear of miscegenation', in Shani D'Cruze, ed., *Everyday Violence in Britain, 1850-1950: Gender and Class* (Harlow, England: Longman, 2000), 185–95.

87   Elizabeth Miller, *The New Woman Criminal in British Culture of the Fin de Siècle* (Ann Arbor, MI: University of Michigan Press, 2008), 5.

88   Lizzie Seal, *Women, Murder and Femininity: Gender Representations of Women Who Kill* (London: Palgrave Macmillan, 2010), 164.

89   Lisa Downing, 'Murder in the feminine: Marie Lafarge and the sexualisation of nineteenth-century criminal woman', *Journal of the History of Sexuality* 18 (2009): 122.

90   Downing, 'Murder in the feminine', 121–37.

Further reading

D'Cruze, Shani. *Crimes of Outrage: Sex, Violence and Victorian Working Women.* London: UCL Press, 1998.

D'Cruze, Shani and Louise A. Jackson. *Women, Crime and Justice in England Since 1660.* London: Palgrave Macmillan, 2009.

Gartner, Rosemary and Bill McCarthy, eds. *The Oxford Handbook of Gender, Sex and Crime.* New York: Oxford University Press, 2014.

Gross, Kali N. *Colored Amazons: Crime, Violence and Black Women in the City of Brotherly Love, 1880-1910.* Durham, NC: Duke University Press, 2006.

Knepper, Paul and Sandra Scicluna. 'Historical criminology and the imprisonment of women in nineteenth century Malta'. *Theoretical Criminology* 14 (2010): 407–24.

Kowalsky, Sharon. *Deviant Women: Female Crime and Criminology in Revolutionary Russia, 1880-1930.* Dekalb: Northern Illinois University Press, 2009.

Laite, Julia. *Common Prostitutes and Ordinary Citizens: Commercial Sex in London 1885-1960.* London: Palgrave Macmillan, 2011.

Saunders, Frances Stonor. *The Woman Who Shot Mussolini.* London: Faber and Faber, 2010.

Van der Heijden, Manon. 'Women and crime, 1750-2000', in Paul Knepper and Anja Johansen, eds, *The Oxford Handbook of the History of Crime and Criminal Justice.* Oxford: Oxford University Press, 2015.

Van der Heijden, Manon. 'Women as victims of sexual and domestic violence in seventeenth-century Holland: Criminal cases of rape, incest and maltreatment in Rotterdam and Delft'. *Journal of Social History* 33 (2000): 623–44.

CHAPTER EIGHT

Empire and colonialism

Much of the history of crime has been written in national or more local contexts. There are some practical reasons for this. The institutions that generate the sources for the study of crime have been established by national governments, states and provinces, counties and cities. But some forms of crime and criminal justice practices transcend national boundaries.

This chapter reviews historical writing about crime in colonial contexts. We will deal with the British Empire because the lion's share of what has been published (in English) has to do with this. The British Empire covered a long period of history, and its influence can be seen in former colonies and territories. Thinking about colonial contexts raises questions about connections between activities, networks of people, transfer of knowledge and diffusion of models. Further, colonial history can be seen as part of global or world history, an effort to grasp relationships between events at the micro level in relation to macro structures and processes. Interest in crime and criminal justice within the British Empire has increased in recent years, although much of the emerging scholarship remains to be integrated within the historiography of crime.

Our purpose here will be to see how crime and criminal justice have figured into major perspectives in colonial history. Part 1 examines the history of colonial criminality with a look at the thugs of India. Part 2 samples the 'old' and 'new' imperial history with reference to colonial policing. Part 3 introduces the subaltern studies approach, as developed by Anand Yang and others in South Asia, and also with reference to the convict origins debate in Australia. Part 4 discusses post-colonialism prompted by Edward Said and its implications for colonial crime, police and prisons. Part 5 examines the mixed legacy view of empire proposed by David Cannadine and Niall Ferguson using the rule of law as a focus. Part 6 presents work on links between empire and international crime, specifically, trafficking in women.

Colonial criminality

The first generation of colonial historians wrote while the British Empire was underway. These historians were colonial officials who produced histories in the course of measuring, charting and categorizing overseas possessions. They saw imperialism as a guiding force in historical change in various colonies, and they concentrated on the successes and failures of colonial rule. They aimed to reach an audience back home.[1]

Crime, or more specifically, thuggism, became the subject of colonial history because of its capacity to attract readers with strange, curious goings-on in exotic locations overseas. Edward Thornton, a member of the civil service in British India, at first in tax collection and later a magistrate, wrote several histories, including a multi-volume history of the British in India. *Illustrations of the History and Practices of the Thugs* (1837) documented the existence of the 'thuggee', a specifically Indian form of bandits. Thugs befriended travellers, gained their confidence, and then, strangled, robbed and buried them. In different parts of India, thugs acquired different names based on the method by which they dispatched their victims. *Thugs*, meaning 'deceivers', operated in the northern provinces; in the southern provinces, the *phansigars* or 'stranglers' predominated. Thornton explained how the British government gained awareness of the thugs in 1799 when the army apprehended several hundred of them in Bangalore, but did not realize they represented 'a distinct class of hereditary murderers and plunderers, settled in various parts of India' until 1807. Thornton offered chapters on the varieties of thugs, examples of their religious beliefs and superstitions, followed by a collection of anecdotes about the misadventures of different gangs.[2]

For his knowledge of thuggism, Thornton relied on Major-General William Henry Sleeman. During the course of a murder investigation, Sleeman captured an Indian bandit who confessed to multiple murders. The informant took Sleeman to a grave site containing more than 100 bodies, told him about the cult of Kali and named the individuals responsible. Sleeman started a campaign against the thugs in the 1830s and in 1839 became superintendent of the new Thagi and Dacoity Department. Drawing on statements made at trials, as recounted in Sleeman's reports, Thornton offered a picture of this uniquely sinister band of criminals who perfected techniques for using a scarf to strangle their victims, burying the bodies in chosen locations near roads, after dismembering them to speed decomposition. This remained the common view into the twentieth century. In the 1920s, Frederick de L. Booth Taylor, Commissioner of the Salvation Army in India, echoed Sleeman's understanding of the thuggism in his account of criminal tribes. In most countries, he said, crime was committed by individuals, but not so in India where crime resulted from tribes, communities and gangs trained into it from childhood as profession.[3]

The images remained part of India's criminal history even after colonial rule had ended. Historians discussed thug organization, activities and origins. George Floris described the persistence of notorious bandit leaders in the 1950s who began their career under the British Raj. He described the efforts of the Joint Dacoity Operations Command in the 1950s to suppress Raja Man Singh, 'king of the dacoits', said to have committed 200 murders and 1,000 robberies. He also reported on 'Sister Putli', the 'fiercely attractive dacoit queen', who became mistress to a gang leader and leader of her own gang. There were, Floris said, modern 'Chicago-style gangsters' in India's big cities, but the largest portion of crime in the country was committed by a 'traditional type of criminals' rooted in India's pre-colonial past. Once owners of land, the dacoits had been dispossessed by successive invaders and rejected by Hindu society as 'untouchable'. They committed themselves to waging an eternal war of revenge on the society that wronged them.[4]

Stewart Gordon, a historian at the University of Michigan, revised these views in a paper he published in 1969. Gordon portrayed thugs as a feature of the chaos and socio-economic disruption following the decline of the Mughal Empire and expansion of British rule. He pointed out that many of the 'primary' documents had been the product of an ambitious army officer who was hardly objective. Sleeman portrayed the thugs as a culturally distinct group stretching across the subcontinent. Gordon insisted that rather than focusing on organization of thug bands, it was more meaningful to examine the process by which thug bands developed. What the British perceived as a national fraternity of murderers united by their adherence to ancient customs amounted to several families which had been murderers for several generations. These roving bands had been recruited by the rajahs, and others determined to acquire their own kingdoms, following the dislocations of the last decade of the eighteenth century. Thug bands had survived into the nineteenth century by preying on traders and pilgrims travelling roads. Thugs took on a national character of a religious conspiracy through Sleeman, who attached a word to a poorly understood social institution. Understanding the thugs, Gordon said, required situating them in their historical and geographical setting and viewing them in the context of the formation of power.[5]

Sandria Freitag agrees. The thugs came into view only when looking through a spyglass manufactured by colonial administration. She examines how the British applied the criminal law to this 'extraordinary crime'. The rule of law in India *looked* much like that of English society because it ostensibly dealt with the behaviour of individuals. But there was alongside this a parallel and covert legal structure to deal with 'collective crime', actions judged by the authorities to be anti-social. This alternative structure included a special, centralized police force, the Thagi and Dacoity Department, which attempted control of crime outside provincial police departments. It included judicial reasoning that if a particular gang was declared responsible for a certain crime, it was then sufficient to prove that the accused individual was a member of the gang, and not necessarily responsible for the specific offence. Colonial criminal justice involved structures for groups as well as individuals, and by the 1920s, it was difficult to tell the difference between the two.[6]

Martine van Woerkens disagrees. Too many explanations of thuggism have been weakened by the ambition of placing it into an all-encompassing framework that includes Indian and colonial societies. These explanations show the colonizers distorting perspectives as causes and effects.[7] Van Woerkens, a specialist in religious studies at the École Pratique des Hautes Études in Paris, zeroes in on how the thugs understood themselves, that is, from the standpoint of their secret language. The language was built on a lexicon of 600 words which 'inscribe the Thugs into a concrete reality'.[8] She also pursues thugs as they existed in the imagination of others. She read histories of law, anthropologies and ideologies, but also Indian anthropology and folklore, including popular tradition, tales, sacred writings and other texts in Sanskrit. Van Woerkens aims for depth rather than breadth: a few exemplary trials rather than all thug trials. 'I thus give an account of the Thug phenomenon in its multiple dimensions, first between myth and reality, then between science and imaginary.'[9]

Kim A. Wagner, who writes British imperial history, insists that the thug was both more and less than these images. 'Clearly the colonial representation of thuggee cannot be taken at face value,' Wagner argues, yet he maintains 'that there is some correspondence between representations of India and the social reality of India'. Wagner examines the thuggee as an Indian phenomenon and not merely as colonial fantasy. The thugs were part of Indian history before the 1830s when the British introduced their special intervention. Drawing on an extended range of sources, it is possible to see the indigenous conception before the British created the image for export. Wagner examines the response of the colonial state to banditry and highway robbery in early-nineteenth-century India, which shaped views of indigenous crime. But he also prospects for insights into the lives of thuggee apart from the colonial government; their religious and ethnic background; and patterns of organizational structure and interaction. The historical reality of the thugs can be seen in the significance of the myths and tales they told, their sense of honour, and the perception of their associations and networks.[10]

Colonial policing

The second generation of colonial historians emerged in the twilight of the colonial era, at the middle of the twentieth century when it became clear that the British Empire was falling apart. As one former colony after another claimed independence, historians began to take stock of what had happened. Many of these historians had some experience of defending the empire during the war or administering it after. Thinking about the future for Britain, they looked back at what imperial economics, political institutions and social attitudes had been.[11] This reflection on what the British Empire had meant extended to police forces in the colonies.

Sir Charles Jeffries, Deputy Under-Secretary of State for the Colonies, offered his description of colonial policing in 1952. The history of modern policing began, he said, not in Britain, but in Ireland. From the point of view of colonial forces, it was clear that Ireland supplied the model. The Royal Irish Constabulary was a paramilitary organization of armed men, trained to operate as an agency of the central government, particularly in rural areas where communication was poor and violence against the government not infrequent. It suited colonial conditions because it was not a civilian organization policing by consent but a military-like force policing by coercion. It became the template for colonial police forces, and not the London metropolitan experience, which was primarily civilian and local. The RIC served as a depot for recruitment and training of police personnel that would be scattered across the empire, from the Caribbean and Africa to islands in the Mediterranean and Asia.[12] Jeffries embodied what became known and the 'old' imperial history, that is, colonial history that presented the British Empire as separate and apart from the history of Great Britain.

In *Policing the Empire* (1991), David Anderson and David Killingray brought together a collection of essays that explored policing in the colonies as part of broader social, political and economic processes.[13] In their introduction, they take issue with Jeffries and his Irish model. While there are many references to Irish models and English models in colonial documents, it is also true that no colonial force was quite like the Irish or Ulster constabularies. Anderson and Killingray conclude that the 'assertion that colonial police forces followed one or another model tells us precious little about their history and development, and indeed may obscure more than it reveals'.[14] Colonial policing evolved as part of hybrid legal and administrative systems, so the practices in each colony acquired different features. Attempting to construct a colonial model is a waste of time; the realities of policing the empire were too varied to be contained within ideas of policing in Britain and Ireland. Anderson and Killingray advance the idea that the Metropolitan Police provided an alternative (urban) model to the Royal Irish Constabulary's (rural) model, but note the difficulty of sustaining any clear distinction between models.

In support of their position, Anderson and Killingray drew on Richard Hawkins's chapter in the book. As far as Hawkins is concerned, finding evidence for an Irish pattern or influence at work in colonial policing throughout the empire is a formula for the impossible. The police in the British West Indies could be said to have followed the Irish precedent: police were recruited directly from the RIC, and the governor had been an RIC officer. But, Hawkins concludes, 'The more closely one looks at some forces the less they seem to resemble an "Irish model."' There is no evidence that police forces in India, which would have been expected to display the colonial model if there was one, made an effort to adopt the Irish precedent.[15] But others have found some support for Jeffries' idea. Greg Marquis tested the arguments for and against an Irish model with reference to Canada. Centralized police authority associated with state formation in Europe was not common to North America. Nevertheless, in frontier areas and unsettled political situations, colonial authorities organized constabularies that resembled that of Ireland. These organizations contained 'Irish' elements: paramilitary organization, control by national or territorial governments, barracks for special residences for personnel. Further, the experience of policing in Canada revealed a 'basic attitude of coercive colonialism' that native populations could be more effectively controlled by state authority rather than local control. In this sense, the Irish model was 'more than imaginary'.[16]

Georgina Sinclair pointed out that the phrase 'Irish model' has led historians to overlook the significance of other 'models'. She explained how the Palestine Gendarmerie, established in 1920, took over from the Royal Irish Constabulary as the preparatory school for future colonial police. Further, the history and traditions of the Palestine Police followed directly from the RIC. Like the RIC, the organization of the Palestine Police centralized control, took on counter-insurgency work, and after 1926, became the training ground for police sent to other colonies. The Palestine Police deployed 'snatch squads' as a means of tackling the Irgun Zvai, Stern gang and other rebellious colonists, and this led to the 'Farran affair' in which squad leader Roy Farran was implicated in the murder of a young man who disappeared in 1947. (Farran was not convicted and the murder remains unsolved.) In the post-war years, the experience of the Palestine Police was exported to other colonial constabularies through staff, training and tactics, a continuation of the tradition whereby the Palestine Police had become the unofficial training and recruitment centre. From 1926 to 1947, almost 10,000 men passed through Jerusalem. So although the Irish model provided the initial core, the Palestine Police became a 'model' of its own.[17]

Jeffries also laid down a theory of historical progression for colonial forces, based on the experience in the Caribbean, Africa, and islands of the Mediterranean and Asia. First, the police announced their presence by making improvised arrangements for securing the basics of law and order. Second, a semi-military model emerged (inspired by the Irish example) aimed at suppressing crimes of violence and mass disturbances of the peace. The police force reverted to that of a military force in times of war. Third, the semi-military police metamorphosed into a 'quasi-civil' force (following the British example), as the need for crime prevention became more important than maintaining internal security. The process concluded when the force replaced Europeans with a large number of local residents.[18]

Sinclair has questioned this theory. Her study of colonial policing is taken from records at the National Archives in London and interviews with hundreds of former colonial police. The interviews opened up a trove of materials in private collections: diaries, letters, memoirs, handbooks and memorabilia. The evidence indicates a different set of developments. Colonial rule was achieved by a system of law that incorporated some indigenous practices while delegitimating others. She looked in particular at the end of empire, and how Jeffries' theory of colonial policing, centred on leaving a legacy of Britishness, collided with the realities of the end of empire. She looked at policing of conflict rather than law enforcement and crime fighting. She examined the diffusion of the Irish-colonial and metropolitan-English models of policing in the colonies before turning to post-war developments. In the Mediterranean, Middle East and South East Asia, police reforms occurred as a consequence of the end of empire.[19]

Sinclair's interest in colonial policing has brought an awareness of how much 'cross-fertilisation' took place between domestic and colonial policing. On paper, colonial officials in London drew plans for the colonies and sent them to colonial administrators who put them into practice. In reality, colonial administration was an exchange, a continuous interaction between 'home' and 'away'. This involved movement of personnel; technology and equipment; as well as tactics and traditions. The end of empire in Ireland during the interwar period, and deteriorating conditions in Cyprus and elsewhere after the war, raised questions of large-scale movement of police administrators. The circulation of personnel, however, met with racism which prevented non-European rank-and-file from transferring from force to force.[20] The study of cross-fertilization fit solidly within the 'new imperial history'. Historians within the 'new imperial history' rejected the idea of those within the 'old imperial history' (of Jeffries, for example) who saw the history of empire as separate from the history of Britain. The new imperial history presented Britain's history within the context of its empire: Britain and the British Empire as 'one big thing'.[21]

Subaltern studies of crime

In the 1970s, a cluster of English and Indian historians pioneered a kind of colonial history that became known as 'subaltern studies'. The Subaltern Studies Collective saw themselves as outside the mainstream historical establishment, and produced a book series under the editorship of Ranajit Guha, to write about the aspects of colonial history they believed to be important. Rather than frame narratives around the emergence of national identity and formation of the nation state, they tried to situate contexts within global trends related to migration, labour and markets. By raising new questions about otherness and difference, the collective looked at insurgency, national identity, workers movements and agrarian peasants. They redirected the focus from the activities of administrators and settlers to the lives of people pushed into the margins by these activities.[22]

Subaltern studies modelled their approach on the 'history of the bottom up' as developed by the British Marxist Historians. Anand A. Yang brought subaltern studies to crime history.[23] His *Crime and Criminality in British India* (1985) includes studies on the increase of dacoity after colonial settlement in Bengal, on social banditry in western India in the nineteenth century and on the effects of criminal tribes legislation on the people designated as members. As Yang explained, Guha had demonstrated the importance of examining the aspirations and activities of those of humble social status. 'Turning things upside down', by looking for acts of social protest among violence and criminality, was necessary in order to reveal the 'judgmental process' in the extension of colonial legal order.[24] Subaltern studies increased the number of historians interested in reconstructing the lives of ordinary people through links with 'crime'. The movement encouraged historians to excavate social layers of crime, to study the incidence of crime, and forms of criminality, at the local, regional and national levels. Further, it encouraged historians to see more intricate designs in the fabric of legal rule, to see political authority and criminal law in relation to indigenous society.[25]

John D. Rogers furthered subaltern perspectives with his look at cattle stealing, homicide and riot in colonial Sri Lanka.[26] He found that unlike most societies, the social profile of persons treated as criminal was not weighted towards the poor. Crime was committed by Sinhalese adult men of respectable caste. 'What is striking about crime in Sri Lanka is the relatively high economic and social status of criminals.'[27] Although certain crimes served, to some extent, to level power and income, other crimes had the opposite effect. Illegal activities aided high-status groups in maintaining their social standing. Rogers showed that the social and economic changes associated with this pattern preceded the infusion of colonial power. Both the expansion of the market economy and the construction of colonial institutions took place in the context of long-established and complex structures that formed the social arrangements to appear in the colonial period. This challenged a basic assumption of colonial history: that colonial intervention initiated the most significant period in historical development of these societies. Rogers also pointed out that British rule failed to deliver the rule of law. Although courts did matter, they often failed to operate in ways intended by British policymakers. A resilient, indigenous culture grew up around the courts, and attempts by colonial officials to remove it were unsuccessful. The colonial courts, despite their formal structure modelled on British lines, were far less foreign to the ordinary Sri Lankan than to the average Englishman.

Anand Yang and David Arnold pioneered the history of the colonial prison. Taking their inspiration from subaltern studies, they presented prisons as sites of resistance to colonial rule. Yang uncovered the opposition of prisoners in Bengal to introduction in the 1840s of a shared set-up for taking meals. Prisoners had been allowed to purchase and prepare food themselves which preserved caste distinctions and reduced the dullness of prison routine. In an effort to make prison more of a deterrent, the government decided that prisoners could eat only food prepared by staff and would eat together regardless of caste. Despite protests, strikes and riots, the authorities managed to impose coercive power.[28] Arnold saw more room for prisoners to succeed. Prisoner diaries and memoirs, and other notes intercepted by officials, reveal colonial confinement to be more contested than coercive spaces. In addition to outright rebellion, prisoners displayed resistance through laxity and ineptitude, evasion and intrigue. The episodes of open defiance demonstrated the difficulty of maintaining discipline. Far from a captive space in which discipline reigned supreme, prison disputes spilled over into neighbouring communities. The prison became a symbol, especially during the nationalist era, for breaking British rule. The prison represented a site of 'everyday resistance' to the power of the colonial state over its subjects.[29]

Lanver Mak's look at the lives of ordinary members of the British community in Egypt included a look at crimes. He found inspiration in the 'history from below' and the two-way interaction between metropole and colonial society. By focusing on the lives of non-elites, or subaltern groups, he presents alternative imperial history. In Egypt, foreigners received special rights and privileges, including the exemption from local Egyptian courts. All criminal cases involving a foreign defendant were heard in the consular court of the defendant's country of origin. Using records from the British consular courts of Cairo and Alexandria, Mak examines crime from 1882 to 1922. He audits the factors which contributed to British crime and misconduct and conflicts ordinary Britons had with the authorities. He describes cases of professional misconduct and negligence, personal/domestic crimes, assault and libel; fraud, embezzlement, theft and extortion; and sexual crimes, rape and prostitution. What motivated Britons to turn to crime? Certain key words in the files, 'unemployed' and 'drinking', suggest personal economic crises and addictions led to crime, or at least to financial crimes.[30]

As suggested by Mak's look at Egypt, subaltern studies spread from India to other colonial contexts. Historians interested in Australia's convict origins have found it useful. In Australia, there is much at stake in the debate over convict origins. It is a debate about national identity, about the role of women and about the legacy of British colonial rule. But it has also developed subaltern themes of labour, migration and markets.

The convict origins debate goes back at least as far as George Wood in the 1920s. Wood, the chair of history at the University of Sydney, examined historical records concerning transportation. He concluded that most convicts sent to Australian colonies were victims of an unjust legal system which disproportionately represented the interests of the aristocracy. The convicts were 'more sinned against than sinning', condemned by 'blustering ruffians on the bench'. Conflicts arose in the colony, not because convicts were 'more immoral' than aristocrats and administrators, but because convicts disturbed the comfortable order. Wood justified the convicts' crimes as acts of rebellion or temporary solutions to poverty. Nothing the convicts did before transportation or after their arrival was as immoral as the decisions of judicial authorities and the system of punishment that sent them. 'The greatest English criminals', he emphasized, 'remained in England on the court benches and the House of Lords.'[31]

In the 1950s and 1960s, historians revisited Wood's claims about the convicts' former lives. The idea that they were more 'sinned against than sinning', Manning Clark said, offered fuel to Australian nationalists and families worried about discovering a convict in their family tree.[32] These sorts of considerations had distorted efforts to find out about the origins of the convicts and the effect of their background and experiences in Australia. Wood had offered an 'extreme view without qualification', and to obtain a more credible story, it was necessary to avoid generalizing too far from the First Fleet to Botany Bay or particular ships of political criminals and agricultural rioters. Clark presented information from convict ships and descriptions of convicts from observers at the time. 'The evidence', Clark said, 'shows quite clearly that the convicts in the main were recruited from the criminal classes of Great Britain and Ireland.'[33] They were one section of working class for whom crime was an occupation such as carpentry, plumbing, etc. They took pride in their criminal record, tried to avoid physical labour, maintained a loyalty to one another and viewed Australia as their best chance of redemption.

Lloyd Robson added to Clark's depiction with a sketch of women convicts, drawing on a sample of women sent to the Australian colonies.[34] The fact that most female convicts came from cities, the number and character of their offences, and glimpses of their circumstances surrounding crimes in press accounts confirmed Clark's overall picture of a coarse lot of low reputation, accustomed to a low standard of living, drunk and indecent. 'The picture presented of the women convicted and transported to Australia is not an attractive one.'[35]

A collection edited by Stephen Nicholas, *Convict Workers: Re-examining Australia's Past* (1988), brought economic theory and quantitative analyses to the convict origins debate. The contributors disputed the view of convicts as a class of 'professional and habitual criminals' and portrayed them instead as 'convict workers'. They rejected the findings of the earlier generation of researchers because they failed to dig deeply enough into convicts' past, and for wrongly assuming that because they were professional and habitual criminals they were inefficient workers. The question of convict origins had been pursued within the insularity of Australian history, which situated transportation and convict status in an artificial context. *Convict Workers* presented evocative conclusions about the backgrounds, experiences and significance of convict migration. The convicts transported to Australia contributed to a global system of forced migration. They were ordinary British and Irish working class, fit and healthy, who brought useful skills, and were better educated than the working population at home. The labour system succeeded in the economic sense: it matched the right workers with the right jobs, workers who adapted to new conditions and who generally enjoyed better working conditions than counterparts back home.[36]

Deborah Oxley brought this perspective to female convicts. Colonial officials denigrated them as far worse and more difficult than the men; they had not only violated the law, but feminine nature. Authorities complained that they were loud, rebellious, disobedient and indecent. The women may have been rude and rebellious, Oxley admits, but asks what this really told us. It did not signal membership in a criminal class. Rather, it meant that historians needed to stop repeating nineteenth-century impressions. Perceiving them as prostitutes and criminals, as Robson did, created a conundrum. Most female convicts could read and write. They made good mothers. Many found jobs as domestic servants. They ran businesses, employed others and practised skilled trades. So, if they came from the lowest orders of society, how did they manage to adapt so well to Australian conditions and contribute to economy? The records of women in New South Wales from 1826 to 1840 proved most of the women to be first-time lawbreakers transported for relatively trivial crimes. They arrived young and healthy, and in combination with their work skills and literacy, made exceedingly good root stock for a future society. Oxley argued for an understanding of convict women that recognized their economic worth. They contributed to making Australia an economic success that made it possible to break free of empire.[37]

The significance of the *Convict Workers* collection, Stephen Garton has said, is the evidence the contributors present on health, literacy and occupation. Nicholas and associates found that, on the average, convicts in Australia were healthier and more literate than workers back in England. The convicts, both men and women, possessed a range of occupational skills comparable to the working-class population. This means that the first European settlers of Australia were not members of an urban criminal class but members of ordinary working class who ran counter to the law. Garton worries, however, that *Convict Workers* put too much confidence in indent records, the lists made when convicts arrived on transport ships. Unemployed workers often stated their occupation as one they had before unemployment or would have declared trades they had only apprenticed in or had not practised for years. Further, the evidence for female occupation cannot be taken as not being prostitutes. Given the casual nature of prostitution in nineteenth-century Britain, it was not impossible for a woman to be both a skilled worker *and* a sex worker.[38]

Post-colonial studies

Alongside subaltern studies, there was another movement underway, post-colonial studies, which grew out of literary theory. Post-colonial studies applied techniques of textual criticism such as Derrida's 'deconstruction' and post-structuralist concepts such as Lacan's 'the other' to colonial history and its legacy. Foucault's discourse analysis was also very important. Edward Said combined these in his influential book *Orientalism* published in 1978.[39]

Orientalism had referred to a specialized study of Asian cultures. Said claimed that the 'Orient' did not exist, but was a creation of the West. He used Orientalism to signify those areas of the world the West identified as the 'Orient', a body of knowledge that offered nothing about the people or places, but revealed much about the West's relationship to the Orient. Specifically, it revealed how the means of power used by the West to impose itself on the Orient relied on a cultural system, imprinted on the minds of the colonizers and the colonized. This system survived after the Second World War, to the extent of Western academics who claimed to be engaged in objective research. The task of *post*-colonial theory was to expose the repertoire of domination within colonial discourse and to spotlight the hollowness of Western theories of knowledge. The difference between subaltern studies and post-colonialism is that while subaltern studies attempted to write a history of indigenous peoples ('the other' of colonial discourse), post-colonialism rejected the possibility of historical knowledge obtained by historicist methods altogether.[40]

From the post-colonial perspective, it does not make sense to speak of colonial criminality except as an invention of the colonizers to justify their policies. The thugs – to return to an earlier discussion – were not discovered by the British, but created by them. Meena Radakrishna traces the origins of the Criminal Tribes Act (1871) to demonstrate some general aspects of British social policy in India. The concept of hereditary crime was never really linked to biological determinism as in Europe. The Act originated in local structures of government rather than concerns of escalating crime. The need of practical governance led to the search for a 'social scientific' explanation of crime in India; it was connected with new forest policy, repeated famines and displacement caused by the introduction of railways. The British targeted the Koravas, who were said to have turned to criminality when deprived of their livelihood. British administrators emphasized criminal tribes to justify to constituencies back in England how Indian criminality made the colony ungovernable from time to time.[41]

Similarly, Henry Schwarz, a professor of English, argues that thugs were the product of the colonial imagination. He charted British social attitudes leading to formation of criminal tribes policy and resistance to it on the part of those categorized. He developed a social constructionist perspective in which British officials manufactured the modus operandi of the thugs and conducted their campaign against Indian peoples as a rationale for imperialist conquest. In highly public trials between 1829 and 1840, the British government in India tried almost 4,000 thugs. They were convicted and sentenced to deportation or hanged. He pointed to the contradiction in criminal tribes policy. Ostensibly, criminal tribes were predisposed by birth to commit crime and incapable of reform, yet the Colonial Office spent considerable resources settling them, putting them to forced labour and carrying out intricate means of surveillance over them in order to alter their character.[42]

Colonial policing has also afforded an opportunity for post-colonial analysis. As demonstrated by Randall Williams, the idea of the 'Irish model' has particular appeal. He maintains that 'criminalization of the labouring poor' served as a means of justifying middle-class support for the institution of professional policing that Peel introduced in Parliament, and that this criminalization flowed from attempts to control and subjugate colonial subjects. Ignoring the wider historiography about the suitability of models, Williams stresses that Ireland served as the 'primary colonial laboratory for the development of modern policing'. Colonial administrators branded the Irish as an exceptionally violent population, unable to govern themselves and therefore in need of colonial rule. The establishment of a national police force, civilian by appearance but militaristic in reality, sought to destroy all ways of living that threatened the resource extraction on which colonial capitalism was based. 'Conditions in Ireland served as the basis upon which new conceptions of policing and repression began to circulate throughout the British Empire.'[43]

Florence Bernault's edited volume brings themes from post-colonial studies to prisons in Africa. In her opening essay, she characterizes the prison as an 'early instrument for the subjugation of Africans'.[44] Colonial authorities built prisons as one part of an arsenal of asylums, hospitals and work camps. It did not replace, but rather, augmented 'public violence'. Contrary to the idea of the prison as a penal reform, it did not prevent colonial governments from using corporal punishments, including flogging. The colonial prison prioritized economic objectives, based on forced labour, over any ambition of reforming criminals. In southern Africa, the De Beers company became the first non-state entity to make use of massive convict labour. The authorities viewed Africans as a degenerate race and made race the key device for prison management. Across Africa, architectural plans for prisons always provided for separate cells and courtyards to separate Whites from Blacks. The colonial prison 'sought to maintain the racial and judicial hierarchies upon which colonial rule was founded, thus reproducing a violent, personalized, and subscribed power'.[45]

David Killingray's contribution to the Bernault volume reviews colonial penal policy in more detail. Killingray presents the colonial view with one eye on interaction with African societies, and the other on inconsistences, contradictions and limitations in colonial administration. British colonial rule brought new ideas to Africa, not only of law and crime, but also of punishment. These were meant as an improvement over what they viewed as barbaric practices, which included reparations and compensation, but also beating, ordeal by poison, mutilation, torture, enslavement and banishment. The penal system established in Africa mirrored the experiences and practices within the United Kingdom, modified by the experience of colonial rule in India and the West Indies. But officials continually second-guessed themselves: Was prison the right method of punishment for Africans? Was it a deterrent? Were there more economical ways of punishment? What was the best place to remand prisoners, many of whom would not be convicted? The pattern that emerged in most of the colonies by the 1930s was for central prisons, usually in capitals, supported by a lower tier of lock-ups and jails attached to police stations. In Nigeria and Uganda, colonial penal practice included a dual system of native authority prisons. The authorities wanted to keep these under supervision of European administrators, but in practice knew very little of their operations. Colonial officials differed in their view of flogging, a common practice in nineteenth-century Britain. Some colonial officials were 'floggers', some were not.[46]

Frank Dikötter and Ian Brown offer a view of the 'global prison' with their collection of essays on prisons in Africa, Asia and South America. The prison was not a windfall of some globalization process, nor imposed by dark forces of advanced capitalism or cultural imperialism. Rather, it was an institution continually reinvented and altered by local governments. Elites around the world chose to build prisons to associate themselves with the Enlightenment views of Beccaria, Bentham and Locke, and saw prisons as a means of demonstrating their country's progress towards achieving these ideals. Governments poured large sums, often more than they could afford, into prison architecture in order to advertise their membership in the 'advanced nations' of the world. The prison became ubiquitous because of its flexibility; governments of South America, Russia, Japan, China and India adapted it to suit their own visions. Even within colonial contexts, there was never a 'model' that was planted in the colonies. In Burma, the colonial authorities decided that prison was not an effective reform and looked for alternatives. In Vietnam, they decided it could reform criminals, but French, not native criminals. 'The colonial state, in short, could participate in the spread of the vision of the person as a rational, responsible and equal individual – native or otherwise.'[47] Dikötter and Brown emphasize that the penitentiary project as it emerged was rather different from the ideal envisioned by planners. Prison staff did not impose a regime on unwilling subjects. To achieve a fragile control, prison staff had to negotiate a 'customary order' with prisoners. Further, the prison environment was never an isolated order, cut off from the world. Instead, prison walls were only ever a porous barrier; ideas and objects moved in and out of confined areas.[48]

The rule of law

By the 1990s, the memory of British Empire had become too embarrassing to recall. British historians chose to concentrate on Britain, almost as if the empire had never existed. In fact, the headquarters for writing about the British Empire had relocated to the United States where an increasing number of American scholars joined in the post-colonial critique. But, other historians, such as David Cannadine, Niall Ferguson and Kwasi Kwarteng, pursued another way of approaching Britain's colonial past. They refused to accept that the British Empire was completely bad. 'We need to recognize', Cannadine has insisted, 'that while there was much about the British Empire that strikes us as evil and abhorrent, it was far from being wholly devoid of virtue.'[49] At the risk of being accused of defending or apologizing for imperialism, they called for understanding the mixed legacy of the British Empire.

Cannadine and Ferguson can be taken as practitioners of the new imperial history, but their approach was less a revision of the old imperial history than a reaction to post-colonial studies. Following Said's lead, post-colonial studies emphasized Britain and its colonies as a cultural unity. Cannadine and Ferguson saw the British Empire as a social system and wanted to unearth the footings on which it was built. For Cannadine, the foundation was class. Colonial authorities attempted to recreate the hierarchical social order of the English countryside in the colonies, which meant that colonial elites did invoke a notion of social equivalency in which not all colonized peoples were seen as inferior.[50] Like Cannadine, Ferguson recognized that indigenous peoples were very much part of the empire. Post-colonial writers assumed there was a single 'imperial project', which emanated from London, and which was as powerful as it was evil. He presented a colonial social system founded on the rule of law, that among other things, brought some benefit to colonies.[51]

Kwasi Kwarteng, a historian and elected Member of Parliament, agrees with Cannadine about the importance of class in colonial hierarchy and disagrees with Ferguson about the empire as a model of liberalism and democracy. But he shares the 'mixed legacy' perspective: the British Empire cannot be categorized as wholly good or bad, but understood on its own terms. The British Empire did bring a measure of justice and order to anarchic parts of the world, but it invested too much power in the hands of individual administrators. They shared a common belief in their own superiority, but had very different ideas of government and administration. There was too much opportunism, individualism and improvisation in colonial government to implement a coherent ideology. The empire rejected ideas of human equality and put power into the hands of an elite that acted according to their own whims, and brought about instability, disorder and chaos.[52]

So, what of the rule of law? Using Said's techniques of analysis, Vinay Lal has argued that the rule of law had benefits in British India, but only for the British. The law not only allowed, but provided for extreme forms of, sanction meant to degrade and humiliate Indians. Lal studied the legal response to the disturbances in the Punjab in 1919 involving the murder of an English woman at Amritsar in 1919. Brigadier-General Dyer, who caused the deaths of 400 people when he ordered his troops to fire on a gathering of protestors, issued the 'crawling order' which forced Indian men to cross the road where the murder had happened on their hands and knees. Lal emphasized that this measure was not atypical of the rule of law, but a revealing example of a legal regime established to reinforce British superiority. For Indians, British law did not mean 'innocent until proven guilty' but the 'infinite substitutability of the native' which allows colonial officials to punish Indians for the alleged offences of unknown others.[53]

Lal has also observed two murder trials in India in the late nineteenth century in which men were convicted on the testimony of children. To understand how courts reached these judgements, which were later overturned, it is necessary to know something about the 'cultural psychology' of colonial justice in India. As Lal explains, the British dismissed Indian adults as liars and storytellers. Indian children, however, were seen as innocent and truthful, and therefore more likely to be called to court to give evidence. As things turned out, in both cases the evidence of the children proved unreliable. The trial proceedings were important for the defendants, who escaped the gallows, but such everyday justice in a former colony has been forgotten. Forgotten crimes, Lal proposes, revolving around disputes, conflicts and illicit romance and other passions that inform the lives of people, reveal the manner in which structures of law have meaning.[54]

Jordanna Bailkin investigated a subset of homicide cases that turn up again and again in court records and press reports in India from the 1870s to 1920s: a British man kicks an Indian resulting in death from a ruptured spleen. Was the man wearing the boot a criminal? A cold-blooded murderer? Given the extensive legal violence in colonial governance, when and why were specific acts of European violence regarded as murder? The 'boot and spleen' cases serve as a lens into the broader experience of interracial violence in colonial contexts, in particular, the tension between the colonial executive's desire to control European or White criminality and the judiciary's reluctance to see these as murder. Some Britons were put to death for murdering Indians, and military courts were more severe than civilian courts. But, it was also the case that the number of civilians in court for murder fell as the overall level of violence rose during this period. From the earliest days of the East India Company, the British government was concerned about White violence to create the appearance of fairness. Dealing with crimes by individual Britons, many of whom were off-duty soldiers, obscured any connection between acts of individuals and state-sponsored violence. It was a relationship the

British could see in other colonial empires but too rarely when looking at themselves in the mirror.[55]

Elizabeth Kolsky revisited murder on tea plantations in Assam, a province in the far northwest of India.[56] During the colonial period, Assam was dominated by the British tea industry and (until 1910) included a system of indentured servitude that extended private penal powers to British tea planters to enforce labour contracts. She reconstructs the trial in 1893 of several Indians for murder of a planter. Although violence against European planters was not uncommon, murder was rare. The case is also interesting because no one was punished for the crime. Proceedings in court produced evidence of police torture against the defendants and diverted attention from the question of guilt to questioning the British rule of law. 'Although controlling Indian crime was critical to the maintenance of imperial order, the colonial state accepted the fact that a certain amount of European crime was necessary to keep the plantations going.'[57] As the number of gardens in the area began to multiply, the number of trials of European British subjects decreased. Kolsky emphasizes how legal proceedings combined with racial prejudice to further the tea industry. One strategy was the introduction of scientific testimony. To compensate for the supposed unreliability of Indian witnesses, scientific testimony tended to absolve European planters by showing evidence that disconnected the cause of death from the incident of violence.

Although India has furnished much of the historical understanding, there has been work in other colonies. Tapiwa Zimudzi's study of crime in Zimbabwe (Southern Rhodesia) during the first half of the twentieth century examined the murder of children.[58] The killing of newborn twins brought African women into the high court as offenders or witnesses. These cases referenced the superstition that twins brought bad lack to their parents and community; unless killed after birth, the community would experience drought or other calamities. There were variations in how twins were killed and the ways of disposing of their dead bodies. However, the standard procedure required the mother or mother-in-law to strangle the baby. Zimudzi tells how females accused of twin murders tried to excuse their actions by citing adherence to African culture or ignorance of 'White man's law'. Because British judges viewed murders by African women through a lens of paternalism and gender stereotypes, there was some willingness to accept this. But, these sorts of arguments were less successful by the 1920s and 1930s as judges became more tuned into courtroom behaviour inconsistent with gender stereotypes. Judges believed that by the 1920s, colonial moral and religious values had been sufficiently infused in African society for most women to be aware that killing of twins was morally wrong and a serious violation under colonial law.[59]

Martin Wiener has made clear his desire for a 'third narrative'. He compared cases of interracial murder across six colonial contexts, Queensland, Fiji, Trinidad and Bahamas, India, Kenya and Honduras, over the years between 1870 and 1930.[60] Variations in legal practice across time and place reveal British colonialism as more complex and contested than it has been made out to be. The law was a hammer by which administrators and settlers extended their power over non-White majorities. But it was also a lever by which non-White colonial subjects raised concerns about unfairness and exclusion. Wiener portrays the law as a site of 'inner tension', a place where governors, judges and other officials played for power, as well as the means by which settlers questioned their management. When settlers challenged decision-makers in the colonial capital and London, it signalled the end of colonial rule. Wiener affirms the importance of moving beyond 'celebratory' and 'accusatory' narratives of colonial history. His 'third narrative' of colonial law enforcement does not shelve the first two, but rather serves to emphasize that 'there was never a single colonial project'.[61]

Cannadine and Ferguson have called for more comparative work. Too much emphasis has been focused on the British Empire, not enough on empires before and after. Americans, Cannadine has said, have been reluctant to recognize that the United States has been (and remains) an overseas empire.[62] There has been some historical study of crime and criminal justice in other empires (in English). Jakob Zollman has investigated law enforcement in German South West Africa, where the question of what the colonialists were trying to do, and how well they achieved this, takes on added significance. From 1894 to 1915, imperial Germany controlled territory in what is now Namibia. It has been argued that the ideology of colonial rule lights a clear pathway 'from Africa to Auschwitz'. Zollman points out that the Germans began their colonial rule with little or no idea of how to colonize the African continent, and colonial administrators had to rely on trial-and-error policies to pursue the goal of statehood. The police force was charged with enforcing the 'native regulations' of 1907 which required Africans to carry identity cards. But the actual effectiveness of the police force over colonial territory was limited, as seen by futile attempts to end cattle thefts and banditry. German police did not know native languages, which forced them to rely on native interpreters.[63]

Stephen Toth has looked at French penal colonies or *bagnes* (the word originally referred to dockyard prisons of early modern France and later expanded to overseas penal colonies of French Guiana and New Caledonia).[64] The government intended the *bagne* to have rehabilitative power separate from its social function as punishment. It had been established on the fantasy of regenerative work and labour in faraway lands along the lines of Britain's penal colonies on Australia. The French commenced their colonial venture in 1852, with the first shipment of convicts to Guiana, about the time Britain began winding down colonies in Australia. Both systems shared the idea of making convict labour productive and after a period of probation allowing convicts to establish themselves on the land. But this led to a dilemma: Should the penal colony contribute to economic and political aspects of colonial society or should it be harsh and punitive? Toth explores how individuals in colonial outposts constructed the *bagne*. From the vantage point of daily reports, internal memoranda and administrative correspondence, he uncovers what penal colonies meant to those who experienced them.

Like the French, the Germans drew on the British experience in assessing the value of penal colonies. Louisa Meredith's account of her visit in 1852 to Britain's notorious penal colony of Hobart, in which she said she felt safer than in an English country village, figured into German debates about penal colonies throughout the second half of the nineteenth century. However, while German penologists made use of the experiences of other European empires, they argued for or against penal colonies according to domestic knowledge and imperial priorities.[65]

As for the American Empire, there has been some study of the Philippines. When the United States took control of the Philippines in 1898, it acquired the Bilibid prison at Manila, which had been built by the Spanish. Michael Salman describes the American regime at Bilibid, which put prisoners to work in hemp production, road work and building projects. He also discusses the Iwahig Penal Colony, opened in 1904 at the western edge of central Philippines.[66] Alfred McCoy's study of policing in the Philippines covers the shift from colonial to national policing. He looks at formal and informal, legal and illegal, activities in relation to police, both colonial and national. The national police inherited the problematic legacy of colonial policing. Criminal syndicates, and clandestine security services created to counter them, brought about major corruption before and after the Second World War. A relatively small problem, policing of Philippines, revealed profound issues within the American Empire, constitutional principles and the rise of internal security. It exposed the exercise of American power from imperial rule in one chain of islands to worldwide domination by the start of the twenty-first century.[67]

Gender, empire and trafficking

One of the topics ignored by the old imperial history produced after the Second World was gender. Since the 1980s, however, there have been a number of histories of gender and colonialism.[68] This work not only prised open new subjects for colonial history, but also for crime history, particularly in the area of the trafficking in women.

Edward Bristow broke open the study of traffic in women with his study of Jewish efforts between 1880 and 1939 to suppress the 'White slave trade' as it was known. One of the most prominent organizations, the Jewish Association for the Protection of Girls and Women, was established in London by several members of the Rothschild family. Bristow examined practices of prostitution among Jews in Eastern Europe and the causes of the traffic, which represented an aspect of the migration from the Pale of

Settlement to Europe and the Americas. Buenos Aires became a notorious destination for trafficked women, affirmed by the short story, 'The Man from Buenos Aires', by Yiddish writer Sholom Aleichem. Bristow found materials about the activities of Jewish groups in archives in London, New York, Paris and other places.[69]

Philippa Levine discussed the role of empire in the traffic in women as a prelude to a larger study of prostitution and venereal disease in the British Empire. During the nineteenth century, colonial administrators enacted regulations to stop the rise of venereal disease among soldiers. Virtually every colony enacted contagious disease regulations that identified female prostitutes as the principal source of the contagion, leading to schemes for restricting relations between prostitutes and soldiers. Ostensibly, the regulation was about public health, but as her work in archives concerning Queensland, Straits Settlements (Singapore), Hong Kong and India showed, this effort reflected wider themes of colonialism, gender and race. 'Colonial prostitution, and sexually transmissible diseases believed to be worse in colonial environments, struck a chord in the nineteenth-century imagination far beyond the material damage wrought by disease, and with massive and disruptive consequences for women dependent on the sex trade for their livelihood.'[70] Failure to gain control over native sexuality threatened colonial rule.

Drawing on Levine and subaltern studies, Harald Fischer-Tiné has examined further the links between the white slave campaign and colonialism. Fischer-Tiné looked at prostitution networks in the region of the Indian Ocean, focused on their working conditions, but also the anxieties this class of 'White subalterns' generated for colonial authorities. European prostitution took off in British India after the opening of the Suez Canal in 1869. Even in Bombay, which had the highest population of registered European prostitutes, there were never more than a hundred or so. But the presence of this population of 'White women degrading themselves to the lowest depths' upset the racial and class hierarchy on which British colonial society in India had been built, and undermined the civilizing mission of colonial rule.[71]

Petra de Vries extended Levine's analysis to the Dutch colonial situation. The term 'white slave' was a historical construction, born of a particular sexual danger in a specific social and historical context. She examined the Dutch campaign in the early twentieth century concerning the 'White slave trade'. In the Netherlands, anti-White slavery campaign was interwoven with implicit or colonialist attitudes about sexuality in which white slave narratives projected a White woman as a victim of foreign or exotic men. The woman's body was the mark of civilization, and the 'whiteness' of the sexual slave signified racialized sexual threats to 'our women'. The campaigners also targeted men's sexual relations with native women. The Dutch saw themselves within a racial hierarchy that put the White race at the pinnacle of civilization. The sexual relations in 'primitive' societies such as the Dutch East Indies (Indonesia) constituted a threat to the 'civilized' Dutch Empire.[72]

Micheline Lessard provides a look at how the white slave trade operated in the French Empire. While the problem of traffic in women existed in Vietnam prior to 1885, the scale of the illicit trade increased tremendously during the first fifty years of French colonial rule. Markets for the sale of Vietnamese women and children existed, but examination of French colonial administration reveals that cases increased, along with smuggling of firearms and opium. Colonial rule contributed to human trafficking between 1885 and 1935 in more than one way. During the late nineteenth century, the border areas between Tonkin and China were often battlefields. This gave rise to secret societies such as the Black Flags who kidnapped women and children whom they traded for cash or arms as a means of carrying out resistance to French troops. Warfare also undermined the economy, and led to forms of piracy and banditry which preyed on the vulnerability of women and children. Further, the development of commercial trade through Chinese ports increased the volume of ships entering Vietnamese ports. This made it difficult for French colonial authorities to monitor passengers and permitted illegal businesses including smuggling of human beings.[73]

Daniel Gorman examines the international campaign against trafficking in women. British non-governmental organizations, including the Association for Moral and Social Hygiene, played a leading role, as did British diplomats at the League of Nations, particularly Rachel Crowdy, who headed the League's Social Section. Gorman focuses on the trafficking in women in the 1920s to illustrate the emergence of 'international society', which was furthered by the internationalization of the British Empire. The Social Section, one of the most active of the technical bodies of the League, included the Advisory Committee on the Traffic in Women and Children. Under Crowdy's leadership, the League attempted to establish the means to regulate, or abolish, 'a transnational crime with which domestic governments had long struggled'.[74] To further its ambitions, the League negotiated between national governments and non-governmental organizations, such as the International Bureau for the Suppression of the Traffic in Women and Children. The League's anti-trafficking campaign normalized internationalism and forced the British Empire to examine its attitude towards prostitution in the colonies.

Conclusion

The British Empire produced its own histories of crime, including Thornton's portrait of the thugs and Jeffries' Irish model of policing. These accounts inspired further research, and although disagreements continue, it is clear from work by Kim Wagner, David Anderson, David Killingray and Georgina Sinclair, among others, that the initial conceptions of colonial criminality and colonial policing require substantial revision.

The subaltern studies, post-colonial theory and the mixed legacy approaches provide promising alternatives. As shown by Anand Yang, the subaltern studies perspective adds another dimension not only to crime, but also to police and prisons. Lanver Mak's history of crime in Egypt is significant because of its focus on 'subalterns' within the European population. The 'history of bottom up' in colonial contexts is not about race, White versus Brown, or about indigenous populations, natives versus foreigners, but rather about the relationship to power. This is a point Kwasi Kwarteng makes in his 'post-racial' history of the British Empire. Post-colonial theory is hampered by binary thinking, leading to simplistic conclusions about crimes of empire that are the mirror opposite of colonial criminality. Nevertheless, the post-colonial critique has emphasized the lasting influence of empire and inspired a great deal of interest in colonial history. The mixed legacy model fits the comparative approach, such as that of Martin Wiener. We can appreciate the ways in which the criminal court was not a simple tool of colonial domination. Then again, the mixed legacy approach is to some extent based on the point of view of the colonizers, that is, how the British saw their empire.

The age of empire has had a tremendous impact on the making of the modern world, including crime. Histories of trafficking by Philippa Levine, Petra de Vries and Daniel Gorman show how international crime reflected the politics, economics and culture of empire. As work continues, particularly comparative work, the influence of empire will, I think, becomes apparent in domestic crime and criminal justice. From a satellite view, economic, social, cultural and political trends produce similar patterns across national boundaries, so that few forms of crime are unique or particular.

Notes

1 Robert Van Niel, 'Colonialism revisited: Recent historiography', *Journal of World History* 1 (1990): 110–12 (109–24).

2 Edward Thornton, *Illustrations of the History and Practices of the Thugs* (London: William H Allen, 1837).

3 Frederick de L. Booth Taylor, 'The criminal tribes of India', *Journal of the Royal Society of Arts* 71 (1923): 158–66.

4 George Floris, 'A note on the dacoits of India', *Comparative Studies in Society and History* 4 (1962): 467–72.

5 Stewart Gordon, 'Scarf and sword: Thugs, marauders, and state formation in eighteenth century Malwa', *Indian Economic and Social History Review* 6 (1969): 403–29.

6 Sandria B. Freitag, 'Crime in the social order of colonial North India', *Modern Asian Studies* 25 (1991): 227–61.

7   Martine Van Woerkens, *The Strangled Traveller: Colonial Imaginings and the Thugs of India* (Chicago: University of Chicago Press, 1995).

8   Van Woerkens, *The Strangled Traveller*, 8.

9   Van Woerkens, *The Strangled Traveller*, 9.

10 Kim A. Wagner, *Thuggee: Banditry and the British in Early Nineteenth-Century India* (London: Palgrave Macmillan, 2007).

11 David Cannadine, '"Big Tent" historiography: Transatlantic obstacles and opportunities in writing the history of Empire', *Common Knowledge* 11 (2005): 388.

12 Charles Jeffries, *The Colonial Police* (London: Max Parrish, 1952), 30–1.

13 David M. Anderson and David Killingray, eds, *Policing the Empire: Government, Authority and Control, 1830-1940* (Manchester: Manchester University Press, 1991), 1–14.

14 Anderson and Killingray, 'Consent, coercion and colonial control: Policing the empire, 1830-1940', in Anderson and Killingray, *Policing the Empire*, 4.

15 Richard Hawkins, 'The "Irish model" and the empire: A case for reassessment', in Anderson and Killingray, *Policing the Empire*, 19.

16 Greg Marquis, 'The "Irish Model" and nineteenth-century Canadian policing', *Journal of Imperial and Commonwealth History* 25 (1997): 193–218.

17 Georgina Sinclair, '"Get into a crack force and earn £20 a month": The influence of the Palestine Police upon colonial policing 1922-1948', *European Review of History* 13 (2006): 49–65.

18 Jeffries, *The Colonial Police*, 32–3.

19 Georgina Sinclair, *At the End of the Line: Colonial Policing and the Imperial Endgame 1945-80* (Manchester: Manchester University Press, 2006).

20 Georgina Sinclair and Chris A. Williams, '"Home and away": The cross-fertilisation between "Colonial" and "British" policing, 1921-85', *Journal of Imperial and Commonwealth History* 35 (2007): 221–38.

21 Richard Price, 'One big thing: Britain, its Empire, and their imperial culture', *Journal of British Studies* 45 (2006): 602–27.

22 Vinay Lal, 'Subaltern studies and its critics', *History and Theory* 40 (2001): 135–48.

23 Anand A. Yang, *Crime and Criminality in British India* (Tucson: University of Arizona Press, 1987).

24 Anand A. Yang, 'Issues and themes in the study of historical crime and criminality: Passages to the social history of British India', in Yang, *Crime and Criminality*, 12, 1–25.

25 Yang, 'Issues and themes', 23.

26 John D. Rogers, *Crime, Justice and Society in Colonial Sri Lanka* (London: Curzon Press, 1987).

27 Rogers, *Crime, Justice and Society*, 10.

28 Anand A. Yang, 'Disciplining "natives": Prisons and prisoners in early nineteenth century India', *South Asia* 10 (1987): 29–45.

29   David Arnold, 'The colonial prison: Power, knowledge, and penology in
     nineteenth-century India', in Ranajit Guha, ed., *A Subaltern Studies Reader,
     1986-1995* (Minneapolis: University of Minnesota Press, 1992), 140–78.

30   Lanver Mak, *The British in Egypt: Community, Crime and Crises 1822-1922*
     (London: I. B. Tauris, 2012).

31   George A. Wood, 'Convicts', *Royal Australian Historical Society Journal and
     Proceedings* 8 (1922): 177–208.

32   M. Clark, 'The origins of the convicts transported to Eastern Australia, 1787-
     1852. Part 1', *Historical Studies: Australia and New Zealand* 7 (1956): 121–35
     and M. Clark, 'The origins of the convicts transported to Eastern Australia,
     1787-1852. Part 2', *Historical Studies: Australia and New Zealand* 7 (1956):
     314–27.

33   Clark, 'The origins: Part 2', 327.

34   L. Robson, 'The origin of the women convicts sent to Australia, 1787-1852',
     Historical Studies: Australia and New Zealand 11 (1963): 43–53.

35   Robson, 'The origin of the women', 53.

36   Stephen Nicholas and Peter R. Shergold, 'Unshackling the past', in Stephen
     Nicholas, ed., *Convict Workers: Reinterpreting Australia's Past* (Cambridge:
     Cambridge University Press, 1988), 3–13.

37   Deborah Oxley, *Convict Maids: The Forced Migration of Women to Australia*
     (Cambridge: Cambridge University Press, 1996).

38   Stephen Garton, 'The convict origins debate: Historians and the problem of
     the "criminal class"', *Australian and New Zealand Journal of Criminology* 24
     (1991): 66–82.

39   Edward Said, *Orientalism* (London: Routledge and Kegan Paul, 1978).

40   Dane Kennedy, 'Imperial history and post-colonial theory', *Journal of Imperial
     and Commonwealth History* 24 (1996): 351 (345–63).

41   Meena Radhakrishna, *Dishonoured by History: 'Criminal Tribes' and British
     Colonial Policy* (Hyderabad, India: Orient Longman, 2001).

42   Henry Schwarz, *Constructing the Criminal Tribe in Colonial India: Acting Life
     a Thief* (Oxford: Wiley-Blackwell, 2010).

43   Randall Williams, 'A state of permanent exception: The birth of modern
     policing in colonial capitalism', *Interventions: International Journal of
     Postcolonial Studies* 5 (2010): 322–44.

44   Florence Bernault, 'The politics of enclosure in colonial and post-colonial
     Africa', in Florence Bernault, ed., *A History of Prison and Confinement in
     Africa* (Portsmouth, NH: Heinemann, 2003), 2–3, 1–118.

45   Bernault, 'The politics of enclosure', 38.

46   David Killingray, 'Punishment to fit the crime? Penal policy and practice in
     British Colonial Africa', in Bernault, *A History of Prison*, 98–118.

47   Frank Dikötter, 'Introduction', in Frank Dikötter and Ian Brown, eds, *Cultures
     of Confinement: A History of the Prison in Africa, Asia and Latin America*
     (Ithaca, New York: Cornell University Press, 2007), 8.

48 Dikötter, 'Introduction', 1–13.

49 Cannadine, '"Big tent" historiography', 388.

50 David Cannadine, *Ornamentalism: How the British Saw Their Empire* (London: Pengion, 2002).

51 Niall Ferguson, *Empire: How Britain Made the Modern World* (London: Allen Lane, 2003).

52 Kwasi Kwarteng, *Ghosts of Empire: Britain's Legacies in the Modern World* (London: Bloomsbury, 2011).

53 Vinay Lal, 'The incident of the "Crawling lane": Women in the Punjab disturbances of 1919', *Genders* 16 (1993): 35–60.

54 Vinay Lal, 'Everyday crime, native mendacity and the cultural psychology of justice in colonial India', *Studies in History* 15 (1999): 145–66.

55 Jordanna Bailkin, 'The boot and the spleen: When was murder possible in British India?', *Comparative Studies in Society and History* 48 (2006): 462–93.

56 Elizabeth Kolsky, 'Crime and punishment on tea plantations in colonial India', in Markus D. Dubber and Lindsay Farmer, eds, *Modern Histories of Crime and Punishment* (Stanford: Stanford University Press, 2007), 272–98.

57 Kolsky, 'Crime and punishment', 279.

58 Tapiwa Zimudzi, 'African women, violent crime and the criminal law in colonial Zimbabwe, 1900-1952', *Journal of Southern African Studies* 30 (2004): 499–517.

59 Zimudzi, 'African women, violent crime', 513–14.

60 Martin J. Wiener, *An Empire on Trial: Race, Murder, and Justice under British Rule, 1870-1935* (Cambridge: Cambridge University Press, 2009).

61 Wiener, *An Empire on Trial*, 233.

62 Cannadine, '"Big tent" historiography', 384–5.

63 Jakob Zollman, 'Communicating colonial order: The police of German South-West Africa (c. 1894-1915)', *Crime, History & Societies* 15 (2011): 33–58.

64 Stephen A. Toth, *Beyond Papillon: The French Overseas Penal Colonies 1854-1952* (Lincoln: University of Nebraska Press, 2006).

65 Matthew Fitzpatrick, 'New South Wales in Africa? The convict colonialism debate in imperial Germany', *Itinerio* 37 (2013): 59–72.

66 Michael Salman, '"Nothing without labor": Penology, discipline, and independence in the Philippines under United States colonial rule, 1898-1914', in Vincente L. Rafael, ed., *Discrepant Histories: Translocal Essays on Filipino Cultures* (Philadelphia: Temple University Press, 1995), 113–29.

67 Alfred McCoy, *Policing America's Empire: The United States, the Philippines, and the Rise of the Surveillance State* (Madison: University of Wisconsin Press, 2009).

68 Durba Ghosh. 'Gender and Colonialism: Expansion or marginalization?', *Historical Journal* 47 (2004): 737–55.

69   Edward J. Bristow, *Prostitution and Prejudice: The Jewish Fight Against White Slavery 1870-1939* (Oxford: Clarendon Press, 1982).

70   Philippa Levine, *Prostitution, Race and Politics: Policing Venereal Disease in the British Empire* (London: Routledge, 2003), 6.

71   Harald Fischer-Tiné, '"White women degrading themselves to the lowest depths": European networks of prostitution and colonial anxieties in British India and Ceylon ca. 1880-1914', *Indian Economic and Social History Review* 40 (2003): 163–90.

72   Petra de Vries, '"White Slaves" in a Colonial Nation: The dutch campaign against the traffic in women in the early twentieth century', *Social and Legal Studies* 14 (2005): 39–60.

73   Micheline Lessard, '"Cet ignoble traffic": The kidnapping and sale of vietnamese women and children in French Colonial Indochina, 1873-1935', *French Colonial History* 10 (2009): 1–34.

74   Daniel Gorman, *The Emergence of International Society in the 1920s* (Cambridge: Cambridge University Press, 2012), 12.

Further reading

Brown, Mark. *Penal Power and Colonial Rule*. London: Routledge, 2014.

Brown, Mark. 'Crime, liberalism and empire: Governing the Mina tribe of Northern India'. *Social and Legal Studies* 13 (2004): 191–218.

French, Paul. *Midnight in Peking: How the Murder of a Young Englishwoman Haunted the Last Days of Old China*. London: Penguin, 2012.

Godfrey, Barry and Graeme Dunstall, eds. *Crime and Empire 1840-1940: Criminal Justice in Local and Global Context*. Cullumpton, Devon: Willan, 2005.

Mukherjee, Upamanyu P. *Crime and Empire: The Colony in Nineteenth-Century Fictions of Crime*. Oxford: Oxford University Press, 2003.

Sherman, Taylor C. 'Tensions of colonial punishment: Perspectives on recent developments in the study of coercive networks in Asia, Africa and the Caribbean'. *History Compass* 7 (2009): 659–77.

Sinclair, Georgina and Chris A. Williams. '"Home and away": The cross-fertilisation between "Colonial" and "British" policing, 1921-85'. *Journal of Imperial and Commonwealth History* 35 (2007): 221–38.

Van Onselen, Charles. *The Fox and the Flies: The Criminal Empire of the Whitechapel Murderer*. London: Vintage, 2008.

Wiener, Martin J. *An Empire on Trial: Race, Murder, and Justice under British Rule, 1870-1935*. Cambridge: Cambridge University Press, 2009.

Yang, Anand A., ed. *Crime and Criminality in British India*. Tucson: University of Arizona Press, 1987.

Conclusion

During the past four decades or so, crime has become an important topic of historical writing. What started as a subject of interest to lawyers has been taken up by historians interested in the 'new social history' – by those interested in Marxist social theory, quantitative analysis, urban history, psychohistory and women's history. It has also become a topic for historians following Foucault and the 'new cultural history', and for those interested in the British Empire and colonial history. Having reviewed this work, and the debates, controversies and disagreements over the past 40 years, we might ask: What is next? Where do we go from here? What is the best way forward?

The tradition of legal history established during the Victorian era by James Fitzjames Stephen, and later, William Holdsworth and Leon Radzinowicz, left crime history with two problems: Whig history and institutional history.[1] They produced a legal history focused on the present with the role of the practising lawyer in mind. They depicted law as a closed system, as if it reflected only legal doctrines, judicial decisions and legal practices. Internal legal history did not provide a suitable platform for building the history of crime. But, the lawyer-historians did write about crime. Pike's history of crime in England does not offer a model, but he did get there first. Also, legal history produced an external approach that contributed to social history. Jerome Hall's history of theft opened a 'law and society' path for Lawrence Friedman to make into a road. The problems of Whig history and institutional history continue to haunt crime history, but this does not mean that crime history should have nothing to do with legal history, as the 1980s' clash between John Langbein and Douglas Hay might suggest. Rather, we need the legal definition of crime as a starting point, and the law remains essential when legal texts are read as historical documents.

Quantification has added another dimension, and like legal history, we cannot do without it. Quantification has led to important conversations about the level of violence across Europe over the centuries and the extent of crime in specific places at particular times, such as Dodge City, Kansas, in the 1880s. But the practitioners have since the days of Buckle and the positivists been extremely enthusiastic about what can be accomplished with numbers, and this has raised expectations. In the 1980s, Ted R. Gurr received government funding in the belief that social science history could yield knowledge of use to policymakers. Eric Monkkonen, and more recently, Randolph Roth, have said that statistical analysis can compensate for limitations in historical data. There is no harm in being optimistic. As Lawrence Stone argued, there will never be as much evidence concerning the past as historians would want, so we must make the most of what is available. But there is a danger in promising more than what a 'scientific' approach to history can actually deliver, especially given the superhuman capabilities afforded by computerization. The fact that we can create digital databases and more complex statistical models for use with police records, court records, etc., does not make the numbers involved more valuable as historical evidence. The lesson of the *Annales* historians remains important: it does not require a particle accelerator to crack a nutshell.

Crime history has been interdisciplinary history, and the infusion of ideas from other disciplines has been beneficial. But historians interested in evolutionary biology have much more work to do. David Courtwright, Martin Wiener and others avoid earlier work by Cesare Lombroso, O. W. Holmes and Harry Barnes, and start with recent scientific statements about testosterone levels and the like. Avoiding this earlier work has an advantage in distancing evolutionary psychology from these rough formulations and the problems of reductionism and determinism. But it also has its drawbacks. Beginning with statements along the lines of 'scientists tell us that' simply will not do. The relationship between science and history is more complicated than advocates of evolutionary psychology want to believe.[2] The history of science reveals that culture, politics and economics influence what scientists do. The use of scientific knowledge in society, whether by governments or advocacy organizations, merits historical investigation. Take the eugenics movement for start. So, for evolutionary psychology to be taken seriously in the history of crime, the advocates need to take history more seriously.

The 'civilizing process' has proven to be a popular theory and it makes sense to look to it for an explanation of long-term trends in violence. But whether we can christen it the best explanation, as Pieter Spierenburg has done, requires further work on the theory itself. When fortified by concepts such as 'decivilizing processes', it becomes something more like a 'just so' story that accounts for virtually any aspect of crime trends. A theory so broad and elastic that it can explain any sequence of events explains nothing, because it makes the actual sequence of events irrelevant. So, in order to improve the fit between the theory and the evidence, it would be useful to clarify concepts. For one thing, it would be good to think through what Elias has to offer that is different from what Freud had to offer. If the civilizing process is an elaboration of *Civilisation and its Discontents*, then we have additional concepts from psychoanalytic theory, and importantly, decades of critique, that we can bring to the table.[3] For another, we need to think through how the civilizing process is different from modernization theory. There is an undeniable similarity between these two approaches, and the issues raised, for example, in James Sharpe's critique of Lawrence Stone's use of modernization theory, become relevant.

The British Marxist Historians popularized crime history in a way that few can match. Through their pursuit of social theory as supplied by Marx, they made history relevant to social scientists interested in crime. Historical criminology, as a branch of criminology that seeks to bring history to bear on current issues of crime and justice, owes a great deal to their work. But the greatest contribution certainly has to do with their commitment to 'history from the bottom up'. The idea that the lives of ordinary people matter is an important idea when we are writing the history of crime. It is a point of doing history that transcends the original theoretical framework so that even those not as committed to Marx as Eric Hobsbawm or Edward Thompson can appreciate it. Anand Yang's study of crime within the subaltern studies approach is one example of how far bottom-up history has travelled.

But if we really are interested in ordinary people in relation to crime, we need to spend more time with victims. Given their commitment to Marx, and their interest in finding 'primitive rebels' among labourers, the British Marxist Historians had their own reasons for focusing on criminals. Aside from this, much of the history of crime starts with the activity of criminals and tries to explain it with reference to social, economic, political or cultural factors. This is only half the story. To write a more complete 'bottom up' history, it might be useful to borrow opportunity theory from criminology. Opportunity theory starts with the activity of ordinary people to assess their vulnerability to victimization. Rather than trying to explain why criminals do what they do, the theory tries to explain what potential victims are doing that makes them more or less likely to be targeted. As an interpretative framework for crime history, this approach supposes that the motivation for crime remains constant through time. Crime rates rise and fall because the everyday lives of potential victims open up or close down opportunities for criminal activity.[4] It is an interesting way to think about crime victims: historical actors, not passive recipients of historical processes. They are the motor of crime history so to speak. Criminals react to them, and the police, judges and so on react to the criminals.

Because of the way urban history fit into the new social history, the city acquired a central place in crime history. Historians like Eric Monkkonen, who contributed so much to crime history, started in urban history. The city remains an important context in which to understand the history of crime, whether policing, delinquency or the underworld. For more than one reason (such as availability of historical records, historians' interest in the nineteenth and twentieth centuries), this work will continue. But we need more work on crime outside urban spaces to help separate city issues from crime issues. As Timothy Gilfoyle, Heather Shore and others suggest, the underworld presents interesting issues, from the informal economy to cultural geography, and these can be unravelled through comparative or other methods.[5]

It is hard to know where to begin to assess Foucault's influence on writing the history of crime. In addition to establishing the prison and criminology as worthy topics, he brought new theory and method to historical writing. Foucault's version of post-structuralism brought crime history within the 'new cultural history' and led to a wide array of topics. The extent of Foucault's influence can be seen in research about women and crime, with historians such as Judith Walkowitz and many others interested in narratives about gender and criminality. It can also be seen in the study of crime in the British Empire. Through post-colonial theory, Foucault has shaped the understanding of crime in colonies, as well as colonial prisons. Foucault may have lost his power to startle, amuse and annoy, but this makes him a victim of his own success. So many aspects of his project, such as 'discourse analysis', have become so popular that they have become mainstream.

Foucault's single biggest influence on crime history has been the prioritization of theory over evidence. He combined compelling narrative, vivid images and evocative language to present ideas that were so interesting that his eccentric choice of historical sources seemed quite reasonable. Foucault's account of the 'birth of the prison' has nothing to do with the way prisons actually work, but did not matter.[6] His appeal was always in the realm of theoretical or philosophical history. This has made it difficult to get away with narrow, institutional history, which is a good thing. But, it also led away from archival research (even though Foucault himself spent much of his time in archives). Foucault's theory-driven approach to the past encouraged 'histories of the present' that have more to do with contemporary issues than understanding the past, and there is not much difference between this and the 'history for lawyers' social historians complained about. The conclusions for the present differ widely, but both distort the past through too much enthusiasm for making a statement in the present.

The introduction of themes from women's history has expanded crime history in multiple ways. The discussion about changes in the level of crime among women over the centuries – Malcolm Feeley's 'vanishing female' – is important, not only for what it suggests about theories of women's participation in crime, but also for its implications concerning methodology. Are crime statistics a good way for understanding crime among women? Or, to put it more provocatively, are the methods used to study men and crime suitable for studying women and crime? Garthine Walker makes a significant point about sources when she questions what the statistical proportion of crime by women tells us. Her argument about the value of narrative sources echoes that of J. J. Tobias about Britain's national crime statistics. It also speaks to the larger business about how much crime history has been written as if 'crime' and 'criminal justice' only referred to men. The version of gender history that makes the female criminal nothing more than a virtual figure, an image in the minds of men not unlike a video game, has already said about all it is capable of saying. But Nicole Rafter, Louise Jackson and others, who have written about women, prisons and police, have demonstrated how different the history of crime is with women 'written in', and the study of women and crime holds the promise of even more interesting work to follow.

Crime in the British Empire has attracted an increasing number of historians in the past few years. The point Georgina Sinclair and Chris Williams make about 'cross-fertilization' in policing is an important one, and one that applies to much more than police history. The history of crime in Britain, in the widest sense of including criminal justice, is intertwined with the history of crime in the colonies. The problem so far is that with few exceptions (such as Yang), colonial history has not been integrated with crime history more generally. Much more cross-fertilization, to borrow a phrase, needs to occur between British crime history and the history of crime in the British Empire. At a minimum, this avoids methodological nationalism that leads to incomplete, if not mistaken, histories of crime.

The case for the United States is different because the American Empire was nowhere near as extensive as the British Empire. But this of course depends on how we define 'empire'. The British Empire included a range of legal possessions, but there were also countries over which Britain exercised an enormous influence (such as Argentina). To take this reality into account, some historians have talked about the 'informal empire' or 'British world'. Following this same tack, it becomes clear that the informal American Empire has been extensive, and if we include American influence on international affairs, even more so. I mention all of this to suggest the context in which the emerging study of international crime – drug trade, traffic in women, terrorism – must take place.[7]

Crime history owes its life to the social history of the 1970s. Traditional history would never have allowed such a pretender to the throne to remain alive. But traditional history in the sense of research has more to offer. The techniques of legal analysis, quantification, textual criticism and psychoanalysis have offered alternatives to historicist interpretation of documents in archives. These are supplements, not a replacement. Each has made a valuable contribution, but none provides a substitute for finding documents originating in the period of interest, interpreting the contents in view of what was possible at the time, and trying to appreciate the particulars of what happened. We need document analysis, in the traditional sense, to make the most of legal records and statistical material, to unravel concepts from convict transportation to the underworld and to grasp the significance of crime for women and crime in colonial contexts. So, the paradox of crime history is that it would not have emerged without revolutionary social and cultural history, but the way forward requires an affirmation of traditional, conventional historical research.

Notes

1 Clive Emsley, 'The history of crime and crime control institutions', in Mike Maguire, Rod Morgan and Robert Reiner, eds, *The Oxford Handbook of Criminology*, 3rd edn (Oxford: Oxford University Press, 2002).

2 Randolph Roth, 'Scientific history and experimental history', *Journal of Interdisciplinary History* 43 (2013): 443–58.

3 Peter Burke, 'Freud and cultural history', *Psychoanalysis and History* 9 (2007): 5–15.

4 Martin Killias, 'The opening and closing of breaches: A theory on crime waves, law creation and crime prevention', *European Journal of Criminology* 3 (2006): 11–31.

5 Heather Shore, *London's Criminal Underworlds, c. 1720-c. 1930: A Social and Cultural History* (London: Palgrave Macmillan, 2015).

6 C. Fred Allford, 'What would it matter if everything Foucault said about prison were wrong? *Discipline and Punish* after twenty years', *Theory and Society* 29 (2000): 125–46.

7 Paul Knepper, *International Crime in the Twentieth Century: The League of Nations Era, 1919-1939* (London: Palgrave Macmillan, 2011).

INDEX